Toleration and State Institutions

Toleration and State Institutions

British Policy toward Catholics in Eighteenth-Century Ireland and Quebec

Karen Stanbridge

LEXINGTON BOOKS
Lanham • Boulder • New York • Oxford

LEXINGTON BOOKS

Published in the United States of America
by Lexington Books
A Member of the Rowman & Littlefield Publishing Group
4501 Forbes Boulevard, Suite 200, Lanham, Maryland 20706

PO Box 317
Oxford
OX2 9RU, UK

British Library Cataloguing in Publication Information Available

Library of Congress Cataloging-in-Publication Data

Stanbridge, Karen, 1962–
    Toleration and state institutions : British policy toward Catholics in eighteenth-century
Ireland and Quebec / Karen Stanbridge.
        p. cm.
    Includes bibliographical references (p.) and index.
    ISBN 0-7391-0558-2 (cloth : alk. paper)
        1. Catholic Church—Ireland—History—18th century. 2. Church and
state—Ireland—History—18th century. 3. Religious tolerance—Ireland—History—
18th century. 4. Catholic Church—Quâbec (Province)—History—18th century. 5.
Church and state—Quâbec (Province)—History—18th century. 6. Religious tolerance—
Quâbec (Province)—History—18th century. I. Title.

BX1504.S73 2003
323.3—dc21
                                                                    2003040096
Printed in the United States of America

⊖™ The paper used in this publication meets the minimum requirements of American
National Standard for Information Sciences—Permanence of Paper for Printed Library
Materials, ANSI/NISO Z39.48–1992.

Contents

Chapter 1

Introduction

After the Glorious Revolution, Irish Catholics were subjected to a series of laws restricting their political, economic and social behavior. Although laws inhibiting their activities, religious or otherwise, had been in place since Tudor times, Catholics had enjoyed, if not a legal, at least a practical, toleration of their religious beliefs and practices in Ireland. The situation changed in the 1690s, however, when the Protestant minority in Ireland, in partnership with English officials, began to legislate policy that not only stripped Irish Catholics of most of their political, economic and social rights, but appeared, at least initially, bent on eradicating the Catholic religion in Ireland all together.

These laws are in contrast to the policy of toleration that was extended to Quebec Catholics some seventy-five years later in the Quebec Act of 1774. Although it appeared when France ceded Quebec to Britain in the Treaty of Paris in 1763 that French Catholics in the new colony would be subject to the same restrictive policies as their coreligionists in Ireland and other British territories, the Quebec Act insured that Quebec's majority population would enjoy freedoms unknown to Catholics elsewhere in the empire. The Act specified that Catholics were free to exercise their religion in the province, and that the Catholic clergy were allowed to collect the tithe. Public officials were no longer required to take oaths objectionable to Catholics, opening up the colonial civil service to individuals other than British Protestants. The act required that a few positions be made available to French Catholic élites in the provincial council, which, in the absence of a representative assembly in the colony, had legislative jurisdiction over the region.

In 1778, a Catholic Relief Act was passed in Ireland. The concessions granted to Irish Catholics were not nearly as extensive as those granted to Quebec Catholics. The Act repealed earlier penal legislation that required that Catholics divide their estates among their sons upon their death, and increased the number of years Catholics could lease land from 31 to 999 or 5 lifetimes. Nevertheless, the Act represented the first in a series of measures that eventually saw Irish Catholics acquire citizenship rights commensurate with their Irish Protestant counterparts.

That only four years separated the passage of the Irish Act from the Quebec Act, and that many of the same British officials presided over, or at least contributed to, both decisions, suggests that there may have existed important connections between these measures. The Quebec Act was the first major piece of legislation to extend *concessions* to Catholics in the British empire rather than repress them. To ascertain its influence as a precedent to the Irish Relief Acts that followed it could clarify the circumstances that led officials to begin passing policies more tolerant of Catholics and Catholicism in Ireland and contribute to a better understanding of the more protracted movement toward more charitable treatment of British Catholics.

This study explores linkages between policies directed toward Catholics in Ireland and Quebec during the "long" eighteenth century. It is especially concerned with establishing how state institutions structuring Anglo-Irish and Anglo-Quebec political relations helped or hindered the adoption of measures more tolerant of Catholics in these two peripheries. Its aim is to supplement more traditional approaches to Catholic relief that attribute legislative change to the "growth of toleration" amongst Irish and British élites, or to the more practical demands of securing the allegiance of recusants in the empire. An institutional analysis adds a dimension to the question of Catholic relief that has been little explored, that of how enduring and changing patterns of governance helped to array interests on both sides of the relief issue and so helped to shape policy outcomes.

Traditionally, scholars concerned with Catholicism in eighteenth-century Ireland have drawn few comparisons between the Irish and Quebec legislation. Ireland's "penal era" has been studied with little reference to factors and forces outside Ireland. According to Jacqueline Hill,[1] this insularity can be attributed, in part, to the persistence of the "growth of toleration" explanation for the relaxation of the penal laws in Ireland. The "growth of toleration" argument maintains that the trend toward legislating policy less repressive of Irish Catholics that began in the latter half of the eighteenth century was a manifestation of the changing attitudes of Irish élites. The European Enlightenment encouraged the softening of the traditional ideas about Catholics held by Protestant Ireland, which led to the gradual relaxation of the penal laws. The emphasis on the "growth of toleration" explanation, writes Hill,[2] has "persuad[ed] historians that there is no need to look outside Ireland for the forces at work leading to the relaxation of the penal laws," and fostered an insular approach to the matter.

It is true that the "growth of toleration" explanation was prevalent among early historians such as J. A. Froude and W. E. H. Lecky, who, in the nineteenth century, wrote of "the growing spirit of liberty" and "decline of religious fanaticism among the Protestants" in the latter half of the eighteenth century, a phenomenon that "led shortly to religious liberty."[3] More recent studies, however, have acknowledged that past claims of this approach have been exaggerated and its emphasis on attitudes overstated. Scholars have been inclined to add that the lessening of the Stuart threat with the death of the "Old Pretender" in 1766 and the general decline in the power and influence of the Catholic church in Western Europe by the mid-eighteenth century provided further inducements for a more lenient policy toward Catholics. As well, there has been increasing recognition that the continuity implied by the "growth of toleration" approach is not supported by actual events. Policy toward Catholics did not thereafter follow a smooth and steady course toward greater freedoms. While a majority of Irish MPs may have tolerated the limited reforms contained in the Irish Catholic Relief Act, few supported extending political rights to Catholics into the 1780s. It was not until the following decade that Irish MPs or any significant body of Protestants thought it natural to back such a proposal.[4] And although legislative union with Britain in 1801 promised Irish Catholics that significant concessions would soon be forthcoming, they were forced to wait several decades before they experienced their "emancipation."[5]

While such inconsistencies have been recognized, so embedded is the "growth of toleration" argument in the discourse of the period that historians "have in general been reluctant to abandon the idea of a growth in toleration altogether."[6] Hill herself refers to works by James Kelly and J. C. Beckett that continue to cite changes in the general disposition toward Catholics by the latter half of the eighteenth century as fundamental to the passing of more charitable measures.[7] In a later work, Kelly again draws attention to "the more accommodating liberal strain within Irish Protestantism which favored religious tolerance" and its influence on changes in policies toward Catholics.[8] More recently, Francis James has carried on in this tradition by stressing the significance of attitude change among the Irish peerage to the extension of concessions to Irish Catholics in the later eighteenth century.[9] Thomas Bartlett, while cautious not to attribute policy change to attitudes alone, nevertheless allocates several pages to describing the decline in religious "enthusiasm" expressed by European society in the mid-eighteenth century, a shift "which ultimately had a vital bearing on the progress of the Catholic question in Ireland."[10] And Colin Haydon, to whose doctoral research Bartlett refers as evidence of this shift, is of like mind with respect to the attitudes of British élites in particular.[11] These works align with more general studies that continue to emphasize the impact of Enlightenment thinking on political leaders, attributing policy change to governments seeking "to demonstrate their enlightened credentials."[12]

The continued emphasis by researchers on the importance of attitude change among Irish élites has helped to maintain traditional, insular, approaches to Catholic relief in Ireland. This has discouraged adoption of the broader perspective required to consider the influence on Irish measures of more tolerant legislation in Quebec and elsewhere in the British empire. It has also hindered study of the place of Irish legislation in the more general trend toward policies less repressive of Catholics that is observed over the "long" eighteenth century.

The "Growth of Toleration" and Quebec

The treatment by scholars of penal legislation in Ireland can be compared to research on Quebec and the Quebec Act. To some extent, what Jacqueline Hill writes of Ireland is true of Quebec as well. The "growth of toleration" has found its way into historical accounts of the period, again primarily early ones. Writers adhering to nineteenth-century liberal notions of progress and development "had little use for Catholicism and tended therefore to see the French colony in North America as lost in the misty wafts of clerical obscurantism."[13] To these and like-minded historians of the next century, the conquest of Quebec was a deliverance and the Quebec Act representative of the pioneering spirit of enlightened British administrators toward Catholics in the empire, "the finest product of the benign statesmanship that signified a maturing awareness of the real responsibilities of imperial governance in the early modern period."[14]

The role of the "growth of toleration" among élites in the formulation of the Quebec Act has never featured as prominently in the Quebec literature as in the Irish, however. This is due in part to the early emergence of a French-Canadian literature that challenged nineteenth-century British liberal interpretations of the conquest. Reflecting a view that had been expressed as early as 1840, Jean Bruchesi denied the image of Britons as enlightened liberators of Quebec, arguing instead that Quebec under France had been a full-fledged, almost idyllic, nation in 1760, inhabited by pious, hardworking, fiercely patriotic settlers. After the conquest, charitable policies were not enacted out of British benevolence, but because of the settlers' steadfast refusal to renounce their religion, laws and language. Later Quebec writers emphasized the debilitating effects of the conquest on an emerging French Canadian bourgeoisie. While British liberals maintained that Quebec's inhabitants had been prevented from developing the necessary characteristics – ambition, enterprise, risk-taking, and the political values of liberty and democracy – to prosper economically under French rule, secular-nationalists argued that it was the conquest and subsequent severing of the link between New France and its metropolis that halted the maturation of Quebec's entrepreneurial class. Maurice Séguin, Guy Frégault and Michel Brunet argued that British takeover provoked the "decapitation" of the colony, forcing its most enterprising inhabitants to return to the mother country. Deprived of dynamic leadership and opportunity, the French Canadians that remained retreated to the countryside, so beginning the French-Canadian legacy of agriculturalism.[15] While it has been argued that the Quebec nationalist response to the British liberalist interpretation of the conquest is but a battle of competing ideologies, the debate has long militated against interpretations of the conquest and the Quebec Act as simple corollaries of the "growth of toleration" amongst British élites.[16]

If French-Canadian nationalists undermined attitudinal explanations of the Quebec Act, Quebec's status as a recognized colony of the British empire discouraged insular understandings of the legislation. Crucial in this regard was the looming and constant presence throughout its negotiation of the thirteen colonies to the south and their dispute with the British metropolis. The Quebec Act came less than a year before the outbreak of the American war, and colonists and their supporters in Great Britain were quick to draw connections between the act and the wider framework of British imperial policy. A contemporary American interpretation of the Quebec Act held that the legislation was part of a British plot to do away with representative government in the American colonies and impose a "popish" and despotic rule on the entire continent, a view that continued to inform histories dealing with postconquest America into the twentieth century.[17] Since then, scholars have situated the Quebec Act squarely within the context of Britain's Atlantic empire. The place of Ireland within the empire has not been so clearly delineated. Some have argued that the Anglo-Irish relationship should be understood as a "colonial" one, but this view is by no means uncontested.[18]

Catholic Relief from an Imperial Perspective

It is this tradition in Quebec history, that which links the colony's politics to political activities and decisions taken outside the province, that Jacqueline Hill evokes when she advocates an "imperial approach" to the relaxation of the penal laws in Ireland.[19] As in the case of Quebec, the role of the state – the British state – in Catholic relief is of special importance here. In pondering what was the part played by the British government in the relaxation of the penal laws, Hill stresses the need to remember that Ireland was but part of a larger British empire which, by the latter half of the eighteenth century, encompassed other peripheries with significant Catholic populations. An examination of how British officials treated Catholics in other territories during the same period would broaden understanding of the processes surrounding the extension of concessions to Catholics in Ireland.

Certainly an imperial approach undermines further the traditional "growth of toleration" argument. If the "growth of toleration" as the principle basis for Catholic relief has become untenable with respect to Ireland, it is indefensible from an imperial perspective. Policy toward Catholics varied widely across the empire during the latter half of the eighteenth century. If it was an increasingly tolerant spirit that inspired British administrators to allow such charitable treatment of French Catholics in Quebec in the 1760s and 1770s, it is difficult to reconcile on these grounds the delay of several decades to pass legislation that granted Irish Catholics similar rights. Even more troubling is the fact that they allowed the expulsion of upwards of 10,000 Catholic Acadians from Nova Scotia in 1755,[20] and continued to entertain the notion that those few who remained should be expelled as late as 1765,[21] even while they were tolerating the new Quebec administration's generous treatment of Catholics there. They allowed Catholics in Newfoundland and the Canadian Maritime provinces to be persecuted and excluded from civil life by the administrations and Protestant inhabitants of these colonies until well into the next century.[22] And although French Catholics in Grenada were granted extensive political rights shortly after the conquest, those rights were withdrawn in 1784 when anglicization of the colony began in earnest.[23] Clearly, something other than a charitable attitude was informing the policymaking decisions of British state officials during this period.

An imperial perspective encourages interpretation of Catholic relief in Ireland and elsewhere in more practical terms, "high policy" issues such as war and diplomacy. Indeed, recent works that have adopted a broader view toward the extension of concessions to Catholics in the empire in the eighteenth century have focused on the causal importance of such factors. Colin Haydon, while he does not abandon entirely the traditional reliance on changing attitudes to account for policy change, describes how the "demands of statesmanship" in an increasingly diverse empire compelled British élites to take a more conciliatory stance toward Catholics to insure their loyalty to Crown and country.[24] Samuel Clark, in a larger study of the influence of international competition on the treatment of minorities, argues that conflict between Britain and France was crucial in determining how Catholics were treated in Ireland and Quebec.[25] Variations in policy toward Catholics are thus explained in terms of the military and strategic requirements of each territory.

Irish history is not entirely bereft of analyses that acknowledge connections between legislation affecting Catholics in Ireland and the larger empire. Maurice O'Connell's classic monograph on Irish politics in the late eighteenth century linked the Quebec Act and the Irish Catholic Relief Act in a more or less natural progression of events leading to the "dawning of a new day" for Catholics in the British empire.[26] More recently, David Dickson and Thomas Bartlett stress the importance of situating the English and Irish Catholic Relief Acts of 1778 in the context of the British-American conflict.[27] In support of this view, both make reference to Robert Donovan's excellent study that reveals the acts were part of a larger plan to extend concessions to Catholics all over the British Isles to encourage their enlistment in the British army.[28] Works such as these draw attention to the part played by the British state in the promulgation of policy toward Irish Catholics during this period, and the influence of practical concerns of governance on the policymaking process. Donovan's study in particular, his detailed account of how individuals and groups in and on the periphery of Anglo-Irish politics responded to the demands of war to help give rise to the English and Irish Relief Acts, demonstrates how an imperial perspective can help to refashion understandings of past events.

Problems with the Imperial Perspective

An imperial approach has helped researchers to begin to move away from their reliance on the "growth of toleration" and traditional, insular understandings of Ireland's penal laws. There are, however, a number of difficulties with the way in which the perspective has thus far been applied, not only to the Irish but to the Quebec situation as well.

Prescient Politicians

In maintaining that the "demands of statesmanship" were the basis of the more charitable measures extended to Catholics in the British empire in the later eighteenth century, researchers overemphasize the capacity of political élites to formulate policies in accordance with the military and security demands of each territory. Such studies accept that British administrators had the wherewithal to effectively take stock of circumstances and apply policy that was best suited to that particular situation. Such a view, however, portrays British officials in the early years of empire as more rational and prescient than evidence allows. Certainly there is no evidence that British administrators were acting in accordance with a coherent "grand scheme" of empire when deciding the policies that should be put into place. It is difficult to imagine a cohesive imperial strategy that simultaneously calls for the partial inclusion of Catholics in the political system in one province (Quebec), and their full inclusion in another (Grenada); the continued repression of one population of Catholics (Ireland), the outright expulsion of another (Acadia) and the total disregard of yet another community of Catholics under British rule (Newfoundland).

Yet even when the actions of officials are less circumscribed and administrators are allowed to deal with situations on an ad hoc basis, it is difficult to demonstrate that "considerations of empire" were fundamental to the promulgation of a given policy. It is one thing to harken back on a situation and assign causal importance to such factors; it is quite another to make the case that these were the reasons behind those directives being implemented. The expulsion of the Acadians, for example, may appear politically prudent from a security perspective. There were far fewer Acadians – at the most 10,000 versus the estimated 65,000 to 80,000 Catholics in Quebec – making expulsion more feasible. Further, the Acadians had long refused to take an oath of allegiance to the British king; they insisted on retaining their neutrality. Quebec Catholics made no such demands. Acadians were also in an area that was strategically more important than Quebec.

But the notion that British administrators in London weighed all these considerations carefully then decided that expulsion was the best option suggests that the Acadian situation was handled in a much more deliberate and rational way than it actually was. The decision to expel the Acadians was not made by officials in Britain at all. Rather, the local governor took it upon himself to do it. By the time London officials learned of the expulsion it was well underway. It is true that administrators had discussed the option of removing the Acadians before. It is also true that officials in England did nothing to stop the deed once it had started. But the act did not involve any careful taking stock or calculated implementation of the most logical course of action.

The Grenadian case provides another example. When ceded to the British by the Treaty of Paris, the "white" population of the island of Grenada was about half French Catholic. These Catholics were granted full civil rights in 1768 and were allowed to vote, sit on the assembly and council and occupy important positions in the administration and defense of the island. Most of these French Catholics were wealthy landowners and planters on an island where the black slave population vastly outnumbered the white. A conventional understanding of British actions presumes that these Catholics were granted full political rights because it was necessary for the white, landowning Protestant and Catholic populations to present a united front in case of a slave uprising.

But this explanation for the legislation does not tell the whole story. The instructions that accompanied the new governor of the colony, Robert Melville, ordered him to call an assembly in the province as soon as he thought feasible. This assembly, however, like other assemblies in the British empire, was to be a wholly Protestant body. The French Catholic planters protested, insisting that they be allowed to participate fully in the political life of the colony. Upon consideration of their demands, Melville decided to let them vote for, but not sit in, the assembly. This was not enough for the French planters, who petitioned the British government asking that they be allocated positions in the provincial council and the assembly. It is true that the French planters pointed out to officials the importance of a united élite in a colony with a majority slave population, but this was not the only matter concerning the British Privy Council.[29] By this time, governor Melville had already called an assembly in the province. There would have been an outcry from the British inhabitants had the government tried to suppress the assembly to avoid having to deal with the French Catholic situation. At the same time, the French planters made up such a significant and important number of the island's population that British administrators could not leave them out of the civil life of the island as the British planters wanted. The Privy Council decided to allow most of the French planters' demands. These actions might have had the effect of better securing the island against a slave revolt and helped to bind the French inhabitants to the new regime. But considerations of this type were not the primary reason why these decisions were taken. As in the Acadian case, the actual process was much more complicated than an imperial considerations argument suggests.

The notion, then, that policies promulgated in the British empire in the latter half of the eighteenth century were the result of practical decisions taken on the part of British administrators who consciously and purposely sought to achieve imperial ends is empirically untenable. What appears when events are examined more closely is that the treatment of Catholics during these early years of empire was much less deliberate than the approach suggests.

Parochial to Pandemic

Another related problem concerns the apparently spontaneous change in the mindset of British politicians in the late eighteenth century. There is a sense here that the expansion of the empire wrought by the Seven Years' War was accompanied closely by a shift in thinking amongst British officials away from a parochial perspective that advocated blanket use of anti-Catholic measures, to a harder-headed approach that recognized the practical advantages of permitting British Catholics in some areas certain rights and freedoms. The shift is often assumed rather than explained, leaving important causal influences unexamined.

In studies concerned with the relaxation of the penal laws in Ireland, this view is most evident in their treatment, or more correctly, their nontreatment, of the place of the Quebec Act relative to the English and Irish Catholic relief acts. The Quebec Act is given little attention, despite the fact that it preceded the Anglo-Irish legislation, was widely discussed in Britain and Ireland with respect to Irish Catholics and that many of the same legislators were responsible for promulgating all three relief policies. David Dickson, reflecting traditional insular approaches to Catholic relief, deals with the American conflict and the Quebec measure only so far as they served to stimulate the Irish patriot activity and Catholic agitation that contributed to the concessions.[30] Thomas Bartlett takes a broader perspective. Following Donovan, Bartlett groups the Quebec Act with the Acts in England and Ireland as measures designed by British officials to encourage the loyalty of Catholic subjects in a time of war.[31] Aside from acknowledging that the Quebec Act preceded the English and Irish legislation, however, he makes no effort to explore the actual relationships between the measures, making only bracketed reference to the Quebec measure and its place in the triad of policies.[32] Donovan himself, while he mentions the Quebec Act as an indication of "[a] shrewd attitude toward the possible usefulness of Catholics" in British government, fails to explain from where this new posture originated.[33] The Quebec measure remains outside the purview of Anglo-Irish politics, a stimulus to domestic activities perhaps, but largely external to events unfolding on the Island or in the metropolis.

Neglect of the Quebec Act has allowed these researchers to avoid answering what is surely the crucial question with respect to Catholic relief in the British empire: how did British officials come to think of the Catholic question in imperial terms? It may be true that toleration-in-exchange-for-allegiance became a policy practiced regularly by officials by the nineteenth century; indeed, toleration of indigenous institutions is considered by some historians as an "innovation" of the eighteenth century that was applied in other territories in which Britons wished to create goodwill such as India and the Cape Colony.[34] In the 1770s, however, when this strategy was apparently in its early stages, British élites were operating in an environment in which anti-Catholic sentiments were almost universal, and where for generations Catholics and Catholicism had been actively and purposefully suppressed by the state. Although the toleration-for-allegiance exchange makes practical sense from a modern perspective, the question remains as to how contemporaries came to make the link between these issues, let alone formulate and pass policy rescinding established anti-Catholic measures to realize that relationship. The conceptual "leap" that linked concessions to the demands of empire was not as automatic as is generally assumed.

Certainly the "leap" had not yet been taken in 1763. When France ceded Quebec to Britain in the Treaty of Paris, the possibility that Quebec would be governed any differently than any other colony in the British empire was barely discussed. The Quebec Proclamation issued by the British government in 1763, as well as the commission and instructions to Quebec's first governor, James Murray, contained the same sorts of stipulations concerning religion as those contained in other colonial documents: the Church of England was to be the established church in the colony, anglicization of the French Catholic population was to begin in earnest, and all office holders, including members of the representative assembly, were required to take the standard oaths. Public office and political power was thus restricted to the 5 percent of the population who were British Protestants. The notion that a more tolerant stance toward Catholics by British administrators grew readily out of the expanded demands of empire after the Seven Years' War is difficult to substantiate.

By simply citing, rather than establishing, the Quebec Act as a precedent to relief Acts in England and Ireland, these authors allow that the shift from a parochial to a more practical approach to the Catholic issue by British officials had already somehow occurred by 1778. Decisions taken with respect to Catholics were by then directed by imperial concerns; the notion that concessions could be extended in exchange for allegiance already established. Now was the challenge to conceive of policies that politicians in Britain and Ireland would swallow. Thus the crucial question of how the transition came about is circumvented. The idealized image of British administrators as officials transformed is perpetuated while the factors and forces that encouraged them to think about Catholic relief as a tool to promote empire are left unexamined.

Given the tenacity of the "growth of toleration" argument, it is perhaps not surprising that researchers grappling with the shift have fallen back on attitudes to help deal with it. As mentioned, Colin Haydon goes some way toward qualifying the traditional argument in his investigation of anti-Catholicism in eighteenth-century England/Britain, emphasizing that whatever spirit of toleration that existed at that time was sporadic, and confined largely to British élites and not expressed by the British populous.[35] Nevertheless, it was that spirit that contributed to the willingness of British government officials to consider extending concessions to Catholics in the empire to secure their loyalty. Their anti-Catholicism tempered by enlightenment ideals, British administrators were more inclined to entertain political strategies that granted freedoms to Catholics rather than restricted them. Haydon thus combines old and new approaches to the question, stressing the concurrence of imperial demands and the development of more tolerant attitudes as crucial to the policy shift.

Reliance on the "growth of toleration" to help account for the turnaround in British policy toward Catholics in the 1770s and for the unevenness of legislation into the nineteenth century has appeal, but is ultimately unsatisfying. Attitudes are a slippery thing to grasp at the best of times, let alone when the individuals whose sentiments are being gauged lived over two centuries ago. There is also the problem of what "toleration" meant to Protestant Britons and Irish in the late eighteenth century. There is a vast difference between a "softening" in attitudes toward Catholics because of the removal of external dangers such as the Stuart threat, and the belief that Catholics should have rights commensurate with Protestants; between conscientious opposition to religious persecution, and the extension of concessions to recusants. Haydon himself acknowledges the problem when he writes that, in England at least, toleration may have been developing amongst élites "but a relaxation of the penal laws was not seen as a prelude to their complete abandonment."[36] Finally, demonstrating an actual link between attitudes and behavior is also problematic. Even if Protestants became more indulgent of Catholics and Catholicism over time, it does not mean their indulgence translated to political action.

The imperial approach as it has thus far been applied to the study of policy toward Catholics has generated a number of loose ends. Attention has been drawn to the influence of the demands of war and statesmanship on the promulgation of policy toward Catholics in Ireland, yet traditional insular approaches to Catholic relief are perpetuated by continuing to treat these matters as factors largely external to the Irish situation; the role of British politics and politicians in the formulation of relief policy is recognized, but those politicians are represented as more rational and prescient than evidence allows. And while the need to understand the "practical" origins of Catholic relief is emphasized, the pragmatism of officials toward Catholic legislation in the 1770s is either accepted as a natural corollary of an expanding empire, or attributed to changes in the attitudes of British administrators. Thus a perspective that sought to move away from the "growth of toleration" explanation of the relaxation of the Irish penal laws ends up resurrecting it to account for the less parochial approach required to institute policy more in line with imperial concerns.

An Alternative Approach

The preceding raises a number of questions. From where did the more tolerant approach characterizing late-eighteenth-century policy toward Catholics originate? British administrators appear not to have initially made the connection between toleration and security in Quebec. The "shrewd attitude" toward Catholics that Donovan mentions was evident during negotiation of the Irish Catholic Relief Act did not arise complete out of the Seven Years' War; it took hold only over time. What conditions helped to bring about this change? And how did the "movement" toward emancipation become established? The image portrayed by the imperial perspective of late-eighteenth-century British administrators, their provincial views of Catholics shattered by the new demands of an expanded empire, consciously and purposefully extending greater and greater freedoms to recusants to secure their allegiance, cannot be substantiated. Upon closer examination, whatever "movement" toward Catholic relief that can be discerned in the eighteenth century appears to have happened much less smoothly, more haphazardly, than existing studies suggest. The imperial perspective as it has thus far been applied is hard pressed to address these matters.

The current study offers a different approach. It does not deny the main tenets of the imperial perspective, that which state that British administrators, in the main, came to adopt a more practical, less parochial, view of Catholics in the empire during the late eighteenth century. Neither, for that matter, does it reject studies that maintain that there occurred a "growth of toleration" among government officials in Britain and in Ireland. These and other contributions have done much to clarify *why* officials grew to be more accommodating of Catholics over time. Rather, the current study seeks to supplement these approaches by examining *how* these changes were actually manifested in policy toward Catholics. In emphasizing the "how" over the "why" the analysis asks that consideration be given to aspects of the question of Catholic relief that have thus far largely been neglected. In doing so, it attempts to overcome some of the limitations of existing approaches and provide a picture of policy toward Catholics that better aligns with events in the way that they unfolded.

The Influence of Institutions

To ask "how" a particular policy came into being, there must occur a shift away from exploring the *rationale* for the measure, to the *political mechanisms* that contributed to its realization. Existing studies adopting an imperial perspective, indeed those employing the "growth of toleration" argument as well, have neglected to specify these mechanisms. Underlying both approaches is the notion that government legislation was essentially the straightforward manifestation of the intentions of British government officials. Whether their judgments concerning the Catholic situation stemmed from their attitudes, or from concerns over imperial matters, these perspectives suggest that administrators were able to translate their policy intentions into legislation, directly and purposively, through government channels. That political institutions may have militated against the ambitions of British officials and ended up shaping policy and its effects in ways that administrators may not have intended is not always appreciated.

An example is a recent work by Colin Haydon.[37] Haydon attempts to clarify the relationship between the attitudes of government officials and legislation that remained ambiguous in his previous research. He attributes the "changing perceptions" by the British Parliament toward Catholics in the eighteenth century principally to the "demise of jacobitism" as evinced by the disinclination of British Catholics to participate in the 1745 rising and the death of James Stuart. These events "put an end to serious political concerns" regarding Catholics. Henceforth, Catholicism became an "increasingly insignificant matter in the eyes of the legislature" which paved the way for more tolerant legislation.

While Haydon's study sheds further light on *why* the anti-Catholicism of British members of Parliament may have begun to erode, it fails to address *how* those changing perceptions were translated into policy via government mechanisms. It ignores how the institutions surrounding policymaking may themselves have repressed or promoted a more tolerant approach to Catholics in the empire. Early relief measures like the Quebec Act and the Irish Catholic Relief Act were preceded by a century of legislated anti-Catholicism. Laws were in place restricting Catholics in the empire in all manner of ways; discrimination was embedded in the day-to-day activities of those engaged in the political realm by means of well-established norms and political practices. The question remains as to how these structures were modified or superceded to allow concessions to be extended. Further, the inertia embodied within these institutions would have militated against any departure from precedent and discouraged fresh approaches to the Catholic question. Haydon's reformulation does not address these matters.

For example, the British state held a very different political relationship with Ireland than with Quebec in the 1760s and 1770s. Ireland had a Parliament; Quebec was not granted representative institutions until 1791. Irish policymaking adhered to centuries-old principles and procedures; Quebec did not join the empire until 1763, so there were no established guidelines for British administrators to follow when formulating policy affecting the province. Variations in the institutions governing policymaking affected the nature of the policies directed at Catholics in the two peripheries, independent of, or in combination with, the personal attitudes and more pragmatic intentions of British officials. To address "how" certain policies came about it is necessary to consider the impact of these institutions.

Toleration: A Novel Idea?

Another factor to be considered when pondering "how" given policy was enacted concerns the distribution of competing interests. While institutions affected policy by establishing the "bounds" of political activity, the distribution of rival interests, the way in which "pro" and "anti" forces were arrayed in the political realm, influenced the nature of the policy outcome.

The imperial perspective, as well as the "growth of toleration" argument, imply that there were few competing ideas on the matter of the treatment of Catholics before the 1770s. Both perspectives suggest intolerance was a universal sentiment that only disappeared in the late eighteenth century. Hence the focus of these perspectives on ascertaining the forces in the *latter half* of the century that promoted that change, such as the "growth of toleration," the demands of statesmanship, the decline in Jacobitism, and so forth.

But the notion that Catholics should be treated more charitably, particularly for reasons of English/British security, was hardly novel. Tolerant Protestant monarchs and officials existed in England/Britain before the 1770s. It has been argued that William III, for example, the monarch still celebrated by many Irish Protestants for saving Ireland from "popery" by defeating James II at Limerick in 1691, was conspicuously tolerant of Catholics. Many of his personal servants and military officers were Catholics; he even allowed mass to be sung everyday in his army.[38] Other monarchs as well were often compelled to treat Catholics within their boundaries charitably or else jeopardize military alliances struck with countries inhabited by majority Catholic populations such as France and Spain. Samuel Clark supplies us with a number of examples from the seventeenth and eighteenth centuries in which minority populations – Catholics and others – were tolerated in circumstances of international competition.[39]

This is not to suggest that anti-Catholicism did not undergo a "softening" over the course of the eighteenth century in the British Isles; a larger number of Protestants became more accommodating of Catholics over time as a result of the forces already described. But powerful political actors were promoting, in many cases successfully, policies tolerant of Catholics in the empire far before the first relief acts were passed in Quebec and Ireland. Perspectives that represent toleration as a phenomenon peculiar to the late eighteenth century have difficulty accounting for these outcomes.

A change in focus away from *why* policies toward Catholics became increasingly charitable during the late eighteenth century, to *how* those policies were actually enacted allows the question of Catholic relief to be framed in new terms. By acknowledging the influence of political institutions, and the presence of both pro- and anti-Catholic interests in government *throughout* the eighteenth century, policy toward Catholics may be examined through a fresh "lens" so to speak. The analysis is no longer concerned with identifying what factors late in the century induced a more charitable approach to Catholics, but with understanding how, and under what circumstances, toleration was extended to recusants at any particular time and place. Policy toward Catholics in the eighteenth century becomes not a straightforward manifestation of the intentions of officials, but the outcome of a contest between pro- and anti-Catholic forces interacting within a particular institutional environment. The "movement" toward Catholic relief is no longer a steady march from restrictive to more charitable policies, but a series of discrete events in which the option of extending concessions to Catholics became more regular and recurring while other alternatives were increasingly discarded or ignored. The goal is to examine closely these discrete events, grasp the conditions that encouraged the emergence of a particular policy, and discern whether the factors surrounding that outcome affected subsequent measures and how.

Such a recasting is better able to absorb discrepancies in the treatment of Catholics across the empire in the eighteenth century. The process leading to Catholic emancipation is allowed to follow its actual, rockier path; policy is permitted to take steps "backward" occasionally as well as "forward" even while the overall trend is toward concessions. Officials are not required to extend freedoms in a purposeful and rational manner; neither are they required to have undergone a transformation from a provincial to a more practical mindset by the 1770s. Rationality and practicality as applied to legislation toward Catholics become learned responses, born of particular circumstances, and confirmed by past decisions, but not applied automatically to all situations once tried. The picture that emerges resembles less a smooth progression of events than a "build up" of a more tolerant treatment of Catholics in the empire.

The specificity demanded of this approach requires that particular pieces of legislation be examined closely to ascertain the distribution of interests and how the institutions and other factors surrounding the process of negotiation affected policy outcomes. The cases that will be examined, and the framework within which the investigation will take place, are the subjects of the next chapter.

Notes

1. Jacqueline Hill, "Religious Toleration and the Relaxation of the Penal Laws: An Imperial Perspective," *Archivium Hibernicum* 44 (1989), 98-109.

2. Hill, "Religious Toleration," 100.

3. Thomas Bartlett, *The Rise and Fall of the Irish Nation: The Catholic Question 1690-1830* (Dublin: Gill and Macmillan, 1992), 66.

4. Hill, "Religious Toleration," 107.

5. Thomas Bartlett, "The Origins and Progress of the Catholic Question in Ireland, 1760-1800," in *Endurance and Emergence* (Dublin: Irish Academic Press, 1990), 15.

6. Hill, "Religious Toleration," 99.

7. James Kelly, "Interdenominational Relations and Religious Toleration in Late-Eighteenth Century Ireland," in *Eighteenth-Century Ireland* 3 (1988), 41; J. C. Beckett, "Introduction," in *A New History of Ireland* (Oxford: Clarendon Press, 1986), liv. Kelly refers to a growing liberalism in Irish Protestantism and that writes that "the first tangible result of this disposition towards toleration was the 1778 Catholic Relief Act." Beckett writes that "Tolerance, which earlier ages had regarded as a sin, came to be regarded as a virtue. This more charitable attitude . . . prepared protestant opinion for a gradual relaxation of the penal code."

8. James Kelly, "The Genesis of Protestant Ascendancy," in *Parliament, Politics, and People: Essays in Eighteenth-Century Irish History* (Dublin: Irish Academic Press, 1989), 97.

9. Francis James, *Lords of the Ascendancy* (Dublin: Irish Academic Press, 1995), 164-65.

10. Bartlett, *Rise and Fall*, 66-72. See also Bartlett, "The Origins and Progress of the Catholic Question," 7-8.

11. Colin Haydon, *Anti-Catholicism in Eighteenth-Century England, c. 1714-1780* (Manchester: Manchester University Press, 1993).

12. Martin Fitzpatrick, "Toleration and the Enlightenment Movement," in *Toleration in Enlightenment Europe* (Cambridge: Cambridge University Press, 2000), 41.

13. Susan Mann Trofimenkoff, *The Dream of Nation: A Social and Intellectual History of Quebec* (Toronto: Gage Publishing Ltd., 1983), 20.

14. Philip Lawson, "'Sapped by Corruption': British Governance of Quebec and the

Breakdown of Anglo-American Relations on the Eve of the Revolution," *Canadian Review of American Studies* 22, no. 3 (1991): 301. See also R. Coupland, *The Quebec Act* (Oxford: Clarendon Press, 1925); Francis Parkman, *France and England in North America: 10 volumes* (Boston: Little Brown & Company, 1851-1892).

15. Dale Miquelon, ed., *Society and Conquest: The Debate on the Bourgeoisie and Social Change in French Canada 1700-1850* (Toronto: Copp Clark Publishing, 1977). Miquelon provides an overview of the French-Canadian nationalist literature.

16. Karen Stanbridge, "The French-Canadian Bourgeois Debate: History and the Ideology of Colonialism," *International Journal of Comparative Race and Ethnic Studies* 1, no. 1(1994): 127-33.

17. David Milobar, "Quebec Reform, the British Constitution and the Atlantic Empire: 1774-1775," in *Parliament and the Atlantic Empire,* ed. P. Lawson (Edinburgh: Edinburgh University Press, 1995), 73-79.

18. Nicholas Canny, *Kingdom and Colony: Ireland in the Atlantic World, 1560-1800* (Baltimore: John Hopkins University Press, 1988); S. J. Connolly, *Religion, Law and Power: The Making of Protestant Ireland, 1660-1760* (Oxford: Clarendon Press, 1992); C. D. A. Leighton, *Catholicism in a Protestant Kingdom: A Study of the Irish Ancien Regime* (New York: St Martin's Press, 1994).

19. Hill, "Religious Toleration."

20. John Bartlet Brebner, *New England's Outpost: Acadia Before the Conquest of Canada* (Hamden, Connecticut: Archon Books, 1965).

21. G. P. Browne, "James Murray," *Dictionary of Canadian Biography IV, 1771-1800* (Toronto: University of Toronto Press, 1979), 571. In 1765, the Governor of Quebec, James Murray, recommended that the Acadians remaining in Bonaventure be removed.

22. John Garner, "The Enfranchisement of Roman Catholics in the Maritimes," *Canadian Historical Review* 34, no. 3 (1953): 203-18; Hans Rollmann, "Richard Edwards, John Campbell, and the Proclamation of Religious Liberty in Eighteenth-century Newfoundland," *Newfoundland Quarterly* 80, no. 2 (1984): 4-12.

23. Beverley Steele, "Grenada, an Island State, its History and its People," Caribbean Quarterly 20, no. 1 (1974): 5-43. France recaptured Grenada in 1779 during the American war. The island was returned to Britain in 1784 by the Treaty of Versailles. This time, French Catholic inhabitants were denied all political rights. The oath against transubstantiation was resurrected, closing off Catholic access to Grenada's assembly Roman Catholic churches and church properties were confiscated and conferred to the Protestant church or the crown. And all "popish emblems" – statues, altars, etc. – were ordered put to flames.

24. Haydon, *Anti-Catholicism in Eighteenth-Century England,*169-72.

25. Samuel Clark, "International Competition and the Treatment of Minorities: Seventeenth-century Cases and General Propositions," *American Journal of Sociology* 103, no. 5 (1998): 1267-1308.

26. Maurice O'Connell, *Irish Politics and Social Conflict in the Age of the American Revolution (*Philadelphia: University of Philadelphia Press, 1965), 107.

27. David Dickson, *New Foundations: Ireland 1660-1800* (Dublin: Irish Academic Press, 2000); Bartlett, *Rise and Fall.*

28. Robert Donovan, "The Military Origins of the Roman Catholic Relief Programme of 1778," *The Historical Journal* 28, no. 1 (1985): 79-102.

29. C. S. S. Higham, "The General Assembly of the Leeward Islands, Part II," *English Historical Review* 41, no. 163 (1926): 375n.

30. Dickson, *New Foundations.*

31. Bartlett, *Rise and Fall.*

32. Ibid., 83. Bartlett writes, "it was felt that Catholic Relief Acts in Scotland, England and especially Ireland (*Quebec had already got its 'Relief Act' in 1774*) would not only help recruitment but would also fix the allegiance of the different Catholic populations...." (emphasis added).

33. Donovan, "The Military Origins," 90.

34. Robin E. Close, "Toleration and its Limits in the Late Hanoverian Empire: the Cape Colony 1795-1828," in *Hanoverian Britain and Empire: Essays in Memory of Philip Lawson*, ed. S. Taylor et al. (Woodbridge: The Boydell Press, 1998), 299-317; Philip Lawson, *The East India Company: A History* (London: Longman, 1993).

35. Haydon, *Anti-Catholicism in Eighteenth-Century England.*

36. Ibid.,181.

37. Colin Haydon, "Parliament and Popery in England, 1700-1780," *Parliamentary History* 19, no. 1 (2000): 49-63.

38. Stephen Baxter, *William III* (London: Longmans, 1966), 130-31. See also Wouter Troost, *William III and the Treaty of Limerick (1691-1697): A Study of His Irish Policy* (Leiden: Wouter Troost, 1983), *passim.*

39. Clark, "International Competition and the Treatment of Minorities."

Chapter 2

Approach and Historical Cases

When asking *how* policy toward Catholics became more charitable over the course of the eighteenth century, attention should be paid to two neglected areas: the political mechanisms by which policies were promulgated in a particular region of the empire, and the distribution of influence between pro- and anti-Catholic forces during policy negotiations. The first addresses the tendency in the literature to treat religious policy as the direct manifestation of the intentions of officials and ignore the impact of the structures surrounding the political process on policy outcomes. The second acknowledges that religious policy was, at all times during the century, a *negotiated* outcome and not the result of unilateral decisionmaking on the part of officials who were either intolerant (in the first half of the century) or tolerant (in the latter half of the century). To explore these issues, the current study will make use of the *institutional approach*. The analysis will apply the approach to three pieces of legislation that occupied strategic locations in the "movement" toward Catholic relief to ascertain how institutions shaped the formulation of those specific directives and the ways in which they contributed to the larger trend toward policies more tolerant of Catholics in the empire.

The Institutional Approach

The past twenty years has seen a resurgence in the interests of social scientists in the influence of institutions on social life, a rediscovery, writes John Campbell that "has become somewhat of an academic growth industry."[1] "Institutionalists" have appeared in most of the social sciences all sharing the general conviction that complex organizations are more than the sum of their parts, and the institutions that comprise organizations affect human behavior to a greater extent than is often allowed by agential approaches.

Beyond this basic assumption, however, institutionalists vary widely in their subject matter and methodology. One chronicler of the "new institutionalist" movement has identified no less that seven distinct schools of institutionalist research.[2] This internal diversity can be explained, in part, by the fact that the institutionalist schools in each discipline have emerged and developed in relative isolation. Hence, economics has produced "rational-choice institutionalism," sociology a peculiarly "sociological institutionalism," and so on.

Sociology has, of course, had a long and rich tradition of institutional research, and so it is not surprising that it has been influenced by this movement. Indeed, in the most recent classifications of perspectives comprising "the new institutionalism," sociological institutionalism is invariably treated as one of the most promising and vigorous areas of study. Although many areas of sociology have been affected,[3] it is researchers who study organizations and organizational behavior that seem to have responded most strongly to the trend.

According to Peter Hall and Rosemary Taylor, sociological institutionalism emerged as a critical response to traditional approaches that understood organizational uniformity – in particular, the widespread and consistent adoption of bureaucratic structures in diverse areas of modern society – as the manifestation of a rationality or efficiency inherent to the structure itself.[4] Skeptics argued that these institutional forms emerged and were fostered not because they were the most functional or efficient; rather, they comprised sets of culturally specific practices that were promulgated via the same processes that transmit cultural practices in general. These critics maintained that, to understand institutions, it was necessary for analysts to look to cultural factors; to capture why institutional forms and procedures are so similar in such different types of organizations, researchers needed to grasp how these forms were transmitted and diffused by means of culture, rather than assume their commonality represented the culmination of an evolutionary trend of institutional development.

The notion that institutional structures are created, that they emerge, endure, change and disappear, as the result of the actions of individuals interacting within a particular cultural milieu, is perhaps sociology's greatest contribution to institutional research. But while the focus of sociology's institutionalists has to this point been on organizations of the "middle-range," they have largely neglected the state as an object of study, preferring to treat it as an external pressure or influence.[5] This is problematic from the standpoint of the current study as it is the origins and formulation of state policy toward Catholics with which it is most concerned. In contrast, the state figures prominently in the work of institutionalists in political science who use the institutional approach to explain the policy outcomes of modern states.

Perhaps the institutionalist school most closely aligned with political science is the *rational choice tradition*. Like other adherents to rational choice theory, rational choice institutionalists focus on the utility-maximizing individual. They recognize, however, that actors may realize that the most effective way to achieve their goals is by means of institutions, and so will shape their actions to align with those structures. "Thus," writes Guy Peters, "in this view, individuals rationally choose to be to some extent constrained by their membership in institutions, whether that membership is voluntary or not."[6] Arising originally out of investigations of American congressional behavior, rational choice institutionalists in political science have gone on to research how other political institutions, such as political parties, cabinets and bureaucracies, structure actor behavior and policy outcomes.[7] Peters includes within the general rubric of rational choice institutionalism "empirical institutionalism," a school of institutionalism in the political sciences that seeks to measure empirically the impact of institutions on individuals participating in a particular institution.[8]

But while the institutionalisms of political science focus squarely on the state and its structures, they are not without their difficulties. Scholars adhering to a more "sociological" approach to political decisionmaking have questioned the primacy that rational choice institutionalists assign to self-interest as a motivator. They argue that cultural factors such as norms and ideology exert as great an influence on individual decisionmaking as utility maximization.[9] Further, if sociological institutionalism emphasizes the interaction of individual agency and institutions to the neglect of the state, approaches in political science emphasize the state at the expense of such reflexivity. Rational choice and empirical institutionalist perspectives are static and unidirectional compared to their counterpart in sociology, concerned with explaining how institutions affect behavior, but not as concerned with how that behavior influences institutions. Clearly, a framework that seeks to combine the best features of each "school" would be desirable.

"Historical institutionalism" is an approach that begins to address some of these issues. John Campbell classifies historical institutionalism as a form of institutionalism, along with organizational analysis, that has arisen in political studies to counter the "calculus" approach to institutions that accentuates "cost-benefit" analyses of institutional behavior. Historical institutionalism "argues that actors are driven more by concerns for doing what is institutionally possible or culturally appropriate."[10] Political "decision-making and institutional change is driven less by quests for efficiency than by a path dependent process in which previous decisions and institutional arrangements constrain and facilitate the emergence of new ones."[11]

Historical institutionalism is characterized by a number of features that suggest it is a framework suited to the current investigation of religious toleration. Historical institutionalism does not require that political actors behave "rationally," an assumption that was shown to be difficult to substantiate when the circumstances surrounding the passage of certain measures were examined closely. While the perspective does not deny that individuals act strategically or purposefully, it recognizes that behavior is shaped by the "path dependence" of previous institutional arrangements. This point is lost in accounts that assume legislation was the direct manifestation of the intentions of officials and ignore how the inertia contained in over a century of legislated anti-Catholicism affected the inception and unfolding of the "movement" toward Catholic relief. It recognizes that a policy of toleration was not simply a function of the changing perceptions of administrators, but was affected by past choices and so may not have constituted itself as readily as has often been implied. Historical institutionalism also emphasizes how "institutional possibility" can influence political outcomes by affecting power relations. Institutions "distribute power unevenly across social groups" and "give some groups or interests disproportionate access to the decision-making process."[12] The approach thus acknowledges competing interests and can serve as a framework to explore how pro- and anti-Catholic forces were arrayed during policy negotiations. Finally, its materialist position highlights the importance of close examination of historical evidence to substantiate any claims concerning the policy toward Catholics in this period, an approach that can help to stave off erroneous assumptions concerning the origins of policies and linkages between them.

While historical institutionalism is more befitting of the current investigation than the rational choice perspective, it still poses some difficulties with respect to the reflexivity issue. It nevertheless provides a good place to start. A more detailed description of the historical institutionalist method is preceded by a clarification of concepts and terms shared by the institutionalist literature.

Some Definitions[13]

Institutionalists in the political sciences argue, very basically, that "the state" has an influence on policymaking independent of the individuals and groups involved in the formulation of state policy. It exerts this influence by means of institutions or "institutional factors."

"Institution" as it is used by institutionalists, historical or otherwise, has been criticized for its imprecision, and it is true that it remains a fairly open concept.[14] It does not, however, defy definition. Peter Hall's is probably the most widely accepted. He defines institutions as "the formal rules, compliance procedures, and standard operating practices that structure the relationship between individuals in various units of the polity and economy."[15] Guy Peters provides a down-to-earth example:

> Individuals may decide to meet for coffee one afternoon. That could be very pleasant, but it would not be an institution. If they decide to meet every Thursday afternoon at the same time and place, that would begin to take on the features of an institution. Further, if those people are all senators then the meeting may be relevant for our concern with institutions in political science.[16]

The basic characteristics that emerge from Peters' example establish that an institution is *structural*, in that it "transcends individuals to involve groups of individuals in some sort of *patterned interactions* that are *predictable* based upon *specified relationships among the actors*."[17] Further, those patterned interactions have to exhibit some *stability* over time. Finally, the institution must *affect individual behavior*. Peters' "coffee klatch" may be entirely voluntary. Nevertheless, the very regularity of the coffee break/institution comes to affect the activities of the individuals involved. It may also have an influence on individuals and events outside the people directly involved. The restrictions and responsibilities associated with such a routine are, of course, very informal. Nevertheless, the routine actions of the individuals, this "institution" of the coffee break, comes to affect the way in which the people involved, and even those less close to the situation, behave, independent of other factors like personal will. They are not forced to comply with the institution, and may even choose noncompliance, but they must at least take it into account when framing their activities. To move the discussion more directly on to the state, when individuals come together in organizations like government, their activities in various areas often become regular and recurring. When these patterns of interaction are repeated, they become institutionalized, that is they become accepted as "the way things are done." Institutions are then patterns of behavior that have their origins in past interactions, and that have acquired a certain durability, or "stickiness," enough to require that contemporary actors abide by them, or at least take them into account, when formulating policy.

Institutions can be formalized. The most formal institutional factors in the political realm are written laws and the state constitution. They make up the foundation of the policymaking process and define its fundamental bounds. Institutions can remain informal. Informal institutional factors are organizational norms, routine procedures and so forth. They may not be quite as rigid or enduring as formal factors, but informal institutional factors can have an important influence on policymaking activities.

Historical Institutionalism

Historical institutionalists maintain that institutions influence policymaking in two main ways. First, they help determine which actors are eligible to participate in the policymaking process, and the distribution of power amongst those actors. They have an important impact on policy outcomes because they constrain or enable the capacity of some actors over others to have a say in the political process. Second, they structure the relations and activities surrounding policymaking, defining the "rules" by which the actors must play when formulating policy. In other words, institutions influence who can take part in the policymaking process and define the bounds of what they can do when they are there.

All other things being equal, state officials will hold the most power in the policymaking process. This is because the organization they represent holds jurisdictional dominance; "the state," by whatever means, has procured the right to promulgate policy in a particular area. Jurisdictional dominance, however, does not mean that these officials can act autonomously or that institutional factors will always benefit state administrators. Depending on how policymaking was organized in the past, current administrators may find that, because of institutional constraints, they must abide by procedures or take into account demands that are detrimental to their interests or contrary to their own opinions. On the other hand, by defining the institutional responsibilities of actors and their relationship to other actors, institutional factors help actors to formulate their aims and determine how best to approach any given policymaking process. Institutional factors may, for example, create circumstances that are unfavorable to a certain set of actors, but may also assist those actors in devising their best course of action.

This last point demonstrates how institutions, while they certainly *delimit* behavior, can also *empower* actors in various ways by shaping their aims and strategies, even their preferences, interests and other motivations. They do this by influencing the ways in which these actors come together, their patterns of interaction and opportunity structures.[18] This is not to say that institutions compel political actors to believe in certain things, or behave in rigid and prescribed ways, although the more formal the institution certainly the more predictable the approach of the actors with respect to that institutional context will be. The picture that emerges, rather, is one of actors exercising "choice within constraints." Individuals and groups are "free-willed," they choose how they will act and respond to various political circumstances. Those choices, however, are not limitless; they are constrained to some extent by the institutions characterizing the political environment and the cultural precedents that they support. Depending on how power is arrayed within a particular institutional context, actors can manipulate their impact on policymaking procedures in a number of ways. They can work with the institutions surrounding the process, work around them, formulate strategies or modify their makeup to improve their chances of succeeding within them, even attempt to change them. Of course their success in any of these endeavors will be influenced by the actions of other actors, including state officials, in the policy domain, as they too try to better their chances relative to the institutions governing the policymaking process.

Clearly, the emphasis of the historical institutional approach is on structure. Its primary aim is to show how state institutions, by shaping the activities of the individuals involved in policymaking, come to affect policy outcomes. The approach does not claim, however, that institutions are the only factors that cause policy outcomes. It does not deny that other factors, such as human agency and historical contingency, such as socioeconomic development and the diffusion of ideas, have a role to play in the policymaking process. "In this respect," write Hall and Taylor, "[historical institutionalism] posit[s] a world that is more complex than the world of tastes and institutions often postulated by rational choice institution-alism[s]."[19] These factors, however, must be considered within a particular institutional context. By influencing the way in which the policy process is conducted, by constraining, enabling and otherwise affecting the actors taking part in the process, institutions have an important effect on government directives. Although institutions are the focus, the institutional approach requires that the other factors and forces impacting on policymaking are specified in order to assess how and to what extent institutions affect them and so affect policy.

Historical Institutionalism and Social Change

The capacity of the historical institutionalist approach to help to explode the "black box" of the state and reveal how particular government policy is formed is one of its greatest strengths. Historical institutionalists have demonstrated the importance of specifying the institutions affecting government policymaking to acquire a grasp of why and how certain legislation came to be. Studies by Theda Skocpol, Peter Hall, Grace Skogstad, Michael Atkinson and William Coleman, and numerous others have shown how the institutional approach can help us to understand the expansion of pensions for Civil War veterans and survivors and the implementation of social policies for mothers in the nineteenth century[20]; why different Western nations chose such different policies and political strategies to deal with similar economic problems in the early 1980s[21]; the reasons agriculture was included in the Canada-U.S. Free Trade negotiations in the late 1980s and how and why different commodities were incorporated[22]; and the kind of industrial policy that would be most suited to Canada's economy.[23] Historical institutionalists are also unique in their adoption of a more "sociological" approach to the study of institutions. Judith Goldstein, Margaret Weir, Peter Hall and others, for example, explore the linkages between the nature of political institutions and prevailing ideas or beliefs.[24] The results of these and other studies have shown how paying attention to the institutional context surrounding policymaking can cast new light on conventional views of how state policy is formed.

Historical institutionalists have been less prolific in the areas of institutional and policy *change*, however. Indeed, it is their relative quiescence on the matter of institutional change that has garnered them the most negative attention from critics. Institutionalists have produced more works demonstrating how stable institutions influence behavior and policy in the short term. This focus has prompted critics to charge that the approach is static and structurally deterministic, concerned more with how institutions endure and how they constrain human behavior than with how human behavior and action give rise to and/or alter institutions, and in turn government policy, over a more protracted period.[25]

As Hall and Taylor have pointed out, this is to some extent an empty criticism; institutionalists have never hidden their predilection for the structural. The charge, for example, that historical institutionalism is prone to a "latent structuralism" lends a false intrigue to what has always been a manifest feature of the framework.[26] Indeed, to preserve the "analytical distinctiveness" of the approach, ". . . institutionalists must remain structuralist at least in the sense that they seek to reveal how institutions shape social and political life."[27] Nevertheless, the absence of a dynamic element in historical institutionalism presents a problem to the current study, as it seeks to explore linkages between policy toward Catholics in the eighteenth century and institutional variation and change in the political realm.

Criticisms have prompted proponents of the historical institutionalist approach to explore the sources and character of institutional change. Early attempts presented institutions as stable until they were disrupted by some exogenous force (war, revolution, global economic changes). At these times, the usual "path dependency" of existing institutions, i.e., the "inertial tendency" for institutions to persist once they have been established, was destroyed.[28] Once the new institutions that emerged from these unsettled periods were stipulated, they acquired a "stickiness" of their own, and set the bounds for future action.

This "punctuated equilibria" approach to institutional change has been refined considerably in recent years. As Elisabeth Clemens and James Cook report the "causal imagery of some external force or legislative *deus ex machina* smacking into stable institutional arrangements and creating indeterminancy" has been replaced by more sophisticated representations of institutional change.[29] Many still focus on "critical junctures" or "constitutive moments" in the existence of institutions, but these "moments" are not prompted only by factors outside the institutional arrangement. Culture, idealistic motivations, individual agency, internal contradictions, as well as the *mutability* (i.e., the degree to which an institution can accommodate heterogeneity of action) of institutions and the *density* (i.e., the degree to which different institutions overlap with respect to the behavior that they encourage) of the institutional networks to which they belong can produce institutional change.[30]

These types of studies demonstrate attempts by historical institutionalists to tackle the reflexivity issue; to clarify not only how institutions affect individual behavior, but how individuals, along with other factors and forces, shape and alter institutions. They recognize that, although institutions influence the people engaged in the policymaking process, institutional factors are not fixed. Because they arise out of human interaction, all are subject to modification, or even elimination, by human activity. New choices and decisions on the part of individuals continually transform existing institutions. These changes can be purposive (as are those that occur when a government administration introduces modifications to an existing system) or involuntary (as a result of continual minor modifications to routine behavior), incremental, or dramatic (as in the case of revolution). Furthermore, events outside the immediate institutional context help to shape how institutions and individual action interact by helping determine whether patterns of behavior are perpetuated and institutionalized. It is true that some institutions will be more susceptible to change than others. Formal institutions such as the legal code or the constitution are less likely to change because they tend to be entrenched in the political system in very tangible ways and so require more effort, purposeful or otherwise, to alter them. Informal institutional factors are more vulnerable to change because of their less ceremonious nature. The goal in all cases, however, is to locate the sources of change, interpret its nature and establish how changes in turn modify subsequent behaviors.

Historical institutionalists continue to refine their conceptualizations of institutional change. The inductive approach to the material, although it represents a fundamental feature of historical institutional analysis, has militated against the rapid development of a concise "theory" of change, however. Consequently, there exist few statements of the institutionalist approach to change. Nevertheless, it is on these newer studies that explore institutional formation and change and their association with policy change that the current study will draw.

Institutionalism and Catholic Relief

Having outlined the general approach taken by historical institutionalists in the study of the state and institutional change, there remains the challenge of applying the framework to the investigation of policy toward Catholics in the British empire during the eighteenth century. This work will focus on three pieces of Catholic legislation: the bill to ratify the Treaty of Limerick (1697), an anti-Catholic measure, and two relief measures, the Quebec Act (1774) and the first Irish Catholic Relief Act (1778). All three measures have been identified by writers concerned with Irish and/or Canadian history as precedent-setting. The Treaty of Limerick ratification bill signaled the onset of the penal era in Ireland; the Irish Catholic Relief Act represented the "beginning of the end" of that era; and the Quebec Act was the precursor to the more tolerant measures that were to follow in succeeding decades in the rest of the empire. These policies occupy crucial positions in what has been viewed as the long-term trend toward Catholic relief in the empire. This is especially true of the Quebec Act and the Irish Catholic Relief Act, which have been understood to form the foundations of the more general movement from repressive to more tolerant religious policy. The links between these policy events have, however, been largely assumed rather than demonstrated. As a result, their nature has remained somewhat obscured.

By focusing on critical Irish legislation at the beginning and latter half of the century the interaction between institutions and policy change in Ireland can be observed over time. The inclusion of the Quebec Act permits comparison of concurrent legislation toward Catholics in two different areas of the empire and exploration of why religious policy varied so dramatically across territories, particularly in the latter half of the century. Further, conditions surrounding the promulgation of the Quebec Act were broadly similar to those in place at the time of the passage of the Treaty of Limerick bill. Both the Treaty and the Quebec bills were preceded by "revolutions" of sorts. The Treaty of Limerick bill followed the so-called Glorious Revolution of 1688 that saw William III and Mary assume the English throne and represented a crucial stage in what is understood to be the "rise" of the English Parliament relative to the English Crown. The Quebec Act came after the "revolution" in imperial governance wrought by the end of the Seven Years' War and the expansion of the British empire to include many new, far-flung and diverse territories. In both situations, government officials were confronted with questions concerning governance in a periphery inhabited by a majority of Roman Catholics. Assessing the role that institutions, both stable and developing, played in the processes surrounding the passage of each Act may help to explain why and how events unfolded so differently in each place.

Institutions

The institutions that will serve as the focus and form the bounds of this investigation belong to the polity. Whether formal or informal, they are structures that shaped the actions of individuals and groups engaged in political pursuits in important ways.

Institutions identified as formal are invariably institutions that were explicitly defined, either in the form of a constitution, or in the legal code. Formal institutions are the most durable of the institutions aligned with the political realm, and specify the fundamental bases of the relationships between political actors. Although their formality demands that their existence must always be taken into account, their ambiguity, to the extent that they do not specify exact or day-to-day relationships or actions, allows for some freedom of action within their bounds.

Informal institutions are the norms, rules and standard operating procedures that guide the behavior of individuals and groups within the political realm but are not specified by the constitution or legal code. These include established patterns of interaction between ministers, between ministers and departments, between departments and politicized groups in larger society and so forth. While they must comply with the formal institutions setting the bounds of political activity, informal institutions are considerably more "fluid" with respect to their makeup.

The very formality of formal institutions makes them relatively easy to describe and define. The "birth" of a constitution or the passage of a law can be dated, the contents of each referred to explicitly. Changes and/or additions to formal institutions can be readily ascertained. Not so in the case of informal institutions. Although they, like formal institutions, arise out of the patterned interactions of individuals and groups engaged in political pursuits, informal institutions are never "born" so much as they develop or are adopted, sometimes refined and maintained, at other times abandoned or replaced. The whole process is much more nebulous and so is more difficult to specify. Hence, those portions of the historical cases that deal with the emergence and perpetuation of informal institutions affecting legislation are more prolonged, the description of factors contributing to their creation and maintenance often more detailed, than in the case of formal institutions.

Chapter Outline

The following chapters present analyses of the Treaty of Limerick ratification bill (chapter 3), the Quebec Act (chapters 4 and 5) and the Irish Catholic Relief Act (chapter 6). In each case, the historical material will be presented roughly as follows. First, a brief sketch of the events surrounding the formulation and passage of the legislation will be provided. Then the fundamental formal and informal institutions associated with government policymaking will be described. Next, the major actors involved in the legislation process as defined by these institutions will be identified, and their sentiments concerning Catholic policy – so far as they can be ascertained – assessed to determine how pro- and anti-Catholic interests were arrayed. Finally, the events surrounding the formulation and passage of the particular legislation will be examined in detail, ending with an evaluation of how institutions influenced the policy outcome. These sections will place special emphasis on identifying and explaining institutional formation and change, why and how new institutions were created and perpetuated, or existing ones modified or eliminated, and how these changes affected the strategies and aims of the players involved in the policy processes and so influenced resulting legislation.

The conclusions will bring together the results of all three sections to determine how a historical institutional approach to legislation affecting Catholics in the eighteenth-century British empire can help to clarify the circumstances surrounding the adoption of any particular policy, and elucidate the linkages between the events that comprised the trend toward legislating policies more tolerant of Catholics and Catholicism in these two peripheries. By exploring *how* officials instituted toleration, the analysis seeks to provide a supplement to studies focusing on *why* a policy of charity came to overtake one of repression, contributing to a fuller picture of the overall "movement" toward Catholic relief.

Notes

1. John Campbell, "Recent Trends in Institutional Political Economy," *International Journal of Sociology and Social Policy* 17, no. 7 (1997), 15.

2. B. Guy Peters, *Institutional Theory in Political Science: The 'New Institutionalism'* (London: Pinter, 1999).

3. William Dugger, "Comparison of Marxism and Institutionalism," *Journal of Economic Issues* 28, no. 1 (1994), 101-27; Gunnar Grenstad, "Cultural Theory and the New Institutionalism," *Journal of Theoretical Politics* 7, no. 1 (1995), 5-27; John T. Harvey, "Symbolic Interactionism and Institutionalism: Common Roots," *Journal of Economic Issues* 26, no. 3 (1992), 791-812; Roland Hoksberger, "Postmodernism and Institutionalism: Toward a Resolution of the Debate on Relativism," *Journal of Economic Issues* 28, no. 3 (1994), 679-713.

4. Peter Hall and Rosemary Taylor, "Political Science and the Three New Institutionalisms," *Political Studies* 44, no. 5 (1996), 936-57.

5. Lynn Zucker, "Institutional Theories of Organizations," *Annual Review of Sociology* 13 (1987), 443-64.

6. Peters, *Institutional Theory in Political Science*, 44.

7. Hall and Taylor, "Political Science," 942-46; Peters, *Institutional Theory in Political Science*, chapter 3.

8. Peters, *Institutional Theory in Political Science*, 145-46.

9. John Campbell, "Recent Trends in Institutional Political Economy," *International Journal of Sociology and Social Policy* 17, no. 7 (1997), 15-56.

10. Ibid., 16.

11. Ibid., 16.

12. Hall and Taylor, "Political Science," 941.

13. The following is a synopsis of the descriptions of and ideas associated with the (historical) institutionalist approach provided by Campbell, "Recent Trends"; Elisabeth Clemens and James Cook, "Politics and Institutionalism: Explaining Durability and Change," *Annual Review of Sociology* 25 (1999), 441-66; John Dearlove, "Bringing the Constitution Back In: Political Science and the State," *Political Studies* 37, no. 4 (1989), 521-39; Peter Hall, *Governing the Economy: The Politics of State Intervention in Britain*

and France (Cambridge: Polity Press, 1986); Hall and Taylor, "Political Science," 936-57; Peter Hall and Rosemary Taylor, "The Potential of Historical Institutionalism: A Response to Hay and Wincott," *Political Studies* 46, no. 5 (1998), 958-62; G. John Ikenberry, "Conclusion: An Institutional Approach to American Foreign Economic Policy," *International Organization* 42, no. 1 (1988), 219-43; James G. March and Johan P. Olsen, "The New Institutionalism: Organizational Factors in Political Life," *American Political Science Review* 78, no. 3 (1984); and Peters, *Institutional Theory in Political Science.*

14. Peters, *Institutional Theory in Political Science*, 65.

15. Hall, *Governing the Economy*, 19.

16. Peters, *Institutional Theory in Political Science*, 18.

17. Ibid. (emphasis added).

18. Campbell, "Recent Trends," 22.

19. Hall and Taylor, "Political Science," 942.

20. Theda Skocpol, *Protecting Soldiers and Mothers: The Political Origins of Social Policy in the U.S.* (Cambridge, Mass.: Belknap Press of Harvard University Press, 1992).

21. Hall, *Governing the Economy.*

22. Grace Skogstad, "The State, Organized Interests and Canadian Agricultural Trade Policy: The Impact of Institutions," *Canadian Journal of Political Science* 25, no. 2 (1992), 319-47.

23. Michael M. Atkinson and William D. Coleman, *The State, Business, and Industrial Change in Canada* (Toronto: University of Toronto Press, 1989).

24. Judith Goldstein, "Ideas, Institutions, and American Trade Policy." *International Organization* 42, no. 1 (1988), 179-217.

25. Campbell, "Recent Trends"; Colin Hay and Daniel Wincott, "Structure, Agency and Historical Institutionalism," *Political Studies* 46, no. 5 (1998), 951-57; Peters, *Institutional Theory in Political Science*, 70.

26. Hay and Wincott, "Structure," 952.

27. Hall and Taylor, "Political Science," 959.

28. Peters, *Institutional Theory in Political Science*, 63.

29. Clemens and Cook, "Politics and Institutionalism," 447.

30. For examples of recent research that explores institutional change, see Sven Steinmo, Kathleen Thelen and Frank Longstreth, eds., *Structuring Politics: Historical Institutionalism in Comparative Analysis* (Cambridge: Cambridge University Press, 1997).

Chapter 3

The Treaty of Limerick Ratification Bill

The Treaty of Limerick signaled the end of the Jacobite war in Ireland. Protestant alarm at the blatantly pro-Catholic stance and conduct of the Irish administration appointed by James II turned to religious warfare soon after news reached Ireland of William III's landing in England in November 1688. Louis XIV recognized an opportunity to tie up William's forces in Ireland and so improve France's prospects on the continent. He urged James II, who had fled to France on William's arrival in England, to go to Ireland and take over control of the predominantly Catholic Stuart forces from his lord deputy in the field, the earl of Tyrconnell. When James arrived in Ireland four months later with a bevy of French troops, the kingdom was drawn irrevocably into the larger disputes concerning the English constitution and the rivalry between England and France.

The war in Ireland was a thorn in William's side, an "exasperating sideshow" writes J. G. Simms, to his campaigns against Louis XIV and his allies. William wished to bring the Irish war to a speedy end to free up troops for battle on the continent. By the spring of 1690, however, Williamite forces had failed to induce the Jacobite surrender the king had hoped for. He left the continent for Ireland to take care of matters himself.

William landed near Carrickfergus on 14 June 1690 with enough troops and artillery to overwhelm his opponents. William's defeat of the Jacobite forces at the Boyne on 1 July 1690 was decisive, but he was premature in thinking that he had destroyed his opposition. The Boyne victory was followed by successes at Cork and Kinsale, but the Williamite advance continued to be hampered by Jacobite resistance. As the conflict dragged on, William (who had left Ireland in September) implored his general in the field, Godard van Reede van Ginkel, to negotiate an end to a war that had already tied up his troops for too long. Ginkel spent the winter and spring of 1690/91 trying to come up with a settlement that would satisfy both sides. He was unsuccessful.

Fighting resumed that summer. Athlone, Aughrim and Galway were taken by Williamite forces in July. The Jacobite army congregated in Limerick. Uncertain of his ability to take the city, and loath to spend another winter in the field, Ginkel continued to press for a settlement. A negotiated settlement became the priority of an increasing number of Jacobites too, as many began to question the wisdom of Tyrconnell's determination to stand firm against William's army and wait for French assistance.[1] Tyrconnell's death in mid-August further undermined the pro-French position. A bloody show of Williamite force on 22 September outside the city finally destroyed the Jacobite resolve to resist. With the presence of an English fleet in the Shannon and no sign that French help would arrive, Jacobite leaders decided that a negotiated settlement would be in their best interest. On 23 September, they approached the Williamite camp and asked for a capitulation and a cease-fire. After ten days of talks, terms were agreed. The Treaty was signed on 3 October 1691.

The Treaty of Limerick comprised both military and civil articles. The military terms provided for the transport of French troops back to the continent, as well as for any Irish soldiers who wished to enter service abroad. The civil articles stipulated, among other things, that Irish Catholics could continue to exercise their religion, provided it be "consistent with the laws of Ireland" or as those laws existed in the reign of Charles II. They also granted a general pardon to all those surrendering to William in the five counties under the control of the Jacobite army at the time of the Treaty, allowing them to retain their lands, regardless of their religion, provided that they remain in Ireland and take an oath of allegiance to the new rulers. Further, the Treaty stated that William and Mary would do their best to have the articles of the Treaty of Limerick ratified by the Irish Parliament.

The terms of the military articles were carried out by Ginkel without much fanfare. Over the course of the next few months, 11,000 of the 14,000 Irish troops were dispatched to the continent. The civil articles, however, were to prove more contentious. Trouble began shortly after the Treaty's signing when it was discovered that the version of the Treaty sent to England for approval failed to include "all those under their protection in the said counties" as beneficiaries of the terms granted to individuals surrendering in the five counties. Whether this "missing clause" had indeed been part of the original text of the Treaty, as the Irish and the Treaty's authors insisted, or whether, as Protestants claimed, it was a ploy on the part of vanquished Irish Catholics to wrest more assurances from the victors than they were entitled to, was hotly debated. It proved to be a sticking point that contributed to the delay in the ratification of the Treaty that William III and his officials, not to mention Irish Catholics, sought.

The Treaty as it was finally passed by the Irish Parliament in 1697 bore little resemblance to the agreement signed on the battlefield six years earlier. The bill "For the confirmation of the articles made at the surrender of Limerick" contained no reference to the allowances made in the Treaty for the practice of the Catholic religion; neither was there any mention of the article that specified that only the oath of allegiance be demanded. It also altered considerably the terms under which land claims were to be heard, and the controversial "missing clause" was absent. In the six years that it took to ratify the articles of the Treaty of Limerick, the tolerant spirit that had characterized the original Treaty had been suppressed. An examination of the institutions surrounding the events preceding the passage of the Treaty bill will help clarify the circumstances that led to this outcome.

Formal Institutions Characterizing Anglo-Irish Policymaking after the Glorious Revolution

Institutions are the organizational rules or patterns of interaction that constrain and enable the players involved in the policymaking process in various ways. *Formal institutions* are more enduring, more explicitly defined, and less variable than *informal institutions*, such as operational norms and procedures. Although formal institutions are, like all institutions, subject to modification or replacement, they tend, except in the case of revolution or other extreme occurrences, to be slower to change, embedded as they usually are in the constitutional and legal spheres of the polity.

There were two important and connected *formal* institutional arrangements governing Irish policymaking in the late seventeenth century. The first pertained to the constitutional and legal existence of the Irish Parliament, the second to the operation of a statute known as Poynings' Law.

Ireland's Parliamentary Tradition

At the time of the Treaty's signing, Irish policy fell under the jurisdiction of the English state. England ruled Ireland through a Crown-appointed administration and a Parliament consisting of a House of Lords and an elected House of Commons. Originating in the Middle Ages, the Irish Parliament, like its English counterpart, was instituted by Norman conquerors to facilitate communication between the central government and local power holders, men on whom the political center depended to rule in the name of the Crown in the localities.[2] Its potency as a tool of the ruling élite varied over time, however. The Irish Parliament depended on élite participation, and at all times represented a potential locus of opposition to English power over the island.

Participation was the issue in the early years of its existence. Although they exercised considerable influence over the island initially, the Normans had neither the numbers nor the support from English kings to secure and maintain their authority in conquered territories. The native Irish began to retake the parts of Ireland that the Anglo-Normans had seized, gradually reducing the size of the area over which the invaders exercised control.[3] By the fifteenth century, most of Ireland was being ruled by independent magnates, native Irish and "Old English" (as the descendants of the Anglo-Norman invaders came to be called) lords. The power of the royal government was confined largely to the counties surrounding Dublin, an area that was to be referred to as "the English Pale."[4] As Norman power over

Ireland diminished, so too did the jurisdiction of the Irish Parliament. By 1495, the Irish Parliament spoke for only four counties of the English Pale.[5] Furthermore, it was dominated by Old English magnates; the native Irish were not represented. The Tudors improved the representative nature of the Irish Parliament somewhat: native Irish chieftains were allowed to attend Henry VIII's Parliament in 1542, and Elizabeth created a number of new counties during her reign.[6]

While the numbers and area represented by the Irish Parliament expanded, however, its power as a center for local resistance was circumscribed as sessions became less frequent. An Irish Parliament that met almost annually from 1461 to 1494 met only eight times from 1494 to 1536.[7] Henry VIII called his Irish Parliament just six times during his long reign; Mary held one Parliament in 1557-1558, and Elizabeth only three, the last in 1585-1586. The Irish Parliament did not meet again until 1613 under James I.[8]

The frequency of meetings did not improve over the course of the seventeenth century – only four official sessions were held before William III called his first Irish Parliament in 1692. Its authority was limited further as successive monarchs manipulated its composition to enhance their power. To insure that he obtained approval of legislation that would have been opposed by an assembly in which sat a majority of Old English representatives, James I, through his representative in Ireland, Thomas Wentworth, remade the Irish Parliament to his liking. He created 40 new boroughs, most in areas where Protestant English or Scottish had recently settled, and installed 106 new men in the Irish House of Commons, all of whom were loyal to the Crown and "the religion of the court."[9] Many objected to James' actions, especially since most of the new boroughs were "rotten," with few or no inhabitants, and their "representatives" were chosen from the largely Protestant Irish administration. Yet their maintenance was important to the preservation of a "court party" in the Irish Parliament and their validity was confirmed by successive monarchs.[10] This strategy of "Protestant-packing" continued; by the Parliament of 1640, the proportion of Catholics in the Irish Parliament had been reduced by a third since the previous sitting in 1634.[11]

Although its membership was managed for political and religious reasons, although it was often unrepresentative of the élite population and met only sporadically before 1692, the Irish Parliament nevertheless represented a long history of participatory governance in Ireland. Its presence empowered Irish élites and represented a formal restriction on the autonomy of the Crown-appointed administration and on the jurisdiction of English monarchs and ministers over Ireland. It is true that the import of that restriction varied. The primary reason for calling for a session of the Irish Parliament was to vote supplies, and if the hereditary revenues voted in the previous meeting were sufficient to sustain the Irish administration, army and other costs of government, no assembly would be summoned. This was why the Irish Parliament did not meet for twenty-six years after Charles II's Parliament was adjourned in 1667.[12] The Crown was still bound, however, to summon the Irish Parliament periodically. And if the capacity of Parliament to check the authority of the English administration was not always realized, its existence offered the potential for opposition, a formal institution by which Irish élites could exercise some control over legislation affecting Ireland.

Poynings' Law

If the Irish Parliament represented an avenue through which Irish élites had the potential to challenge the power of the English executive, another formal institution was in operation that restricted their competence. From 1495 onward, the power of the Irish Parliament to legislate for Ireland was circumscribed by Poynings' Law. Poynings' Law was instituted in response to the Yorkist leanings of the chief governor of Ireland, the earl of Kildare. In 1487, Kildare called an Irish Parliamentary assembly to declare the Yorkist pretender, Lambert Simnel, the true king of England and lord of Ireland. Although Simnel's attempt to seize the Crown failed, the incident demonstrated that Kildare's power over the Irish Parliament could be a threat to Henry VII. Kildare was dismissed and in his place, Henry installed an Englishman, Sir Edward Poynings. Poynings was assigned the task of consolidating English authority over the Old English on whom the king depended to rule Ireland on his behalf, and refashioning the relationship between the Irish and English governments to prevent any future Irish chief governors from using the Irish Parliament as a cover for treasonable activities. The result was the passage by the Irish Parliament of Poynings' Law.[13]

Poynings' Law stipulated that the Irish Parliament could not originate legislation, pass bills, or even meet, without the approval of the English government. The Irish chief governor and his council were required to submit bills to the monarch and the English Privy Council as grounds for a session. Once the meeting was sanctioned, the English Privy Council and the monarch could accept, modify or reject the bills. Those that were not suppressed were sent back to Ireland where they were voted on by both houses of Irish Parliament. If passed, the Irish chief governor was empowered to give them royal assent and the bill then became law. The bills returned from England could only be accepted or rejected, however; neither house had the power to make amendments to the legislation.[14]

Opinions vary concerning the extent to which Poynings' Law actually restricted the powers of the Irish Parliament. R. Dudley Edwards and T. W. Moody maintained that it was the Irish Parliament, and not the English government, that benefited from Poynings' Law during the first century or so of its existence. Irish MPs exploited the tangle of procedures to obstruct the legislative programs of the administration.[15] Brendan Bradshaw, however, has pointed out that the establishment of the Poynings procedure coincided with an abrupt reduction in the frequency of Parliaments, a decline in the judicial functions of the Irish Parliament and a fall in the volume of significant legislation being tabled,[16] suggesting that Poynings' Law succeeded in its intent of circumscribing the activities of the Irish Parliament. Certainly Poynings' Law was used by the Irish and English administrations to limit the power of Irish MPs during the lord deputyship of Thomas Wentworth in the 1630s and thereafter.[17]

By the end of the seventeenth century, the Poynings procedure had gone through some modifications that had implications for the distribution of power governing Anglo-Irish relations. During Mary's reign, the Crown allowed that the Irish Privy Council could draft and submit bills to the English Privy Council while the Irish Parliament was in session. After the Restoration, the Irish Parliament drew up legislation itself in the form of "heads of bills," which it presented to the Irish administration for review, where, if they were not suppressed by the Irish Privy Council, they became bills and were transmitted to England.[18] Although these adjustments represented a partial expansion of the powers of the Irish Parliament and streamlined the process somewhat, it nevertheless remained quite convoluted, "and served effectively to qualify the authority of the Irish Parliament" throughout the greater part of the eighteenth century.[19] The power that Poynings' Law granted the English Crown over Irish policy was expressed in a memorandum to William III in 1690: "to present a government bill to the Irish Parliament 'was no more in effect than referring it to yourself, since by the constitution of the government the acts made must be first approved here [Westminster], before they can be admitted or debated there.'"[20]

The centuries-long existence of an Irish Parliament and Poynings' Law were the main *formal* institutions that governed the political relationship between Ireland and England and influenced the Irish policymaking process in the years immediately following the Glorious Revolution. Together, they defined the basic structure of Anglo-Irish policymaking: who were the actors authorized to participate in the process and the principal "rules" these individuals were required to follow or take into account when negotiating policy.

Political Actors

The Irish Parliamentary tradition insured the Irish Parliament some degree of participation in Anglo-Irish policy negotiations. The Poynings procedure required the involvement of the English monarch and his Privy Council, as well as their representatives in Ireland, the Irish chief governor and his council. How both pro- and antitoleration sentiment was arrayed amongst these actors had implications for the policy outcome. Following is a description of each along with an assessment of their sentiments and intentions concerning the Treaty bill.

The Monarch

Undoubtedly, the most important player in the English government in the Treaty bill process was the king, William III. It was William who had encouraged his officer in the field to negotiate an end to the Jacobite war, who had approved of the terms granted, and who had agreed to do his best, along with his queen and co-regent, Mary, to have the Treaty ratified by the Irish Parliament. By insisting on the early conclusion of the war, William played a seminal role in the creation of the Treaty of Limerick and it appears that he intended to make good on its terms.

Whether William's dedication to the Treaty stemmed from his relief that a troublesome war had finally been brought to an end, or from a genuine desire to see Catholics treated fairly and equitably, is more difficult to discern. Certainly there is ample evidence that the Treaty was struck for largely pragmatic reasons. William had not always been keen on granting such generous terms to the Jacobites. He would have much preferred their unconditional surrender, or, if that were not possible (as became increasingly clear as the war dragged on), a negotiated settlement that did not allow for too many concessions.[21] His declaration at Finglas in the summer of 1690, for example, demanded that the leaders of the Jacobite forces simply submit; it said nothing about granting toleration to Catholics.[22] But William's resolve to secure a surrender without concessions had less to do with religion than with his desire to get hold of Jacobite land. He wanted their estates to help pay for the war and pay back his Protestant supporters in Ireland and his friends in England.[23] When finally William was forced to forgo the estates in the interests of ending the war, he did not protest to the charitable terms recommended by Ginkel. In William's view, it was only logical to allow religious toleration in Ireland to secure the support of the majority of the population.[24]

William's military ambitions also required that he take a tolerant stance towards Catholics in Ireland. Alliances with Catholic countries were required to do battle with France. It was often necessary when negotiating with Catholic allies to assure charitable treatment of Catholics in his own realm as an indication of good faith. This was, in fact, a situation in which William found himself during the years preceding and following Treaty bill negotiations. When in 1695 Irish Catholics learned that a bill for the suppression of monasteries and the banishment of all the Catholic regular clergy had been transmitted by the Irish administration to England, they turned to William's ally, Emperor Leopold, for assistance in blocking the legislation. Through his envoy, the emperor cautioned William that passage of the bill could jeopardize the whole alliance and asked that the bill not be laid before the English Privy Council. William complied.[25]

More practical considerations aside, it may be that William was simply more tolerant of religious differences than many of his contemporaries. Although raised in the Netherlands as a strict Calvinist,[26] he grew up in a country where different religions coexisted relatively peacefully,[27] a situation that may have, if not erased his devoutness, tempered his Protestant leanings. Most of his friends were apparently tolerant of Catholics, and many of his personal servants and military officers were Catholics. He even allowed mass to be sung everyday in his army.[28] According to Gilbert Burnet, one of William's advisors, the king was unequivocal in his support of toleration in his discussions with William Penn: "no man was more for toleration in principle than he was: he thought the conscience was only subject to God: and as far as a general toleration, even of papists, would content the king, he would concur in it heartily."[29]

There are strong indications that William III was pro-Treaty and, it appears, he intended to see through its passage by the Irish Parliament. Certainly approval of the Treaty in its original form would have benefited the king practically, as a reassurance to Irish Catholics and his Catholic allies. It may have satisfied him personally as well, as a reflection his comparatively tolerant nature.

The English Privy Council

The English Privy Council dates back to the reign of Henry III (1216-1272) although it was under Edward I (1272-1307) and Edward II (1307-1327) that it acquired the title "The King's Ordinary or Privy Council."[30] It was, in theory, an advisory body comprised of trusted men chosen by the monarch with whom he or she consulted before making any important decisions. Although the monarch was under no obligation to confer with these men or even heed their advice, the Privy Council was an accepted part of the government machinery, and was considered by the English Parliament as the only proper body to give advice to the monarch, aside from Parliament itself.[31]

Privy Council membership was at the discretion of the Crown, "a reward for services rendered, an authority accompanying an executive position, or the consequence of rank."[32] This method of appointment encouraged the number of Privy Councillors to swell over time to a point where the council became quite large. Under the Stuarts, membership rose from twenty-seven at the Restoration to forty in 1664 and to fifty in 1675. Granted, Privy Council meetings never approached full attendance. The quorum was set at only four in 1675, an action that facilitated the efficiency of these gatherings.[33]

As the reign of the Stuarts progressed, and the workload of the council increased, the sixteenth- and seventeenth-century practice of assigning Privy Council work to smaller committees became prevalent.[34] Separate committees were appointed to deal with foreign affairs and intelligence, the military, trade and commerce and with Ireland. With more and more of the responsibilities of the Privy Council falling to committees, the power of the Privy Council proper declined. Decisions were often made without its knowledge, and Charles II repeatedly ignored its counsel, dissolving Parliament and dismissing council members as he liked.[35] Gradually, the actions of the Privy Council were reduced to little more than the rubber stamping of decisions made by other government departments or council committees.[36] Meanwhile, monarchs turned increasingly for advice to a smaller body of ministerial advisors who were influential in Parliament and could be depended on to support government policy. Members of this group, the king's chosen ministers, could usually be found at council meetings and most meetings of council committees. Because of their close association with the monarch, and the exclusive knowledge that relationship afforded them, these men exerted a disproportionate amount of influence at council and committee gatherings and hence on the Privy Council. Their functions, however, were not specific and their position relative to the monarch, the English Parliament and the Privy Council was undefined, a situation that unnerved English MPs but, because of the monarch's authority to appoint his own executive and consult whomever he or she chose, they were powerless to change.[37]

William III maintained the Stuart practice of conferring with a smaller group of special advisors of his own choosing who continued to control the council and its various committees. But the character of the English Privy Council nevertheless changed after the Glorious Revolution, the result of broader changes to England's Parliamentary system wrought by the Revolution itself. The Glorious Revolution and the "settlement" that emerged from it altered forever the relationship between the English Parliament and the Crown. The two acts that comprised the revolutionary settlement, The Bill of Rights (1689) and the Act of Settlement (1700 and 1701), reduced considerably the personal power of the monarch who henceforth had to work with the English Parliament to establish his or her authority. Together, they signaled the end of the "personal rule of the monarch" and a key stage of a process that saw the English Parliament, or more specifically, the dominant faction or party therein, exert more and more control over English governance, particularly over the monarch's choice of ministers.

The revolutionary settlement had no direct influence on Ireland and Anglo-Irish policymaking. Poynings' Law was unaffected: the same groups and individuals decided Irish policy; directives were still channeled through the same cumbersome process. The place and power of the English Parliament relative to the Irish government remained undefined. The settlement did, however, open the door for the English Parliament to shape Irish policy *indirectly*. English ministers influenced the king in his decisions concerning whom to appoint to the positions of the Irish Lord Lieutenancy, the Irish Privy Council. And they of course sat on the English Privy Council through which all Irish policy passed. As the English Parliament came to exercise more power over the individuals assigned to these posts, its disposition was to have an increasing influence on most of the major actors involved in Irish policymaking and hence on Irish policy itself.

A key change in English Parliamentary politics during this time was the emergence of party politics. Although parties were not as well defined as they are in modern politics – their membership was comparatively fluid and MPs could not be guaranteed to support one side or the other on every issue – a Whig or "country" interest and a Tory or "court" party could be clearly discerned in the English Parliament by the end of the seventeenth century. The views of these two parties differed widely on many issues, including religion. Whigs tended to be more tolerant of Protestant Dissenters than of Catholics. In contrast, Tories, although they were not by any means completely accepting of Catholics, held a comparatively charitable attitude towards them. The bulk of Tory wrath was saved for Protestant nonconformists.

None of this interested William III when he took the English throne. Preoccupied with his war with France, he was determined to steer clear of English party politics in order to avoid their influence. As E. L. Ellis puts it, "his aim was quite simple: he wanted the maximum amount of national unity as the best foundation for successful war abroad; he was not seriously interested in English-men's domestic concerns, nor their personal and party feuds, except insofar as these promoted or hampered the military effort."[38] Initially at least, William believed his best strategy was to remain neutral and maintain a balance of parties in his administration. Accordingly, he appointed a mix of Tories and Whigs to the various ministerial positions at his disposal.[39] This tactic proved unsuccessful, however, when party squabbles resulted in political confusion and immobility. The Whigs especially were offended by the king's "balanced" approach to politics. A number expressed their displeasure to William in very pointed terms, conduct that no doubt contributed to William's decision to favor the Tories over the next three years.[40] International objectives continued to inform his domestic decisions, as became clear during the 1692-1693 Parliamentary session when the Tories decided to go against William's appeal for an increase in army expenditures and back instead a "blue water" strategy aimed at strengthening the English navy. Despite William's "personal distaste" for many Whig leaders,[41] the king had little choice but to approach the opposition for support of his war measures. His move bore fruit, as Parliament approved an enlargement of the English army in the following year's session.[42] Thereafter, William tended to appoint a preponderance of Whigs to his administration.

Thus, despite the king's attempts to remain aloof from English party politics, the growing powers of the English Parliament compelled him to consider the disposition of the assembly when making ministerial appointments. As a result, the complexion of the English Privy Council and its various committees, like the rest of William III's government, turned increasingly anti-Catholic over the course of Treaty negotiations.

The Irish House of Commons

The Glorious Revolution confirmed what came to be known as the "Protestant Ascendancy" that began in 1660 in Ireland.[43] William III's victory in the Jacobite war destroyed Irish Catholics' hopes of seeing James II restored to the English throne and ruined the Catholic interest in Ireland. From 1690-1691 and throughout the eighteenth century, positions of power in the Irish government were monopo-lized by an Irish Protestant élite who belonged to the (Anglican) Church of Ireland. All this while Protestants were a religious minority in Ireland, a group whose members were outnumbered by Catholics by an estimated four to one.

The Irish House of Commons consisted of 300 elected members. After the Glorious Revolution, the Commons was dominated by representatives of the Protestant victors.[44] These Irish MPs were in the main intolerant of Catholics and Catholicism, an attitude influenced by their recent experiences under James II and the Jacobite war, as well as the long career of religious turmoil that characterized Irish history.

The most immediate concern of MPs was that the majority Catholic population in Ireland would attempt to overthrow the newly installed Protestant leadership, alone or in concert with French invaders. Their fears were fueled by reports that Irish expatriates living in France, and even local populations, were financing or assisting French privateers targeting English ships off the coast of Ireland.[45] They were also alarmed at the postwar increase in offenses committed by "rapparees," bands of Catholic outlaws who victimized mostly Protestants.[46] But the main issue was land. At the beginning of the seventeenth century, Catholics had owned most of the land in Ireland. The confiscations that occurred under Cromwell in the 1650s reduced the proportion of land owned by Catholics dramatically, from an estimated two-thirds to four-fifths of total profitable land in 1641, to one-third to one-fifth by the Restoration.[47] Protestants believed that a Catholic Ireland would mean that land confiscated in the past would be forcibly returned to their original Catholic owners, and that the Protestant owners would, as a result, suffer a loss of power and liberty. Indeed, Jacobite Ireland had made clear that the land question was still an important one during the meeting of the so-called Patriot Parliament under James II in 1689. A Parliament dominated by Old English interests had passed legislation repealing the restoration land settlement and authorizing Catholics who had lost their lands during the Cromwellian confiscations to take steps to recover their property. The proceedings and acts passed by the Patriot Parliament were nullified by the Williamite Parliament of 1695 and its records burned. Nevertheless, it served as proof to anxious Protestants that their property would be in peril in a Catholic Ireland.[48]

The activities of Catholic and Jacobite Ireland combined with tales of atrocities committed against Protestants during the 1641 rebellion to increase Protestant apprehensions. In October 1641, native Irish leaders in the north, concerned that the growing intolerance of the English Parliament towards Catholics and Catholicism might lead to their persecution in Ireland, had resolved to overthrow the Irish government. Within months, they had been joined by the Old English of the Pale and other Catholic gentry who, distrusted by the Irish and English administrations because of their faith, saw an alliance (and victory) as the only means to protect their land and status. The conflict, complicated and exacerbated by the Civil War in England, raged for over a decade until the Catholic alliance was finally put down by Cromwell's Protestant Parliamentary forces.[49] But "atrocity stories" describing the slaughter and torture of Protestants at the hands of Catholic rebels lived on into the nineteenth century.[50] The fact that many Catholics suffered the brutality of Protestants during the uprising, or that time and intolerance had likely exaggerated the savagery, did not stop Protestants from propagating the stories as proof of the barbarity of Catholics and the potential dangers of Catholic rule.

Fearful of any legislation that might empower Catholics, the majority of MPs in the Irish House of Commons were opposed to the lenient terms contained in the Treaty of Limerick.

The Irish House of Lords

The Irish House of Lords between 1692 and 1727 consisted of 22 bishops of the established church and a large number of lay peers, about 100 to 125.[51] Most Irish Lords – usually more than two-thirds – resided in Ireland and most were politically active at some levels of government, although fewer than thirty attended sessions during William III and Anne's reigns.[52]

In the years following the Glorious Revolution, the bishops were the most influential. As a minority ruling class, the Protestant-led government suffered for qualified lay people to fill government and administrative positions. The Church of Ireland bishops thus acquired a greater political eminence than their counterparts in England.[53] There was a larger proportion of bishops attending the Irish upper house than in the English: approximately one in five Lords were bishops in Ireland compared to about one out of seven in England. They were more active as well, comprising more than 30 percent of the house during sessions in the first five decades after the Revolution.[54] As a result, they took a leading role in assembly business.[55]

As Francis James[56] has noted, while it is possible to establish attendance of the Irish Lords, it is more difficult to determine the sentiments of individual bishops on political matters. In most cases the records do not provide information on how members voted. Some indication of the disposition of the Lords can be gleaned from an examination of the terms of their appointment and their family histories.

Because of their political influence, it was usual for the Crown to appoint English bishops to the Irish peerage.[57] Indeed, more than half of the spiritual Lords serving between 1692 and 1800 were Englishmen. Of those who were born in Ireland, the majority descended from post-Reformation families, the "New English" interest.[58] Most of the temporal Lords were born in Ireland and had deep roots in Ireland. James has shown that the majority of the resident peers attending Parliament after the Glorious Revolution came from families that were established in Ireland during Charles I's reign or before.[59] The most influential of these peers in the post-Revolution period were those descended from the English and Scottish "Old Protestant" families established in Ireland during the sixteenth and early seventeenth centuries. But a number of others could trace their ancestry to Catholic "Old English" interests.[60]

The Irish House of Lords in the aftermath of the Revolution was dominated by bishops, most of whom were either born in England or came from families only recently arrived from England. Leading members of the Lords thus had strong connections to England, suggesting that they would have supported measures proposed by the English administration. Of the lay peerage, the majority were descendants of the "Old Protestant" interest, families that had been allied with government interests since the interregnum.[61] These lords had a history of supporting English government initiatives and could be expected to maintain that support under William III. Many of the remaining temporal peers were of "Old

English" heritage (or had only recently become Protestant) and so may have been sympathetic to the Catholic interest.[62]

The Irish Lord Lieutenant

The head or chief governor of the Irish administration was known at first as the King's Justiciar or Deputy, then, later, the Viceroy or Lord Lieutenant.[63] The Lord Lieutenant was the monarch's personal representative in Ireland, the head of the Irish executive and the commander-in-chief of the military. His responsibilities were wide-ranging and included delivering commands and directives to troops and civil authorities, and issuing warrants for payments from the Irish treasury and for appointments to high-level positions. His most important task, however, was to insure that bills – supply bills in particular – approved in England were passed by the Irish Parliament with as little fuss as possible.[64]

It was generally an English nobleman who occupied the position of Irish Lord Lieutenant in the early modern period. His appointment usually had less to do with his abilities or knowledge of Ireland than with his association with the current English administration. His tenure depended on the mutability of English politics. Furthermore, at the end of the seventeenth century and throughout most of the eighteenth, the Lord Lieutenant was not a resident of Ireland. He only stayed in the kingdom during Parliamentary sessions, usually for about six months, returning to England once the session was over.[65]

When the Lord Lieutenant was absent, Ireland was governed by one or more Lords Justices.[66] Between 1690 and 1697, Ireland was appointed two Lord Lieutenants/Deputies and several Lords Justices. Their views on the Treaty were at variance. When William III left Ireland in September 1690, he declared Viscount Sydney and Thomas Coningsby as Lords Justices of Ireland. They were sworn in on 15 September and were joined by Sir Charles Porter in December. Both Porter and Coningsby were instrumental in the negotiation of the Treaty of Limerick and were present at its signing on 3 October 1691. Henry Sydney was a loyal friend of William III and supported the Treaty and its terms. He was sworn in as the Lord Lieutenant of Ireland 4 September 1692. Porter and Coningsby stayed on as Lord Chancellor and Vice Treasurer, respectively. When Sydney was recalled the following June, Lord Capel, Sir Cyril Wyche and William Duncombe were sworn in as Lords Justices on 28 July 1693. The trio were representative of the "balanced" approach to ministerial appointments that William was to adopt early in his reign. Henry Capel was known for his anti-Catholic sentiments and Whig tendencies; Wyche, who had come to Ireland originally as Sydney's Chief Secretary, and Duncombe were both moderates. Capel was sworn in as the Lord Deputy on 27 May 1695. He died the following year. Porter was appointed interim Lord Justice on 2 June 1696 but died in December. Charles Powlett, Marquis of Winchester and Henry de Ruvigny, earl of Galway, became the next Lords Justices on 31 May

1697, with John Methuen as Lord Chancellor. Winchester, Galway[67] and Methuen were all considered Protestant hard-liners.[68]

During the six years that it took to ratify the Treaty of Limerick, men tolerant of Catholics were replaced in the offices of Ireland's administration by less tolerant officials. Although the intentions of the early officials may have been clearly pro-Treaty, those of later administrators were less supportive of the original measure.

The Irish Privy Council

Irish Privy Council shared a number of characteristics with its English counterpart. It originated around the same time as the English Privy Council,[69] and acted as the link between the administration and the Parliament, providing advice and assistance to the head(s) of the executive. Similarly, members were appointed not for their consulting or arbitrating skills but as a reward for services rendered or as a perquisite of their position or rank.[70] It was also a fairly large body, its membership totaling thirty-five in 1690, although meetings were only attended by, at most, one-third that number.[71] But whereas the English Privy Council (at least officially) decided policy together with the monarch, the Irish Privy Council was required to play a more supportive role in relation to the Irish chief governor. Councillors were to help him to execute policies transmitted from England by providing counsel or by backing directives in the Irish Parliament.[72] As more than half of the Irish Privy Council's membership sat in the upper house, this support came for the most part from the House of Lords.[73]

In appraising the sentiments of the Irish Privy Council toward the Treaty of Limerick, it is necessary to balance the origins of Privy Councillors with the circumstances of their appointment. On the one hand, the prevalence of Irish Lords in the Privy Council suggests that many Privy Councillors may have been supportive of the Treaty in its original form. On the other hand, members were appointed upon the recommendation of the Lord Lieutenant. Given the supportive role that the Privy Council played in Irish governance, it is likely that its disposition varied with the sentiments of the chief governor. If this is the case, then the membership of the Privy Council became less tolerant of Catholics and the original Treaty as time went on.

Other Actors

In addition to the actors discussed above, there were other groups and individuals in Ireland who, although their positions in the Irish policymaking process were not specified by formal institutions, nevertheless had the potential to influence negotiations by more informal or indirect means. The pressures exerted by these groups could be considered exogenous insofar as they were, formally, "outside" the policymaking process. Their positions at the turn of the century will be discussed briefly here, however, as their influence on Anglo-Irish legislation was to grow during the next 100 years.

Irish Catholics

William III's victory in Ireland ruined the Catholic political interest there. Confiscations of land, chiefly under Cromwell in the 1650s had already reduced the amount of Irish land in Catholic hands considerably[74]; further confiscations occurred under William III so that by 1703 only 14 percent of the land belonged to Catholics compared to 60 percent in 1640. Devastated by years of war, feared and disdained by the ruling "Ascendancy," perhaps what hurt Irish Catholics the most was the loss of their leadership. Most of the Catholic nobles and gentry who had not been killed or exiled had fled to the continent, leaving behind a Catholic populace that, although it comprised a majority in Ireland, was essentially powerless.[75] It is true that Irish Catholics did have some success in delaying a bill for the banishment of Catholic regulars in 1695.[76] But that small victory had more to do with William's desire to maintain good relations with his ally Emperor Leopold than with Irish Catholic power per se.

Irish Dissenters

Protestant Dissenters were another group with the potential to influence Irish policy. Along with the accession of James I came increasing ministerial concern over Ireland's northern province of Ulster. Ulster was the most Gaelic, most "native," area in Ireland, and fears that the region's powerful lords might challenge English authority in the province prompted the English government to launch extensive reforms there. Two of the most powerful lords, the earls Tyrone and Tyrconnell, disenchanted with the loss of their old authority and under the suspicion of the English government, decided to quit Ireland for the continent in 1607. The "flight of the earls" signaled the end of Gaelic Ulster. Six of the nine Ulster counties were declared to be at the disposal of the king and open for colonization.[77]

The Ulster plantation transformed the Gaelic province into an Anglo-Scottish preserve. Lowland Scots made up an especially large proportion of the population settling in the northeast, in Donegal and later in counties Antrim and Down. As a result, these areas took on a strong Scottish character, reflecting the culture and traditions of Lowland Scotland. This included the practice of Presbyterianism which was, at least initially, tolerated, despite the legal primacy of the Church of Ireland.[78]

Although not subject to the same grievous suspicions and treatment as were Catholics, Presbyterian Dissenters did experience discrimination in Ireland. Their opposition to the Church of Ireland did nothing to endear them to the Restoration government. The 1660s saw Presbyterian ministers removed from their incumbencies and congregations harassed. The enactment in Ireland of the Act of Uniformity in 1666 placed Dissenters under more serious restrictions. Throughout the 1670s troops were sent into Ulster whenever there were disturbances in Scotland.[79]

The accession of James II and the pro-Catholic policies of his Irish Lord Lieutenant, Tyrconnell, enhanced the unity of Irish Protestants, as did the ensuing war.[80] Although this unity did not persist after the Revolution – Anglican intolerance soon became apparent, particularly amongst the Irish bishops in the House of Lords and Privy Council[81] – the larger threat of a Catholic insurrection encouraged the indulgence of Irish nonconformists by Irish political leaders. Irish Dissenters were essentially treated as "second-class" Protestants. They could enter the public service (an English Act in 1691 replaced the oath of supremacy, in effect since 1560, with other oaths less objectionable to nonconformists) but they were still subject to the restrictions contained in the Act of Uniformity; their ministers were supported financially by the state, yet they had no legal right to exist.[82] Even so, as Protestants, they were beneficiaries of Protestant rule, and were as opposed to and as fearful of leniency towards Catholics as their Anglican counterparts. Aggrieved by the Irish government, they nevertheless supported it, and did not bring any independent pressure to bear on policy directed toward Irish Catholics.

Anglo-Irish politics at the time of the Treaty of Limerick's negotiation and passing was delimited by two main *formal* institutions, the established presence of an Irish Parliament and Poynings' Law. These institutions helped to define in a general way *who* was able to legitimately participate in Anglo-Irish political decisionmaking, and *what* those actors were permitted to do in the process. In other words, formal institutions determined the extent and limits of their actions, and their responsibilities and powers relative to each other. The formal institutions in operation specified the major actors, or groups of actors, authorized to take part in the process: the Monarch, William III, his Privy Council in England, the Irish House of Commons, the Irish House of Lords, the Irish Privy Council and the Irish Lord Lieutenant. Moreover, these actors or groups of actors can be identified as holding a pro- or anti-Treaty stance during the first years of Protestant rule in Ireland. William III held perhaps the strongest pro-Treaty position. The membership of the English Privy Council, while it became increasingly Whiggish as time went on, nevertheless remained at the discretion of the Crown, tempering somewhat its anti-Catholic leanings. As well, some in the Irish House of Lords and in the Irish Privy Council look to have been supportive of the Treaty in its original form. In contrast, the majority of members of the Irish House of Commons adopted an anti-Treaty stance during negotiations; some Irish Lords, chief governors and privy councillors were also intolerant.

The way in which the formal institutions surrounding Anglo-Irish policymaking arrayed the powers of these actors suggests that the proponents of the Treaty were slightly favored in negotiations. It is true that it was necessary that the bill be passed by an Irish House of Commons that was dominated by ardent anti-Catholics, a daunting prospect. But the existence of Poynings' Law and its stipulation that the Treaty bill, like all Irish policy, be authorized by the (pro--Treaty) monarch and his appointed Privy Council, together with the fact that the Irish administration, regardless of the expressed sentiments of its members, was staffed by Crown-appointed officials dependent upon England for their livelihood, suggests that those supporting the Treaty would have some chance at initiating the civil terms of the bill.

This was, however, far from the case. In order to understand why this was so, it is necessary to outline the *informal* institutions surrounding the case.

Informal Institutions Characterizing Irish Policymaking after the Glorious Revolution

Formal institutions define the basic characteristics of the policymaking process, the individuals and groups that are permitted, officially, to participate in the process and the fundamental rules that those players must follow, or take into account, when negotiating policy outcomes. In many cases, however, these formal factors describe the policy process at a fairly high level of abstraction. Although they supply the basic guidelines for behavior, they do not specify how exactly their conditions should be implemented or met. This is the domain of *informal* institutions, the norms and procedures that arise out of the interactions that occur between actors seeking to influence policy outcomes within the bounds of the more formal structures. *Informal* institutions are less durable, more variable, and have a greater propensity for change than do formal institutions. They represent established approaches to policymaking that, while they govern the behavior of actors, are more readily subject to modification by those actors because they are not as embedded in the workings of the state.

The specification of informal institutions is more difficult than the identification of formal institutions because of their ambiguity. This is certainly true of the informal institutions surrounding Anglo-Irish politics after the Glorious Revolution. Although the formal institutions governing policymaking had changed little since the fifteenth century, the *informal* procedures necessary for the routine operation of Anglo-Irish governance had been disrupted considerably, not only because the Catholic-dominated Irish Parliament that had met under James II had been replaced almost to a man by Protestants. The way in which Irish politics would operate on a day-to-day basis was in a state of flux, and new institutions representative of the new situation had not yet emerged to stabilize governance. New institutions did eventually arise during this period but they were not dictated or imposed. Instead, they grew out of the interactions of political actors in three crucial areas: that which pertained to political relations between the Irish executive and the Irish Parliament; to political relations between the English executive (William III in particular) and the English Parliament; and lastly to political relations characterizing the Anglo-Irish policymaking process itself. How they emerged and what they came to look like will become clear as the events leading up to the ratification of the Treaty are examined.

The Parliamentary Debacle of 1692

The first meeting of the Irish Parliament under William III was held in October 1692. There were a number of reasons why it was necessary that William call a Parliament in Ireland. First, as we have seen, there was the Irish tradition of participatory governance. William needed the support of Irish élites to maintain the English interest in Ireland. It would not have been prudent for him to forgo calling a Parliament in Ireland and provoke the ire of the men who governed the island in his name.[83] Second, the pressure on William to call a Parliament was especially strong because of the principles realized by the revolutionary settlement. Henceforth, it was necessary for the monarch to work through representative assemblies to establish his or her authority.[84] William had pledged several times during the war to summon a Parliament in Ireland once things had settled down,[85] a sign of his commitment to tradition and principle. A third and more practical reason for calling an Irish Parliament was that William needed money. The king's penchant for international warfare meant that eventually the hereditary revenues that had been voted during Charles II's reign would need supplementing. It was necessary that he go to the Irish Parliament to procure the additional supplies required to pay for the costs of war and government.[86] Finally, there was his promise made to the Jacobites in the Treaty of Limerick that he and Mary would "endeavor to procure" ratification of the Treaty by the Irish Parliament "as soon as their Affairs will permit."[87] It is difficult to conceive of how William could have avoided summoning an Irish Parliament if indeed he had wanted to.

Of course whatever constraints any of the above demands placed on William were tempered by the existence of Poynings' Law. The Poynings procedure would prevent the passage of any legislation to which William and his ministers might be averse and insure endorsement of acts that they wished approved. This was true provided that the legislation operated in the way that it was supposed to. For the key to the proper operation of the Poynings procedure was that the Irish Lord Lieutenant have the capacity to usher through the Irish Parliament legislation that had been sanctioned by the English executive. This meant that it was necessary for the Irish Lord Lieutenant to control or at least manage the Irish Parliament to insure passage of the desired legislation.

Opinions varied concerning what the disposition of the Irish Parliament would be once it was called. There is some indication that the Irish Lords Justices, Porter and Coningsby, delayed transmitting bills to England after the decision to hold an Irish Parliament had been made, concerned that the assembly "will not be for the King's service."[88] It is certainly true that Irish Protestants opposed the Treaty of Limerick and were becoming increasingly hostile toward an administration that endorsed and was determined to uphold its provisions.[89] Porter and Coningsby had begun hearing land claims under the Treaty almost immediately. By January 1692, they had restored the estates of sixty people. Porter had also stopped all lawsuits against supporters of James II in accord with the sixth article of the Treaty. These actions were a clear sign that William and his Irish executive were serious in their intent to abide by the conditions of the Treaty.[90] Irish Protestants were fearful that these generous land terms left Irish Catholics with too much power and the potential to again take up their fight for domination of Ireland.[91] Protestants were also disturbed by William's willingness to allow ex-Jacobites into his army, an action intended to help decrease rapparee activity in postwar Ireland, but interpreted as a dangerous trend that could threaten state security.[92] English administrators were well aware of the explosiveness of the Irish situation. A state paper of 1690 wondered whether William should abolish the Irish Parliament and rule the island directly from England.[93]

The new Lord Lieutenant, Henry Sydney, was, nevertheless, optimistic about an Irish Parliament. It is not that he was unaware of the volatile political climate. In a letter to the secretary of state in England before Parliament sat, he expressed his concerns regarding the conflict over preparation of a bill of indemnity that was based on one of the articles in the Treaty of Limerick: "What I fear most is the violence that will be against the Papists, for they [Irish Protestants] do hate them to the greatest degree imaginable."[94] He did not, however, believe that anti-Catholic sentiment would translate into political problems. So confident was Sydney that the Irish Parliament would be conciliatory toward the new administration that, contrary to the intentions of the Crown, he and his council sent over to England three money bills to be considered with the other legislation proposed for the first session.[95]

That Sydney was so upbeat in the face of the growing hostility of Irish Protestants towards the administration and Irish Catholics is somewhat understandable. After all, the Poynings procedure virtually guaranteed the subservence of the Irish Parliament. Besides, having just been delivered by William's army from Catholic domination, how could Irish Protestants be anything but acquiescent?[96] Furthermore, the Irish Parliament had not had much practice challenging the Irish administration and the Crown. It had only met five times before in that century; the last "official" session was held in 1665-1666. It is true that, in all of these sessions, disagreements had arisen, with Irish MPs raising concerns of a constitutional nature. Already in 1460, the Irish Parliament declared that all laws applying to Ireland must be sanctioned by the Irish Parliament.[97] In 1641, the Irish Parliament drew up a list of "queries" to submit to the judges that questioned the validity of laws not accepted and passed by the Irish legislature.[98] The Parliament under Charles II was critical of English acts restricting Irish trade with the colonies.[99] And James II's "Patriot Parliament" of 1689 passed a bill declaring the judicial and legislative independence of the Irish Parliament.[100] But most of these disputes could be explained away. The resistance of Irish recusants in the early seventeenth century could be dismissed as irrelevant now that the Irish Parliament was exclusively Protestant; the constitutional claims of the "Patriot Parliament" could be written off in the same way. And opposition to Wentworth could be interpreted as a struggle against the "tyranny" present in England and Ireland in the last years of Charles I.[101]

Sydney's reading of the situation proved far from the mark. Although the session that opened in October began well enough, with the assemblies confirming their loyalty to William and Mary and promising to proceed with "moderation,"[102] the House of Commons quickly became uncooperative. Only four out of the ten bills that had been prepared for the meeting were ratified by the Irish Parliament and passed into law.[103] Out of the six that were rejected, one was a money bill that Sydney himself had insisted would pass through Parliament without any difficulty. They also voted down a government bill confirming the Acts of Settlement and Explanation from Charles II's reign, and a bill declaring void the proceedings and acts passed by the "Patriot Parliament" of 1689. Both of these bills the Irish Parliament saw as beneficial to Irish Catholics, the first because it legitimized some Catholic landholdings, and the second because it would erase the record of Catholic treachery under James II.[104] But it was not anti-Catholic sentiment that ultimately galvanized the Irish Parliament. Rather, the House of Commons decided that it would assert its "sole right" not only to initiate money bills but to decide the "ways and means" of those bills. The Irish Parliament had been able to introduce "heads of bills," including money bills, since the Restoration. But the insistence of MPs that they had the right to decide how that money was to be raised was new. The Commons' attack challenged directly the power of the Irish and English executive.[105] So demanding and disagreeable was the Irish House of Commons that Sydney prorogued Parliament on 3 November, less than a month after its first meeting.

Clearly, Sydney failed in what was the Lord Lieutenant's primary responsibility: that of insuring the smooth passage through the Irish Parliament of bills approved in England. Sydney had not anticipated the need to establish executive dominance over the Irish Parliament. He and his administration had wrongly assumed that gratitude toward William for his defeat of the Jacobites and the Poynings procedure were enough to ensure that Irish MPs would endorse government-sanctioned bills.[106] The first meeting of the Irish Parliament under William III, although subject to the formal restrictions of Poynings' Law, was characterized by an almost complete absence of any informal institutions that could facilitate the proper operation of the Poynings procedure.

Henry Capel's Solution

The first meeting of the Irish Parliament under William III did not bode well for future bills that were contrary to the will of the Irish Parliament. Any legislation confirming the terms of the Treaty of Limerick would likely have a difficult time passing an anti-Catholic assembly in the mood for a fight, that is, of course, unless the administration could conceive of a method of controlling the Irish Parliament.

That Henry Sydney would be the man to accomplish this was unlikely. It became clear soon after the prorogation that Parliamentary leaders, those who had championed the sole right campaign against the administration, wanted Sydney removed. A number of them left Ireland to air their complaints against the Irish administration in England. They convinced the English Parliament that an investigation into the affairs of Ireland was necessary and in February 1693 an inquiry began. Witness after witness detailed the transgressions of the Dublin administration: quartering abuses, their lenient treatment of Catholics, their alleged mismanagement of the revenue, Sydney's sudden termination of Parliament. The investigation prompted the English Commons to send an address to the king requesting that he deal with matters in Ireland. In June 1693, William III ordered a dissolution of the Irish Parliament and Sydney was recalled.[107]

Sydney was not the only one targeted by the sole right men. Porter and Coningsby were also accused of mismanagement of Irish affairs. Now it was their turn to face the wrath of Irish MPs determined to see them removed from the Irish executive. In December 1693, the English House of Commons was presented with articles of high treason and other crimes and misdemeanors against the lord chancellor and vice treasurer. Included in the list of offenses was the charge that they "openly favoured and supported the Papists in their robberies and their outrages committed upon the Protestants, refusing then to allow them liberty of taking their legal remedies against the Papists," an obvious reference to Porter and Coningsby's commitment to the sixth article of the Treaty of Limerick that forbade private suits against Catholic beneficiaries of the terms of the Treaty. This time, however, the English Parliament ruled against the Irish MPs, dismissing the charges against Porter and Coningsby and ruling against their impeachment.[108]

Henry Sydney was replaced by three Lords Justices, William Duncombe, Cyril Wyche and Henry Capel. It was Capel who emerged as the dominant figure of the three. His success derived from his ability to placate both the English executive and the Irish Parliament. To the king and his ministers, Capel presented himself as a hardworking administrator, committed to establishing good relations between the Irish government and MPs. That it was a role he continued to play throughout his career in Ireland is evident from a letter to Shrewsbury, the secretary of state, in 1695, in which Capel apologized for not having written in some time, having been delayed "by a little journey I took, to run for a plate, the better to discourse with the gentlemen of the country."[109] He always put a positive spin on Irish affairs when writing to English administrators anxious that another Irish Parliament would resurrect the sole right debate, exuding confidence that things could be put right with some skillful political maneuvering.[110] He encouraged the English executive to call a Parliament soon to replenish the depleted coffers of the Irish government.[111]

To the Irish House of Commons, Capel represented himself as their champion. He quickly allied himself with the sole right men – or as Capel called them, the "angry gentlemen" – and set about cultivating their support. For it was the Lord Lieutenant's job that Capel was after. If he could persuade the Irish Commons to support him, he would have a chance at convincing the English executive that he was the most capable of delivering a trouble-free Parliament and win the chief governorship.[112]

By the summer of 1694, Capel's strategy began to bear fruit. In April of that year, the king and his council had told Shrewsbury to ask the Irish Lords Justices for their opinion on the status of the sole right issue. In July, the trio submitted their reports. Wyche and Duncombe predicted that MPs would press the issue, and that there would be problems in the assembly. In their opinion, it would be unwise to call a Parliament. Capel came to the reverse conclusion, asserting that "A good session can take place if the English Protestant gentlemen are convinced that there is a real intention in the Government to do them good."[113]

The calling of the Irish Parliament was already overdue as far as William was concerned. The last session had only approved one of the two money bills sent from England and the king wished to hold a Parliament to vote more supplies and otherwise settle affairs in Ireland. He was irritated that, by waiting so long to submit their opinions, the Lords Justices had forced yet another delay in the summoning of the Irish assembly. William was particularly annoyed with Wyche and Duncombe who William may have suspected put off responding to his request on purpose.[114] Wyche and Duncombe's recommendation that the king proceed with caution convinced William and his ministers that the two would be unable to manage a session if it were called, and they were dismissed.[115]

Capel learned that he was to be appointed chief governor of Ireland in March 1695 and he was sworn in on 10 May. A number of sole right men were appointed to his administration on his recommendations: Robert Rochfort became attorney general and Alan Brodrick was made solicitor general; others were granted posts in the Irish Privy Council, the Exchequer's office, and the judiciary.[116] An announcement was made that a Parliament would be held in Dublin on 27 August and in June, Capel sent some bills to the English Privy Council for approval. Included was a money bill for an additional excise on beer, designed to bring in only a token amount of revenue, about £7,000. The excise bill passed through Parliament without incident. Three days later, the Commons announced that it would raise £163,000. After a month of negotiations, the Commons presented Capel with the heads of three more money bills, one recommending that the excise on beer be extended for another two years, another that a duty be laid on tobacco, and another for a poll bill. Capel had managed to bring about a successful Parliament.[117]

There is disagreement concerning the nature of the "deal" that Capel struck with the leaders of the Irish Parliament to insure their cooperation during the 1695 session. James McGuire emphasizes the political allowances that Capel made during the sitting, permitting the Irish Parliament to initiate money bills and determine the ways and means of raising additional funding.[118] It was Capel's willingness to grant Irish MPs these powers that encouraged their compliance. David Hayton is of much the same opinion, but stresses the importance of the appointments that Capel secured for key members on the sole right faction.[119] Others are of a different mind. Wouter Troost maintains that in order to procure the support of the "angry gentlemen" Capel had to agree to pursue a strong anti-Catholic program once he was appointed the head of the government.[120] Troost believes that it was no coincidence that two anti-Catholic bills – one for disarming Catholics and one prohibiting them from running schools or sending their children to be educated abroad – were introduced at the same time as the excise bill. Charles McGrath agrees, asserting that the bills were "an integral part of the negotiations

. . . for a compromise political solution over the issue of money bills in an Irish Parliament."[121] Indeed, it seems clear that anti-Catholic legislation had a large part to play in Capel's dealings with the leaders of the Irish Parliament. As early as July 1694 Capel had recommended to English ministers that such bills be enacted "for strengthening and securing the English and Protestant interest."[122] Capel prepared and transmitted to England the same legislation in June the following year, and implored William's ministers "not to raise any objections as these laws were absolutely necessary for the security of the Protestant subjects of His Majesty."[123] There is little question that the anti-Catholic members of the Irish House of Commons welcomed the penal legislation. In fact, there were a number in the assembly who felt that the laws were not strong enough. That anti-Catholic measures were on the minds of MPs during the 1695 session was further evinced when both the Lords and the Commons presented Capel with the heads of bills suppressing monasteries and banishing regulars, which Capel duly drew up and transmitted to England for approval.[124] This bill was disallowed by William in response to concerns raised by Emperor Leopold.[125] But Capel's readiness to sanction such legislation (the bill was set to send to England within three days of the Commons' request) suggests that its appearance was not a complete surprise to the Lord Lieutenant.

Capel's bargaining strategy proved a success. It allowed the Irish administration and, by extension, the English executive, to, if not control the Irish Parliament, at least manage it by offering concessions in exchange for compliance.

As the Parliamentary "debacle" of 1692 demonstrated, although the *formal institutions* governing the relationship between Ireland and England after the Revolution were well defined, the *informal institutions* that were necessary to allow the formal structures to function were absent. While Poynings' Law was in place to help the administrations in England and Ireland counter the potential power of the Irish Parliament, the norms and operating procedures that were necessary to insure control were wanting. Capel's bargaining method filled in the gap and established informal procedures that gave the Irish, and by extension, the English, executive some of the authority over the Irish Parliament granted them by Poynings' Law.

Meanwhile in England . . .

William's decision to supplant his original "balanced" approach to ministerial appointments with one that favored Whigs obviously strengthened anti-Catholic interests in the English government. But the influence of English party factions over Irish policy through the Privy Council and other means should not be overstated. The expansion of the power of the English Parliament over Irish, or for that matter, any policymaking, was a gradual process. It is true that William III had to consider the temperament of the English Parliament when making decisions. But compared to the influence that the English Parliament was to have over the appointment of ministers and, hence, government policymaking later in the century, ministers and policy were, to a large degree, still under the control of the monarch and his chosen ministers.

Executive control meant that the policymaking was a fairly "closed" process during this period. As Parliament gained more influence over ministerial appointments and policy, the number of individuals, politicians and others, interested and involved in government policymaking would increase. But for now, major decisions were taken by relatively few officials, who sought information from individuals of their own choosing. It is true that lobby groups did exist at this time.[126] But these groups acknowledged that policy was the charge of the sovereign and his or her executive. The character of these groups reflected the exclusive nature of policymaking at the time. Their membership consisted of men who were well connected to government and the court, all of whom had a direct interest in the matter concerning them. It was uncommon for individuals outside an interest to be included in a lobby. The "public" had not yet found, or been encouraged to find, its voice or the mechanisms through which to express it: the Wood's halfpence demonstrations and the Dublin anti-Union riot[127] were still far in the future; Charles Lucas[128] and John Wilkes[129] were not even born yet. And the methods and manner adopted by lobbies tended to be more conciliatory than confrontational, their appeals more courteous than demanding.

Many of these characteristics were reflected in the activities and membership of what Francis James has identified as the "Irish lobby" that operated during the early eighteenth century in London and Ireland.[130] Contrary to histories that claim that Ireland did not have much political or economic influence during this period, James shows that the Irish did manage to affect government policy with the help of this "lobby." This was no noisy public-interest group, however. James depicts the lobby as made up mostly of politicians and government-appointed officials. While they had some success influencing Anglo-Irish policy, they were representative of the "old school" of government pressure group: connected, influential and more concerned with appeasing administrators than with challenging them.

The exclusive nature of policymaking meant that it was difficult for individuals and groups not directly involved in government procedures and without established connections with government officials to have any significant impact on policymaking. "Out-of-doors" groups representing the Catholic Irish and the Ulster Dissenters for example had a difficult time soliciting the support of English government.[131] It is true that the weakness of Irish Catholics and the incapacity of Dissenters to involve themselves in Anglo-Irish politics contributed to their political impotence. But even if they had the strength or desire to oppose the Irish Parliament on the Treaty, they would have found themselves at a disadvantage in relation to their opposition. Anti-Catholic forces were ensconced in the Irish Parliament and other positions of power that played a direct role in the process of Irish policymaking. To counter this power, not only would the strength of these Irish out-of-doors interests have to improve, but the institutional fabric of political decisionmaking would have to change: the policy process would need to become less restrictive and secretive, more accepting of outside influences, and ministers would have to become accustomed to listening to and heeding the advice (requested or not) of these interests. Many of these changes did occur over the course of the eighteenth century and will be discussed later. For now, however, policymaking, including Irish policymaking and the process surrounding the negotiation and passage of the Treaty of Limerick bill, unfolded within a relatively closed system. It was more or less monopolized by the king and his chosen ministers, and whomever they chose to consult. In other words, the *informal institutions* governing English government policymaking gave the English executive great authority over Irish policymaking, and structured politics in such a way as to favor those players who were most closely related to the executive.

The preceding describes three significant informal institutions operating at the time of the Treaty's negotiation and passing. First, there were the informal mechanisms characterizing Henry Capel's "bargaining method," which defined the way in which the formal conditions of the Poynings' procedure were to be realized, at least for the time being. Second, there were the informal institutions governing the relationship between the English executive and the English Parliament that determined that, despite the changes wrought by the Glorious Revolution, Irish policy was still largely the responsibility of the monarch and his or her chosen ministers. Third, and finally, there were the informal institutions that governed the policymaking process itself, that defined the process as relatively "closed," shielded from pressure from the English Parliament and out-of-doors interests both in England and in Ireland. Only players with established and close connections with the small group of English executives involved could have any real impact on policy decisions concerning Ireland. With these structures in mind, the fate of the Treaty may be examined, the actions and reactions of the various actors involved in the policymaking process to the events surrounding the formulation and passage of the ratification act, and how institutions, both formal and informal, constrained, enabled and otherwise affected their impact on the final outcome.

The Fate of the Treaty

That the Treaty of Limerick did not come before the Irish Parliament until the 1697 session was not because the Treaty or its terms had been disregarded or forgotten. In fact, William had ordered that a confirmation of the Treaty of Limerick be prepared to be presented to the Irish Parliament in 1692. William's order came in response to complaints from the Irish Catholic community that an indemnity bill prepared by Sydney and his council was detrimental to their interests. William quashed the bill, but Parliament was prorogued before the ratification legislation that he replaced it with could be considered.[132] As well, the Lords Justices Porter and Coningsby began hearing land claims almost immediately after the Treaty's signing, so that by 1694, 483 individuals had had their estates restored under the benefit of its articles.[133] Indeed, the Irish executive's determination to adhere to the terms of the Treaty was largely what prompted the Irish Protestant attacks on

Sydney, Porter and Coningsby. It is interesting to note that the Treaty of Limerick was never mentioned by name by the sole right men as a motivation for their offensive against the Irish executive. This may have been because opposition to the Treaty was secondary to the constitutional aims of the Irish Parliament[134] or because the Irish Parliament was hesitant to criticize an agreement that was essentially authored by the king.[135] Their "official" silence on the Treaty does not mean that Irish MPs were unconcerned about the agreement. Its terms represented to Irish Protestants a betrayal by the Irish and English executive of the Protestant cause and informed their actions greatly.[136]

The Treaty of Limerick also came under discussion before and during the 1695 session of the Irish Parliament. Sir Charles Porter, who had been appointed the Irish Lord Chancellor after the impeachment attempt, was anxious to have the Treaty ratified. Disliked and distrusted by Irish Protestants for having helped draft the Treaty as well as bring into effect some of its most contentious terms, Porter felt under constant threat of attack. Only ratification of the Treaty would absolve him and his actions. Capel, on the other hand, was not as enthusiastic about sending over a ratification bill, as his supporters in the Irish Parliament were adamantly opposed to it. Both Porter and Capel wrote to the secretary of state expressing their views regarding the advisability of bringing in a ratification bill at this time. Although the minister agreed with Capel, William came down on the side of Porter and ordered that his wish that a ratification bill be prepared be communicated to Ireland. On 11 October the Irish Privy Council decided, however, to go against the wishes of the king, declaring "that it was not a proper time" to introduce such a bill. Apparently, one of the leading sole right men, Thomas Brodrick, had been allowed to address the council and had convinced its members that "if such a matter should then be brought into the House of Commons it would put them in the greatest disorder." Capel had succeeded in delaying the ratification bill for the present time.[137]

In the meantime, Porter's fears that he might come under attack from Irish Protestants materialized. From 30 September to 25 October 1695, Porter was subjected to the wrath of Irish MPs in the Commons who wished him impeached. The attack apparently came as a surprise to Capel who, although he would have been pleased to see Porter gone, refused to take sides on the issue for fear that he be reprimanded by the king. The Commons decided in a 121 to 77 vote not to impeach Porter, but his opponents immediately began to prepare to present their argument to the English Parliament. To this William objected and ordered the secretary of state to inform the chief governor to prevent this action. Capel managed to stop the proceedings, but only in exchange for appointing three sole right men to high positions in government. Capel's bargaining strategy had once more succeeded in mollifying the "angry gentlemen."[138]

Capel died in May 1696. After some political wrangling, Porter was appointed Lord Justice by the Irish Privy Council over Capel's hand-chosen successors, Robert Wolseley and Lord Blessington, two men who had the confidence of the leaders of the Irish Parliament.[139] But Porter was destined never to hold the position of Lord Lieutenant of Ireland, nor witness the ratification of the Treaty of Limerick that he so much desired. His attempts to convince the English executive to call an Irish Parliament without delay were unsuccessful. He died in December 1696, three months before Parliament reconvened on 16 March 1697.

Twice William had been prevented from introducing Treaty legislation to the Irish Parliament. The *debacle* of 1692 had precluded any real discussion regarding ratification of the Treaty. The 1695 attempt had gone further, but was suppressed by the Irish Privy Council, a victim of the bargaining strategy that Henry Capel had used to bring the Irish Parliament to heel. In April 1697, William met with his Privy Council and gave the order for the Irish Lords Justices to draw up a bill "for confirming so much of the articles of Limerick as the king has promised to endeavour to have ratified."[140] The fate of the Treaty of Limerick would finally be decided.

Charles Powlett, Marquis of Winchester and Henry de Ruvigny, earl of Galway were sworn in as Irish Lords Justices on 31 May 1697, and John Methuen was appointed Lord Chancellor. All three men were known for their anti-Catholic sympathies.[141] Together with an Irish Privy Council dominated by the men of the sole right appointed by Henry Capel, they drew up a bill in response to William's request. A bill "for the confirmation of the Articles of Limerick" was forwarded to the English Privy Council in July. The bill bore little resemblance to the original Treaty. Gone were the references to religious liberties and the article that stipulated that no other oath but the oath of allegiance be demanded. The article forbidding private suits against Catholic beneficiaries of the Treaty remained, but the date on which the war allegedly began was pushed up to 10 April 1689 (rather than November 1688), allowing Irish Protestants to sue for redress for injuries suffered during the Jacobite regime. And the controversial "missing clause" was absent.[142]

Despite its deficiencies, the bill transmitted from Ireland seems to have created little stir amongst the English executive. The only question that arose was whether the "missing clause" should be included in the legislation. The Privy Council decided to ask the king for his opinion on the matter, who, although he had previously certified that it had been a transcribing error,[143] chose this time to defer to the Irish Lords' Justices. Most of the Irish Privy Council agreed that the "missing clause" should remain missing, and William agreed to leave out the clause "which gives so much offence."[144] William and his Privy Council approved the mutilated bill, and it was sent back to Ireland.

It appears that the anti-Catholic sole right men had been in control of the Irish House of Commons in 1692. It is evident by the strong majority that voted against impeaching Porter, however, that by 1695 a fairly large contingent had emerged in the lower house that had come to view the actions of the "angry gentlemen" against the Irish executive as excessively harsh. It is possible that Porter's constant conviction that the Irish Parliament would ratify the Treaty of Limerick would have materialized had the Lord Justice lived to lead his supporters in the following Parliament.

Much of the support that the Treaty of Limerick had in the Irish commons, however, dissolved upon Porter's death. Those MPs who had backed Henry Capel and were averse to any sort of concessions to Irish Catholics came to control the lower house in 1697.[145] It is clear that securing anti-Catholic legislation was a key aim of this Parliament. The bill for the suppression of monasteries and the banishment of Catholic regular clergy that William had blocked in 1695 was among the bills that the Irish Privy Council transmitted to England before the session. This bill was later redrafted to expand the number of ecclesiastics included in its scope. Another bill was drawn up that restricted the property rights of individuals marrying Catholics.[146] All three bills were passed by the Commons without difficulty.

The bill "For the confirmation of the articles made at the surrender of Limerick" came before the Irish House of Commons on 6 September 1697. In contrast to the other anti-Catholic legislation introduced earlier in the session, this bill did not pass the lower house easily. Many MPs thought the legislation was too lenient toward Catholics. But the Lords Justices and the Lord Chancellor managed to persuade a majority of MPs to endorse the bill. It passed the Commons on 14 September.[147]

The bill also had a difficult time in the House of Lords but for different reasons. A number of the Lords in the upper house objected to the absence of the "missing clause" and were opposed to confirming a bill that did not contain any of the terms of the Treaty in their original form.[148] After much debate the bill finally did pass, but by only three votes. Fourteen of those who had been against the bill were so indignant that they signed a formal protest against the vote. They were, however, unable to have the Treaty restored to its original form.[149]

Discussion

The above suggests that anti-Catholic interests in the Irish House of Commons were the clear victors in the process to ratify the Treaty of Limerick. Institutions can help in understanding that success.

From a strictly constitutional, that is formal institutional, standpoint, William III and his executive held the upper hand in these negotiations. Tradition bound the king to call the Irish Parliament to vote the supplies so desperately needed, and so restricted to some extent his autonomy. But there were few indications that the Parliament would be anything but acquiescent, given their recent delivery by William's army from Catholic domination, and their inexperience in challenging the Irish administration and the Crown. Furthermore, Poynings' Law insured that the Irish and English executive would hold the balance of power in Anglo-Irish policymaking. Certain informal institutions benefited the English executive as well. The revolution settlement encouraged the process that would see the English Parliament exert more and more control over the monarch's choice of ministers and by extension English, and Irish, governance. At the time of the Treaty bill negotiations, however, the informal institutions that would allow for this transformation had only begun to develop. The sovereign still held considerable power over the selection of the English administration. Since these were the men who, along with the monarch, decided Irish policy, the Irish policymaking process was still largely under the control of William and his chosen ministers. Irish policy was the policy of the English executive which was the policy of the monarch. It would seem that the manner in which institutions arrayed pro- and anti-Catholic interests at the time would favor toleration.

Yet in the end the English executive acceded to the Irish House of Commons on the terms of the ratification bill. For, in spite of the institutional advantages working for the Crown, there were other institutions, mostly informal ones, that allowed the lower house in Ireland to seize the upper hand in the Treaty bill negotiations. The informal institutions surrounding the process of English policy supported the position of anti-Catholic MPs in the Irish House of Commons. Executive control of the policy process meant that government directives, including those concerning Ireland, were determined by a fairly small group of ministers. Therefore, the number of officials that MPs in the Irish Parliament had to persuade to support their demands was manageable. Moreover, out-of-doors interests did not play as large a role in policymaking as they were to later in the century. Consequently, the Irish House of Commons faced little serious competition from other forces on this issue.

Most importantly, however, the informal institutions surrounding the relationship between the Irish executive and the Irish Parliament were such that they favored intolerant MPs in the Irish House of Commons. For Poynings' Law to operate properly, the Irish executive required enough control over the Irish Parliament to insure that Crown-approved legislation would be passed by both houses: the more control, the more smoothly the Poynings procedure would work, the more power the English executive could exert over Irish governance. But the bargaining process established by Henry Capel was more of a management than a control technique. Although it could deliver an uneventful session, that harmony had to be bought. Compliance could be secured but only in exchange for political appointments, anti-Catholic legislation and other favors. This meant that English administrators often had to strike a compromise with Irish MPs, even bow to their demands occasionally, actions that undermined the Poynings procedure and the power of the executive over Irish politics.

It is likely that the English executive were not aware in the beginning that the informal institutions that came to characterize Anglo-Irish politics after 1695 had the potential to significantly diminish executive authority over the Irish House of Commons. A closer look at the anti-Catholic legislation that was granted to the Irish Parliament during the 1695 and 1697 sessions reveals the English executive ceded very little. The Act for disarming Catholics and an associated bill that prevented Catholics from owning horses worth more than five pounds were essentially confirmations of policies that had been put in place in Ireland by William during the war. Both were measures that were commonly issued during times of crisis. The Act forbidding Catholics from sending their children to schools abroad was to prevent contact between Irish and foreign, particularly French, Catholics.[150] As a military man, it is not surprising that William may have agreed with the leaders of the Irish Parliament that these measures were necessary for the security of the kingdom.

William's apparent abandonment of the Treaty of Limerick to the whims of hard-line Protestants in the Irish government is more perplexing. But by 1697 the ratification of the Treaty of Limerick in its original form was not as important to William as it had been earlier. Relations between William and his ally Emperor Leopold had cooled considerably with the war nearing its end. Although still a concern, it was not as critical for William to uphold the Treaty as a measure of good faith now that the emperor's support was no longer needed.[151] Also, there is some indication that William may have allowed passage of the Treaty bill because he knew that anti-Catholic laws in Ireland could never be implemented effectively. By 1697 William had been on the throne for several years and had developed some understanding of how the English and Irish governments operated in practice. It is possible that William made conscious use of the inefficiencies of the state apparatus to at once mollify intolerant Irish Protestants and ease the concerns of Catholic allies troubled by the treatment of Irish Catholics.[152] When Johann Hoffman, Emperor Leopold's resident in London, approached the earl of Sunderland, one of William's ministers, for assistance in quashing the Bishops' Banishment Act, he was assured that penal legislation was rarely, if ever, enforced in Ireland.[153]

In the end, the Treaty bill itself did not have a significant effect on the condition of Catholics in Ireland. The article in the original Treaty that had guaranteed to Catholics religious liberties enjoyed in the reign of Charles II was so vague that its confirmation would have meant little: the Bishops' Banishment Act, for example, had its foundations in policies put into effect in the 1670s. There was no great wave of private suits after the Treaty's ratification, and no one lost their estates as a result of changes made to the terms or the absence of the "missing clause." In fact, adjudications continued into 1699, the majority of which were allowed.[154] By allowing the ratification of a mutilated Treaty of Limerick, William was able to secure the compliance of the Irish Parliament and still maintain his comparatively tolerant policy towards Irish Catholics by continuing hearing and allowing land claims under its terms. He had little indication that his actions would seriously undermine the power of the executive over the Irish House of Commons and Anglo-Irish politics in general.

But undermine executive power it did. While the Treaty ratification bill may not in itself have affected Catholics too adversely, it, along with the penal legislation passed during the 1690s, was representative of a process that saw an Irish House of Commons dominated by intolerant MPs gain increasing influence over Anglo-Irish policymaking. As the years went on, the informal institutions that had been established in Capel's time compelled William and his executive to cede to the Irish House of Commons on an increasing number of policies restrictive of Irish Catholics. The Bishops' Banishment Act of 1697 was accompanied by legislation prohibiting Protestants from marrying Catholics, and followed in 1698 by an act preventing Catholics from becoming solicitors.[155] The act "to prevent the further growth of popery" passed in 1704 included provisions prohibiting

Protestants from converting to Catholicism, forbidding Catholics from purchasing, inheriting or renting Protestant land and required that land owned by Catholics be "gavelled" (that is, divided amongst male heirs upon the death of the proprietor rather than remain intact). It also prevented Catholics from voting for MPs unless they took the oath of abjuration, an oath objectionable to Catholics.[156] Whatever loopholes Catholics had managed to take advantage of to evade the previous legislation were blocked by an act in 1709 that strengthened the property laws against Catholics and placed further restrictions on the Catholic clergy.[157] These and many other laws limiting the rights and activities of Catholic clergy and laymen continued to be passed until well into the eighteenth century, including an act of 1727 disenfranchising Protestants with Catholic wives,[158] and a measure prohibiting Catholics from voting outright in 1728. Further Acts in 1733 regulated the admission and practice of Catholic lawyers, and barred converts with Catholic wives, or those who were educating their children as Catholics, from the office of justice of the peace.[159] As late as the 1750s, measures were passed restricting the presence of Catholics on juries.

The English executive were, for the most part, less than enthusiastic about sanctioning the anti-Catholic legislation proposed by the Irish Parliament. They were concerned about how the laws would affect England's relations with Catholic allies and whether the legislation was in accord with the articles of Limerick.[160] Occasionally, they appear to have made additions to Irish legislation that would hinder its passing in the Irish assemblies, as when the English Privy Council added to the Act of 1704 an article requiring that Crown and municipal office holders be required to take the sacramental test, a clause to which Dissenting MPs would object.[161] They were, however, bound to abide by the wishes of Irish MPs if they desired a peaceful session.[162] Of this the Irish Parliament was well aware. Bills were known to arrive from Ireland hinting, or even threatening, that the supply bill would be rejected if the proposed legislation was altered in any way.[163] And they were not afraid to follow through on their threats. When in 1713 one of the leaders of the opposition was told by the Lord Lieutenant that he would not cede to the opposition's demand that the current lord chancellor be removed from his office, the House of Commons did not hesitate to reject several government bills and refused to vote a supply for the following year.[164]

The real significance of the Treaty of Limerick ratification bill, therefore, lay not in its immediate impact on Irish Catholics, but in the *informal institutions* that emerged during its negotiation and were strengthened by its passage. These institutions established a new balance of power between the Irish executive and the Irish Parliament that would have a significant effect on the kingdom, and on Irish Catholics in particular.

While he does not employ the language of institutionalism, Charles Ivar McGrath[165] recognizes that the political "compromise" struck by Capel and the sole right men helped to forge a new Anglo-Irish political relationship that served as the basis for future negotiations.[166] According to McGrath, a new constitutional framework evolved in the years following the Glorious Revolution "out of a combination of political conflict and compromise, trial and error, and a mixture of idealism and pragmatism."[167] McGrath underlines the unintentional nature of this "new constitution" noting, for example, that "[t]here is no evidence . . . that anyone participating in the events of October-November 1692 truly realized the full significance of their actions, or that if they did, whether they believed that their aims would eventually lead to a new understanding of the relationship between the executive and legislature in Ireland."[168]

McGrath's excellent study captures the course of institution-building that characterized Anglo-Irish relations after the Glorious Revolution. There is a disadvantage, however, in labeling these events as a process of "constitution construction." There is a significant difference between informal procedures such as the bargaining method established by Capel and his colleagues and true constitutional reform. Constitutional change requires retraction or modification of long-held, usually legally established, political relationships. In contrast, procedural norms are more amenable to change and variation as they do not involve such formal recognition or approval. Informal institutions emerge within the bounds of formal structures out of the interactions of individuals and groups competing to forward their interests. Depending on the mutability of existing structures, informal institutions can take a variety of forms and distribute power amongst political actors in a variety of ways. Yet unless changes are made to the formal structures in which they are embedded, the basic *constitutional* relationship between actors will remain the same. By compounding the two very different forms of institutions, McGrath risks overestimating the depth of change, which has implications for the interpretation of future political developments. While it is true that Capel's "political compromise" redefined the relationship between the Irish Parliament and the Irish and English executive and continued to affect Anglo-Irish relations well into the eighteenth century, the formal relationship between England and Ireland as exemplified by Poynings' Law did not change. Capel's method may have encouraged an understanding of Anglo-Irish policy as a negotiated outcome, but formal institutions continued to affirm the supremacy of the Irish and English executive over Irish MPs. The potential still existed for new informal procedures to emerge that confirmed, rather than countered, the essence of the Anglo-Irish political relationship, a potential that was to be realized later in the century.

Would the Treaty of Limerick have been ratified in its original form had William III and his ministers been more resolute in their efforts to push the legislation through the Irish Parliament? It is of course impossible to say, but social relations only become institutionalized through repeated use, and it is difficult to tell how entrenched were the informal institutional procedures established by Capel by 1697. Certainly each time the English and Irish executive submitted to the demands of the Irish Parliament it strengthened amongst the individuals and groups involved in policymaking (especially the Irish) the notion that Anglo-Irish politics was not a wholly one-sided enterprise, that it was based on a *reciprocal* relationship between governments. When William ceded to the demands of the Irish Parliament and allowed anti-Catholic legislation to pass in 1695 and 1697, he was, however, unintentionally, contributing to the institutionalization of patterns of behavior that confirmed this notion of the Anglo-Irish policymaking process. Whether or not these patterns of behavior were so established that they could have prevented the English executive from pushing through the Treaty in its original form is uncertain. What is certain is that William's allowing the Irish House of Commons to dictate the terms of the ratification bill and then passing the Treaty in a mutilated form did much to validate the idea and the patterns of behavior that said that Anglo-Irish politics was a reciprocal exercise, and helped to establish further the informal institutions that were to serve as the basis for Anglo-Irish relations until well into the next century.

Could the Treaty have been ratified in its original form had other mechanisms – that is, informal institutions – been developed to curb the Irish Parliament? Perhaps. Had the Irish and English executives formulated a way (or alternatively, had events unfolded in such a way as to encourage the emergence of procedures) to *control* rather than simply manage the Irish Parliament, government legislation of all kinds would have had a better opportunity of being approved in the Irish assemblies. It may also have prevented the passage of much of the penal legislation that was to aggrieve Irish Catholics for many generations. The way in which historical contingency interacted with the institutions that emerged during these years, however, militated against this kind of outcome. Poynings' Law required some procedure in place that would allow the Irish executive to insure that bills sent from England be approved by the Irish Parliament. Henry Capel conceived of such an arrangement, although it only permitted the management of Parliament rather than its outright control. That Capel was a Whig contributed to his willingness to include anti-Catholic legislation as part of the negotiations. William III was a monarch who was more interested in doing battle on the continent than looking after domestic affairs. Because he needed supplies to fight his wars, he went along with Capel's arrangement in 1695 even though it meant that he might occasionally have to cede to the demands of Irish MPs. This is not to suggest, of course, that matters may have been different had different conditions been in place. It does demonstrate, however, how institutions, human agency and contingency came together in this particular circumstance to discourage the English executive from taking an alternative, perhaps more authoritative, approach toward Anglo-Irish policymaking at that moment in time.

Notes

1. James II quit Ireland a few days after the Jacobite defeat at the Boyne, leaving Tyrconnell once more in command of James' forces.

2. F. X. Martin, "The Coming of Parliament," in *The Irish Parliamentary Tradition*, ed. B. Farrell (Dublin: Gill and Macmillan, 1973), 38-40.

3. Ibid., 55.

4. J. C. Beckett, *The Making of Modern Ireland* (New York: Alfred A. Knopf, 1969), 14; Art Cosgrove, "A Century of Decline," in *The Irish Parliamentary Tradition*, ed. B. Farrell (Dublin: Gill and Macmillan, 1973), 58-59.

5. Cosgrove, "A Century of Decline," 66; J. L. McCracken, *The Irish Parliament in the Eighteenth Century* (Dundalk: Dundalgan Press, 1971), 5.

6. J. T. Ball, *Historical Review of the Legislative Systems Operative in Ireland from the Invasion of Henry the Second to the Union (1172-1800)* (London: Longmans, Green, and Co., 1889) 13, 15; Francis G. James, *Ireland in the Empire, 1688-1770* (Cambridge: Harvard University Press, 1973), 7.

7. Brendan Bradshaw, "The Beginnings of Modern Ireland," in *The Irish Parliamentary Tradition,* ed. B. Farrell (Dublin: Gill and Macmillan, 1973), 70.

8. David Quinn, "Parliaments and the Great Councils in Ireland, 1461-1586," *Irish Historical Studies* 3, no. 9 (1942): 72-77.

9. Ball, *Historical Review of the Legislative Systems,* 17-18; H. F. Kearney, "The Political Background to English Mercantilism, 1695-1700," *Economic History Review* 11, no. 3 (1959): 90; J. G. Swift MacNeill, *The Constitutional and Parliamentary History of Ireland till the Union* (Dublin: The Talbot Press, 1917), 52-54.

10. Kearney, "The Political Background to English Mercantilism," 92-93; McCracken, *The Irish Parliament in the Eighteenth Century,* 8-9; MacNeill, *The Constitutional and Parliamentary History of Ireland,* 34-35, 53, 55.

11. R. F. Foster, *Modern Ireland, 1600-1972* (London: Penguin Books, 1989), 82.

12. McGuire, "The Irish Parliament of 1692," in *Penal Era and Golden Age,* ed. T. Bartlett and D. W. Hayton (Belfast: Ulster Historical Foundation, 1979), 1.

13. Cosgrove, "A Century of Decline," 64-66.

14. James, *Ireland in the Empire,* 12; MacNeill, *The Constitutional and Parliamentary History of Ireland,* 18.

15. R. Dudley Edwards and T. W. Moody, "The History of Poynings' Law: Part I, 1494-1615," *Irish Historical Studies* 2, no. 8 (1941): 415-24.

16. Bradshaw, "The Beginnings of Modern Ireland," 70-71.

17. Aidan Clarke, "The History of Poynings' Law, 1615-41," *Irish Historical Studies* 18, no. 70 (1972): 207-22; Edwards and Moody, "The History of Poynings' Law," 415.

18. James, *Ireland in the Empire,* 11-12; MacNeill, *The Constitutional and Parliamentary History of Ireland,* 18, 26.

19. James Kelly, "Monitoring the Constitution: the Operation of Poynings' Law in the 1760s," in *The Irish Parliament in the Eighteenth Century: The Long Apprenticeship,* ed. D. W. Hayton (Edinburgh: Edinburgh University Press, 2001), 89-90.

20. Quoted in McGuire, "The Irish Parliament of 1692," 5.

21. J. G. Simms, "The Treaty of Limerick," in *War and Politics in Ireland, 1649-1730,* ed. D. W. Hayton and G. O'Brien (London: The Hambledon Press, 1986), 204.

22. Ibid.

23. David Hayton, "The Williamite Revolution in Ireland, 1688-9," in *The Anglo-Dutch Moment: Essays in the Glorious Revolution and its World Impact,* ed. J. Israel (Cambridge: Cambridge University Press, 1991): 208; J. G. Simms, "Williamite Peace Tactics, 1690- 1." in *War and Politics in Ireland, 1649-1730,* ed. D. W. Hayton and G. O'Brien (London: The Hambledon Press, 1986), 186; Simms, "The Treaty of Limerick," 204.

24. Hayton, "The Williamite Revolution in Ireland," 208.

25. J. G. Simms, "The Bishops' Banishment Act of 1697," in *War and Politics in Ireland, 1649-1730,* ed. D. W. Hayton and G. O'Brien (London: The Hambledon Press, 1986), 237-38; Wouter Troost, "William III and Ireland," in *Fabrics and Fabrications: The Myth and Making of William and Mary,* ed. P. Hoftijzer and C. C. Barfoot (Amsterdam: Rodopi, 1990), 244-45.

26. J. van den Berg, "Religion and Politics in the Life of William and Mary," in *Fabrics and Fabrications: The Myth and Making of William and Mary*, ed. P. Hoftijzer and C. C. Barfoot (Amsterdam: Rodopi, 1990), 21-23.

27. Ibid., 19-20.

28. Stephen Baxter, *William III* (London: Longmans, 1966), 130-31.

29. Quoted in van den Berg, "Religion and Politics in the Life of William and Mary," 31.

30. Ball, *Historical Review of the Legislative Systems Operative in Ireland*, 261.

31. Mark A. Thomson, *A Constitutional History of England, 1642-1801* (London: Methuen & Co., Ltd.,1938), 102, 104.

32. Edith M. Johnston, *Great Britain and Ireland 1760-1800: A Study in Political Administration* (London: Oliver and Boyd, 1963), 89.

33. Thomson, *A Constitutional History of England*, 103.

34. George Burton Adams, *Constitutional History of England* (New York: Henry Holt and Co., 1956), 349-50; Goldwin Smith, *A Constitutional and Legal History of England* (New York: Charles Scribner's Sons, 1955), 356-57, 377.

35. Thomson, *A Constitutional History of England*, 106.

36. Ibid., 105, 211.

37. Adams, *Constitutional History of England*, 350; Thomson, *A Constitutional History of England*, 104-109.

38. E. L. Ellis, "William III and the Politicians," in *Britain After the Glorious Revolution*, ed. G. Holmes (London: Macmillan and Co. Ltd., 1969), 117.

39. Ibid., 120; Henry Horwitz, *Parliament, Policy and Politics in the Reign of William III* (Newark: University of Delaware Press, 1977), 17-19.

40. Ellis, "William III and the Politicians," 122.

41. Ibid.

42. Troost, "William III and Ireland," 242.

43. S. J. Connolly, *Religion, Law and Power: The Making of Protestant Ireland, 1660-1760* (Oxford: Clarendon Press, 1992).

44. McCracken, *The Irish Parliament*, 7, 9.

45. Connolly, *Religion, Law and Power*, 236-37; Charles Ivar McGrath, "Securing the Protestant Interest: The Origins and Purpose of the Penal Laws of 1695," *Irish Historical Studies* 30, no. 117 (1996): 25-46.

46. Connolly, *Religion, Law and Power*, 203-209; McGrath, "Securing the Protestant Interest," 28.

47. J. G. Simms, *The Williamite Confiscation in Ireland 1690-1703* (Westport, Connecticut: Greenwood Press, 1976), 14-17, 160.

48. Brian Farrell, "The Patriot Parliament of 1689," in *The Irish Parliamentary Tradition*, ed. B. Farrell (Dublin: Gill and Macmillan, 1973).

49. Beckett, *The Making of Modern Ireland*, 80; Foster, *Modern Ireland*, 85-103.

50. Thomas Bartlett, *The Fall and Rise of the Irish Nation: The Catholic Question 1690-1830* (Dublin: Gill and Macmillan, 1992), 6-9; Beckett, *The Making of Modern Ireland*, 83; Foster, *Modern Ireland*, 85-86.

51. Francis G. James, "The Active Irish Peers in the Early Eighteenth Century," *Journal of British Studies* 18, no. 2 (1979): 52-69; McCracken, *The Irish Parliament*, 5.

52. James, "The Active Irish Peers," 54, 65; Francis G. James, *Lords of the Ascendancy: The Irish House of Lords and its Members, 1600-1800* (Dublin: Irish Academic Press, 1995), 99 .

53. Connolly, *Religion, Law and Power*, 65.

Chapter 3

54. James, "The Active Irish Peers," 65; James, *Lords of the Ascendancy,* 129.

55. McCracken, *The Irish Parliament,* 5-6.

56. James, "The Active Irish Peers," 66.

57. McCracken, *The Irish Parliament,* 6.

58. James, *Lords of the Ascendancy,* 148.

59. James, "The Active Irish Peers," 60; James, *Lords of the Ascendancy,* 11-12.

60. James, "The Active Irish Peers," 69; James, *Lords of the Ascendancy,* 99-101.

61. James, "The Active Irish Peers," 60-61.

62. Ibid., 68.

63. Ball, *Historical Review of the Legislative Systems,* 6-7.

64. McCracken, *The Irish Parliament,* 15.

65. Ibid., 15.

66. Ibid., 17.

67. Patrick Kelly, "Lord Galway and the Penal Laws," in *The Huguenots and Ireland: Anatomy of an Emigration,* ed. C. E. J. Caldicott, H. Gough and J. P. Pittion (Dublin: Glendale Press, 1987), 239-54. Kelly notes that Galway in particular has been portrayed as an virulent anti-Catholic who contrived to have anti-Catholic legislation brought to Ireland in revenge for the injuries suffered by his fellow Huguenots at the hands of Louis XIV. This characterization does not align with the actual behavior of Galway who from all indications conducted himself as an able politician who sought simply to reconcile the Irish Parliament.

68. T. W. Moody, F. X. Martin and F. J. Byrne, *A New History of Ireland VIII: A Chronology of Irish History to 1976* (Oxford: Clarendon Press, 1982), 254-56; Troost, "William III and Ireland," passim.

69. Ball, *Historical Review of the Legislative Systems,* 7.

70. Johnston, *Great Britain and Ireland 1760-1800,* 89.

71. James, *Lords of the Ascendancy,* 56.

72. Johnston, *Great Britain and Ireland 1760-1800,* 90.

73. James, "The Active Irish Peers," 52; James, *Lords of the Ascendancy,* 56.

74. Foster, *Modern Ireland,* 107-114.

75. Bartlett, *The Fall and Rise of the Irish Nation,* 17; Hayton, "The Williamite Revolution in Ireland," 211.

76. See above, 35.

77. Beckett, *The Making of Modern Ireland,* 43-45.

78. Ibid., 47-48; Foster, *Modern Ireland,* chapter 3.

79. Connolly, *Religion, Law and Power,* 26-27; James I. McGuire, "Government Attitudes to Religious Non-conformity in Ireland 1660-1719," in *The Huguenots and Ireland: Anatomy of an Emigration,* ed. C. E. J. Caldicott, H. Gough and J. P. Pittion (Dublin: The Glendale Press, 1987), 257, 259, 264.

80. J. C. Beckett, *Protestant Dissent in Ireland 1687-1780* (London: Faber and Faber Ltd.., 1948), 25-27; McGuire, "Government Attitudes to Religious Non-conformity in Ireland," 265-66.

81. McGuire, "Government Attitudes to Religious Non-conformity in Ireland," 268.

82. Beckett, *Protestant Dissent in Ireland,* 29.

83. McGuire, "The Irish Parliament of 1692," 4.

84. David Hayton, "Constitutional Experiments and Political Expediency, 1689-1725," in *Conquest and Union: Fashioning a British State, 1485-1725,* ed. S. Ellis and S. Barber (London: Longman, 1995), 281.

85. McGuire, "The Irish Parliament of 1692," 2.

86. Beckett, *The Making of Modern Ireland*, 152; Hayton, "Constitutional Experiments and Political Expediency," 282.

87. Simms, "The Treaty of Limerick," 219.

88. Wouter Troost, *William III and the Treaty of Limerick (1691-1697): A Study of his Irish Policy* (Leiden: Wouter Troost, 1983), 50-51.

89. McGuire, "Government Attitudes to Religious Non-conformity in Ireland," 269-70.

90. Simms, *The Williamite Confiscation in Ireland*, 46; Simms, "The Treaty of Limerick," 213.

91. Connolly, *Religion, Law and Power*, 264-65; McGuire, "The Irish Parliament of 1692," 3; Troost, "William III and Ireland," 231-32.

92. McGrath, "Securing the Protestant Interest," 30-31.

93. Beckett, *The Making of Modern Ireland*, 151.

94. Quoted in Troost, *William III and the Treaty of Limerick*, 51.

95. Beckett, *The Making of Modern Ireland*, 152-53; McGuire, "The Irish Parliament of 1692," 7-8.

96. James, *Lords of the Ascendancy*, 54; Daniel Szechi and David Hayton, "John Bull's Other Kingdoms: the English Government of Scotland and Ireland," in *Britain in the First Age of Party, 1680-1750*, ed. C. Jones (London: The Hambledon Press, 1987), 265.

97. Ball, *Historical Review of the Legislative Systems*, 74; Cosgrove, "A Century of Decline," 62.

98. Beckett, *The Making of Modern Ireland*, 78; Neil Longley York, *Neither Kingdom Nor Nation: The Irish Quest for Constitutional Rights, 1698-1800* (Washington: The Catholic University of America Press, 1994), 13.

99. James, *Ireland in the Empire*, 191.

100. Farrell, "The Patriot Parliament of 1689," 122; J. G. Simms, "The Jacobite Parliament of 1689," in *War and Politics in Ireland, 1649-1730*, ed. D. W. Hayton and G. O'Brien (London: The Hambledon Press, 1986), 70-71.

101. I am grateful to Sean Connolly for enlightenment on these points.

102. Troost, *William III and the Treaty of Limerick*, 57.

103. McGuire, "The Irish Parliament of 1692," 16-19.

104. James, *Lords of the Ascendancy*, 55.

105. Ibid., 19-21.

106. McGuire, "The Irish Parliament of 1692," 29-30.

107. Ibid, 23-26; Troost, *William III and the Treaty of Limerick*, 68-73; Troost, "William III and Ireland," 237, 240-41.

108. Troost, *William III and the Treaty of Limerick*, 81-87.

109. Quoted in McGuire, "The Irish Parliament of 1692," 28.

110. Ibid., 28.

111. Troost, *William III and the Treaty of Limerick*, 91.

112. Ibid., 95.

113. Quoted in Troost, *William III and the Treaty of Limerick*, 94.

114. Troost, *William III and the Treaty of Limerick*, 91. Troost writes that William said to one of his ministers, "the time is elapsed for holding a Parliament this year, whence those two Wyche and Duncombe who were adverse to a session, have indirectly obtained their end."

115. Ibid., 96.

116. James, *Lords of the Ascendancy*, 57; McGuire, "The Irish Parliament of 1692," 28-29; Troost, *William III and the Treaty of Limerick*, 100-101.

117. McGuire, "The Irish Parliament of 1692," 29; Troost, *William III and the Treaty of Limerick*, 112-14; Troost, "William III and Ireland," 243.

118. McGuire, "The Irish Parliament of 1692."

119. David Hayton, "The Beginnings of the 'Undertaker System,'" in *Penal Era and Golden Age*, ed. T. Bartlett and D. W. Hayton (Belfast: Ulster Historical Foundation, 1979), 40-41.

120. Troost, *William III and the Treaty of Limerick*; Troost, "William III and Ireland."

121. McGrath, "Securing the Protestant Interest," 33.

122. Ibid.; Troost, *William III and the Treaty of Limerick*, 93.

123. Troost, *William III and the Treaty of Limerick*, 116.

124. Troost, *William III and the Treaty of Limerick*, 118.

125. See above, 35.

126. Alison Olson, *Making the Empire Work: London and American Interest Groups 1690-1790* (Cambridge: Harvard University Press, 1992).

127. See below, 159, 165.

128. See below, 166.

129. See below, 86-87.

130. Francis G. James, "The Irish Lobby in the Early Eighteenth Century," *English Historical Review* 81, no. 320 (1966): 543-57.

131. Ibid., 545-46.

132. Troost, *William III and the Treaty of Limerick*, 51-54.

133. Simms, "The Treaty of Limerick," 213.

134. McGuire, "The Irish Parliament of 1692."

135. Troost, *William III and the Treaty of Limerick*.

136. Beckett, *The Making of Modern Ireland*, 151; Connolly, *Religion, Law and Power*, 264.

137. Troost, *William III and the Treaty of Limerick*, 121-24; Troost, "William III and Ireland," 246-47.

138. Troost, *William III and the Treaty of Limerick*, 124-34; Troost, "William III and Ireland," 247-48.

139. Troost, *William III and the Treaty of Limerick*, 140-46.

140. Quoted in Troost, *William III and the Treaty of Limerick*, 164.

141. Troost, "William III and Ireland," 251-52.

142. Simms, "The Treaty of Limerick," 213-14; Troost, *William III and the Treaty of Limerick*, 168-70.

143. Simms, "The Treaty of Limerick," 212-13.

144. Troost, *William III and the Treaty of Limerick*, 170-73.

145. Connolly, *Religion, Law and Power*, 296; Troost, *William III and the Treaty of Limerick*, 174-77.

146. Connolly, *Religion, Law and Power*, 269.

147. Simms, "The Treaty of Limerick," 214; Troost, *William III and the Treaty of Limerick*, 179-80.

148. James, *Lords of the Ascendancy*, 60.

149. Ibid.; Simms, *The Williamite Confiscation in Ireland*, 62; Troost, *William III and the Treaty of Limerick*, 181-82.

150. McGrath, "Securing the Protestant Interest."

151. Simms, "The Bishops' Banishment Act," 246.

152. Maureen Wall, *The Penal Laws, 1691-1760* (Dundalk: Dundalgan Press, 1967), 66n. Wall notes that passing draconian legislation then letting it sit on the statute books unenforced was an "unofficial policy" of the English state well into the nineteenth century.

153. Simms, "The Bishops' Banishment Act," 244.

154. Connolly, *Religion, Law and Power*, 270; Simms, *The Williamite Confiscation in Ireland*, 63-65; Troost, "William III and Ireland," 255-56.

155. McGuire, "Government Attitudes to Religious Non-conformity," 271.

156. Edith M. Johnston, *Ireland in the Eighteenth Century* (Dublin: Gill and Macmillan, 1974), 28.

157. Connolly, *Religion, Law and Power*, 273-275; J. G. Simms, "The Making of a Penal Law," in *War and Politics in Ireland, 1649-1730*, ed. D. W. Hayton and G. O'Brien (London: The Hambledon Press, 1986), 267, 276; Wall, *The Penal Laws*, 21.

158. Johnston, *Ireland in the Eighteenth Century*, 36.

159. Thomas P. Power, "Converts," in *Endurance and Emergence: Catholics in Ireland in the Eighteenth Century*, ed. T. P. Power and K. Whelan (Dublin: Irish Academic Press, 1990), 112.

160. Connolly, *Religion, Law and Power*, 272; Simms, "The Making of a Penal Law," 266-68.

161. Simms rejects this argument as an explanation for the addition of the sacramental test. He argues that it was the secretary of state, Nottingham, who, knowing how much the Irish Parliament wished the legislation, simply "saw an opportunity of bringing Ireland into line with England by inserting the test." Beckett provides a compromise. Beckett argues that English ministers recognized that the addition of the test would not prevent the bill's passage in Ireland. They included it to convince their Catholic allies that the responsibility for the bill lay in Ireland not in England.

162. Beckett, *Protestant Dissent in Ireland*, 43-44.

163. Connolly, *Religion, Law and Power*, 273, 277; Simms, "The Making of a Penal Law," 270.

164. McGuire, "The Irish Parliament of 1692," 39-40.

165. Charles Ivar McGrath, *The Making of the Eighteenth-Century Irish Constitution* (Dublin: Four Courts Press, 2000).

166. See also Foster, *Modern Ireland*, 160-61.

167. McGrath, *The Making of the Eighteenth-Century Irish Constitution*, 73-74.

168. Ibid., 80.

Chapter 4

The Quebec Act, Part I

The city of Quebec fell to the British in the early winter of 1759; Montreal capitulated a year later. Thus ended over a century and a half of French rule in Canada. The British victory did not signal the cessation of the larger conflict, however. Britain and France and their respective allies clashed for another three years until 10 February 1763 when the Treaty of Paris finally brought the Seven Years' War to an end. It was not until then that it was decided that Britain would retain the former French colony. Now British officials were compelled to consider how to administer a province in which French Catholics made up 95 percent of the population.

In May 1763, a Royal Proclamation issued by the British government stipulated, among other things, how Britain's new possessions were to be governed. Quebec (as Canada was now called) was to be remade into a traditional British colony as soon as the provincial executive deemed it feasible, complete with British landhold and legal systems, an elected assembly, and an ascendant Protestant church. The position of the Catholic Church and French Catholics was given little consideration. The Treaty of Paris had insured religious liberty to those who decided to stay in the colonies. But this was a vague promise, its ambiguity heightened by the addition of the statement that these freedoms would be enjoyed only "as far as the laws of Britain permit." The Proclamation did not clarify the situation.

The commission and instructions given to the new governor of Quebec, James Murray, however, provided a better picture of how British officials believed religion should be managed in the new province. Members of the future assembly and all those serving the government would have to take oaths of allegiance, supremacy and against transubstantiation, as well as make a declaration abjuring the right of the Stuarts to the English throne. Since most of these oaths were offensive to Catholics, they were effectively barred from holding public office. Anglicization of the French Catholic population was to begin in earnest. The governor was to work to this end by encouraging the establishment of Protestant schools, maintaining Protestant ministers and providing Protestant schoolmasters to promote the conversion of French inhabitants to the Church of England. Whatever religious freedoms had been guaranteed in the Treaty of Paris were to be narrowly interpreted; the Proclamation authorized the provincial government to *tolerate* Catholics and the Catholic Church in Quebec, nothing more.[1]

The Proclamation of 1763 was the only official statement of government policy in Quebec for eleven years. In 1774, the British Parliament passed the Quebec Act. It stipulated that the province was henceforth to be ruled by governor and council only; there was no mention of an elected assembly. Quebec land and legal systems were to conform to French custom; English institutions occupied an ancillary position in the province. Moreover, the Act contained a number of concessions to Quebec Catholics. It guaranteed the free exercise of the Catholic religion in the province, that Catholic clergy be allowed to collect the tithe, and that Catholics not be forced to make any objectionable declarations. The removal of the offensive oaths opened the way for Catholics to hold public office. Indeed, the Quebec Act even stipulated that a few positions be made available to French Catholics in the provincial council, which, in the absence of a representative assembly, had legislative jurisdiction over the region. Protestants and the Protestant church would not hold privileged positions in the province. The Quebec Act placed the Catholic church on almost an equal footing with the established church and allowed Catholics the right to participate fully in the civil life of the colony.[2]

In a little over a decade the position of British officials on Quebec governance and administration had changed drastically. The tolerance granted to Quebec Catholics by the Quebec Act was unprecedented in the British empire. At the time of its passage, penal legislation in Britain and Ireland remained in full force. How and why did it come to pass that Catholics in Quebec were permitted not only to practice their religion without fear of reprisal but actually participate in an official capacity in the governance of the colony, while the activities of Catholics overseas continued to be subject to such severe restrictions? An institutional analysis can help clarify this apparent anomaly.

This chapter will outline the formal and informal institutions structuring Anglo-Quebec policymaking at the time of the Quebec Act negotiations, as well as the major actors involved in the process and their sentiments concerning Catholics and Catholicism. The information will then be used in the following chapter to help analyze the circumstances and events surrounding the Quebec Act's passage.

Formal Institutions Characterizing Quebec Policymaking in 1774

As a colony and dependency of Britain, Quebec was subject to the rule of the British government. Upon British takeover, Quebec and all other territories ceded by the Treaty of Paris became the concern of officials in the British government who were responsible for colonial matters. There were, however, no *formal* institutions in place to specify how Anglo-Quebec policymaking should be handled. Recall that *formal institutions* are the more tangible structures defining the bounds of government policymaking, those guidelines that are more securely embedded in the operation of the state because they are well established, such as the constitution or legal statutes.

In Ireland, the legislative process was governed by a number of centuries-old formal practices. Poynings' Law had been in operation since 1495 and required Anglo-Irish policymaking to adhere to strict guidelines. Ireland had also long been ruled by a Crown-appointed, and since the 1530s English executive, and had a tradition of holding an Irish Parliament, conditions that structured further how Irish policy was formulated and passed. There were no comparable institutions in place to help determine relations between London and Quebec.

Under French rule, Quebec had of course been subject to French institutions. New France had been governed by a royal administration consisting of a governor general, three lesser governors in Acadia, Montreal and Trois-Rivières, an *intendant*, a bishop and five appointed officials. There was no representative body in the province; all laws were adjudicated by the executive and ultimately the French Crown. Justice was dispensed according to French law and land was held on seigneurial tenure. Catholicism was the established religion. The Crown controlled all patronage in the province. Wealth and social status in New France was determined by one's relationship to the Crown as in France. By controlling the main avenues of upward mobility, the metropolis in France insured that officials in New France would maintain their allegiance to the French Crown, an allegiance that facilitated the operation of government in the colony.[3] The system had worked well for the French, and this did not go unnoticed by the British conquerors. James Murray was impressed that France had been able to rule such a vast colony so cheaply and with so few men.[4] Even so, British officials were obviously under no obligation to adopt the institutions of New France.

Although relations between Quebec and the mother country were not formally as well defined as the Anglo-Irish association, British administrators did have at their disposal a few measures that provided, if not a blueprint for the governance of Quebec, at least some formal guidelines to which they could refer. The first was the decision taken in *Calvin's Case* in 1609. The case determined that, in colonies established by *settlement*, colonists would enjoy English laws and institutions. Laws in these colonies could be passed only by the king in Parliament or by a local representative assembly. The institutions of *conquered* or *ceded* colonies, however, were at the discretion of the Crown. Until the Crown decided on the form of governance to be implemented, existing laws and institutions would be maintained.[5] Quebec, having been ceded to Britain from France, fell into the latter category.

The second formal institution was the Declaratory Act, passed by the British Parliament in 1766. Modeled on the Irish Declaratory Act of 1720,[6] this measure established formally the authority of the British Parliament to legislate for the colonies. Although this measure was to have more of an impact on colonies with existing assemblies – indeed, the legislation was passed with the American colonies in mind – it confirmed that the British Parliament had a legal say in colonial policy, including Quebec legislation.[7]

Another formal measure that came to affect Anglo-Quebec policymaking was the decision taken by the Court of King's Bench in the case of *Campbell v. Hall* in November 1774. It was concerned with taxation authority in Grenada. In 1764, an export duty of 4.5 percent was levied by Hall, collector for the Crown in Grenada, on sugar exported from Grenada by Campbell. He imposed this tax on the authority of a letters patent[8] prepared by British officials on behalf of the Crown 20 July. Campbell argued this letters patent was superceded by the Proclamation of 1763 and the Governor's Commission of 9 April 1764, both of which had established that the island was to be governed like other royal colonies, which meant any tax levies had to be approved by a colonial assembly. Although an assembly had not yet been called in Grenada, Campbell maintained that, once the *promise* of a representative legislature had been held out, the monarch did not have the power to impose taxation by prerogative. After several years of deliberation Lord Mansfield, Britain's Lord Chief Justice, came down on the side of Campbell. In addition to confirming the principle laid down in *Calvin's Case* that the laws and institutions of a conquered territory remain in place until they are altered by the conqueror, Mansfield resolved that the monarch could not unilaterally pass legislation in the province after the promise of an assembly had been made. Only the colonial legislature or the British Parliament could henceforth exercise legislative power in a conquered or ceded colony.[9]

Mansfield's final decision came several months after the passage of the Quebec Act in June. But it was a long-running case concerning matters of authority and jurisdiction that had been under consideration for several years. Given its direct relevance to Quebec and the authority of British officials and the Crown to legislate for the new province without recourse to a colonial assembly or the British Parliament, the deliberations surrounding the case came to have an important influence on the way in which government officials were to handle Quebec legislation. Although unconfirmed, the matter was under negotiation and had the potential to constrain them considerably.

While there were no formal institutions governing Anglo-Quebec political relations comparable to those surrounding Anglo-Irish policymaking, there were in place three directives that provided some formal guidelines for Anglo-Quebec governance: the existence of *Calvin's Case* that stipulated conquered or ceded colonies were to retain their existing institutions until the Crown decided otherwise; the Declaratory Act that established formally the legislative jurisdiction of the British Parliament over colonial matters; and the decision in the case of *Campbell vs. Hall*, which determined that only the British Parliament and the colonial assembly could alter legislation pertaining to the colonies after the promise of an assembly had been made. The Crown could no longer act unilaterally on colonial matters.

These formal institutions were not, however, as extensive as those governing the policy process in Ireland, nor did they define the situation as explicitly. Whereas formal institutions specified clearly who were the major actors in the Anglo-Irish policymaking process, as well as their powers and the procedures they were required to follow, the few formal directives that applied to Quebec were much more general. They were not concerned with Quebec specifically so they placed fewer and less stringent conditions on policymakers. Nevertheless, their existence as formal directives was to have a considerable effect on the decisionmaking process.

Informal Institutions Characterizing Quebec Policymaking in 1774

Despite the dearth of precise *formal* institutions surrounding Anglo-Quebec relations, Quebec rule was not entirely unrestrained. Whatever the relations between metropolis and colony lacked in formal guidelines was nearly made up for by the existence of a number of well-established *informal* institutions. These informal institutions helped to structure the governance and policymaking procedures applicable to Quebec. They were not, however, formally established, a fact that was to prove significant to the promulgation of policy in the new province.

The most important *informal* institutions related to Quebec policymaking were those pertaining to the administration of British colonies by metropolitan officials. The other areas in which informal institutions played an important role were in the operation of British politics, specifically, the relationship between the British executive and the British Parliament, and institutions pertaining to the policy process itself; and in the relations between the major actors involved in the process. Following are descriptions of the first two areas. The third requires that the major actors be identified, and so will be discussed after they are introduced.

It should be stressed again that the specification of *informal* institutions can become quite involved, as institutions of an informal nature can only be discerned from observing the behavior of individuals engaged in activities related to the process that is under study. Unlike formal institutions, there is nothing tangible, no written constitution or actual legal statute or bill, that can be referred to that spells out the structures by which actors have to abide. Informal institutions have emerged out of and are manifest in the routine interactions of actors and groups of actors, and so require a greater amount of description, to identify their origins and character.

Informal Institutions Governing Relations between London and Quebec

Although there may not have been many *formal* institutions to help guide relations between Britain and Quebec specifically, there were many unwritten *informal* institutions governing Britain's relationship with *other* colonies, particularly those in America, to which British officials could refer. By the middle of the eighteenth century, the oldest of Britain's colonial possessions in the "new world," Virginia, had existed for a century and a half,[10] and others in North America and in the West Indies nearly as long. During this time, officials in England had waged wars, appointed and directed public officials, collected taxes, pondered legislation and otherwise involved themselves in these distant territories. So long had Britain and the American colonies been affiliated that, by 1763, the practices associated with many areas of colonial management had become quite routine.

"Routine" was hardly the word to describe metropolis-colony relations during the seventeenth century, however. Most of the colonies in North America had been founded by private interests whose authority to establish settlements had been granted them by the Crown. Maryland (1632), the Carolinas, the New Jerseys (1664), and the Bahamas and Pennsylvania (1681) were each established by a grant to an individual or group of proprietors. Virginia (1606) and Massachusetts (1629) were each founded through a Crown grant to a joint stock company. Some colonies, such as Connecticut (1630s) and Rhode Island (1635), were established by colonists without royal sanction. Variations in the type of grant led to the development of different sorts of institutions in each colony and so each colony's relationship to the metropolis was different. The first company charter for Virginia, for example, stipulated that the company would appoint a provincial council to govern but the colony that would remain under Crown control, supervised by a royal council in England. Colonists were guaranteed the "liberties, franchises and immunities" of Englishmen.[11] Three years later the Crown-supervised council was replaced by a *company*-appointed lord governor and a captain general, reducing the amount of Crown control over the colony. In 1619, the Virginia Company surrendered some of their authority to a representative body of settlers, the House of Burgesses. Finally in 1624, the self-governing Virginia colony became a Crown possession, and was eventually given what was to become the standard sort of administration in royal provinces, a royally-appointed governor and council and an elected representative assembly.[12] In contrast to Virginia's experience, the first charter of the proprietary colony of Maryland said nothing about a council; it gave the proprietor absolute power over the colony, "as much authority within his territory as the king had outside it."[13] Connecticut and Rhode Island were on their own as far as their government and administration were concerned. Without a royal grant to their territories, the colonies' founders made do. In Rhode Island, colonists met every fortnight to discuss colonial affairs, agreeing to obey the decisions of the majority of householders. Connecticut decided on an elected governor, magistrates and representatives.[14] In addition to these "colonies of settlement," Britain had collected a number of territories in the west by conquest: Jamaica in 1655, New York in 1664 and Nova Scotia in 1710.[15] These areas had been won from Spain, Holland and France, respectively, and had to be given separate consideration in accord with *Calvin's Case.*

Yet out of this hodgepodge of regimes there emerged, by the early eighteenth century, a collection of colonies with more or less matching systems of governance. Half a century of neglect had been followed at the Restoration by a conspicuous attempt by the English government to establish better control over its colonial possessions. A series of mercantilist trade directives were introduced to help secure the economic interdependence of the many parts of the empire. The responsibilities of existing central agencies such as the Customs Service and the Treasury were expanded to include the colonies and new bodies, such as the Board of Trade, were created to oversee colonial matters. These changes were accompanied by attempts by the English government to acquire greater control over the administration of the colonies. Previous colonial arrangements were revoked and established institutions were abolished with the intention of unifying colonial rule. There was even an effort to make the metropolis-colony relationship more like that between England and Ireland. In 1677, English officials in charge of colonial policy recommended that legislative initiative be taken away from the assembly in Jamaica and a system resembling the Poynings procedure be put in place. They sent along with the new governor, Lord Carlisle, a number of bills to be passed by the Jamaican legislature stipulating that bills were henceforth to be framed by the governor and council of the colony and sent to the British Privy Council for review. Bills approved by council were then to be returned to Jamaica, where the assembly was to give its consent to the directives. The same sort of system was planned for Virginia, whose governor received similar instructions two years later. Had the representatives in the Jamaican assembly reacted to the measures in the same way that colonials in Virginia did, the system would likely have been extended to include other royal provinces. The Virginian assembly passed all the bills necessary to put the system in place. Unfortunately for the Board, however, the Jamaican assembly wanted nothing to do with the new procedures. Opposition to the measures was intense; Jamaican representatives refused to give up their right to initiate legislation. Finally, the Board of Trade had to give in. In October 1680, they restored the initiative to the assemblies in both provinces.[16]

The Glorious Revolution saw the end of the Stuarts' "colonial experiment" and the colonies resumed their separate existences. These authoritative measures were not without their consequences, however. Although the English government failed to consolidate colonial rule, administration became more standardized as the Crown took over colony after colony and put in place in each a system of governance consisting of a Crown-appointed governor, a nominated council and an elected assembly.[17]

This uniformity even extended to the conquered colonies. *Calvin's Case* stipulated that the administrations of these territories were at the disposition of the Crown, and so could have been governed any way the Crown wished. But since the English government wanted to attract settlers to these newly conquered areas, officials decided it would be prudent to grant the same "conditions of freedom" to these territories as were held by the older, settled colonies. So in spite of its "conquered" status, Jamaica received English law and a representative assembly in 1661. Other conquered colonies were extended the same rights for the same reasons.[18]

Administrative uniformity translated into legislative uniformity. By the middle of the eighteenth century, procedures had developed that had made fairly regular the administration of colonial matters. Bills initiated and passed by the two "houses" of colonial government – the representative assembly and the provincial council – were forwarded to the governor. If the governor did not veto the measure, he signed it, at which point the bill became law in the colony. The bill was then sent to the British Privy Council for consideration, where it was confirmed or disallowed. If it was rejected, the governor was informed of the law's reversal and the measure became null and void in the province. Otherwise, the measure received the consent of the king in council and the law remained in effect until it elapsed or was repealed. Occasionally, the British government would require that legislation transmitted from the colonies include a "suspending clause." This was true especially of bills that British officials did not approve of. The suspending clause delayed implementation of the measure until it had received the consent of the king in council.[19] Not surprisingly, most colonial assemblies were reluctant to sanction the inclusion of the suspending clause and only consented to its addition as a "last resort" to secure desired measures.[20]

"Officially" (although not formally), this was the manner in which all colonial policy was considered. In reality the procedure operated somewhat differently. The decisions taken by the king in council were actually adjudicated elsewhere. All colonial legislation sent to the Privy Council was immediately referred to the Board of Trade, the government body responsible for overseeing colonial matters. The Lords Commissioners of the Board would review the act and collect evidence and advice concerning the legislation from relevant documents, government law officers and other sources. It would then submit a report to the Privy Council advising members how to proceed. In many cases judgments made by "the king in council" were just a rubber stamp of the Board's recommendations.[21]

If the procedures surrounding the making of colonial legislation had become routine by this period, so too had the administration of other areas of colonial business. In 1930, Leonard Labaree undertook an examination of the commissions and instructions issued to colonial governors between 1624 and 1783. Although the earlier documents varied widely in detail, around 1670 to 1680 they began to exhibit considerable uniformity. Indeed, Labaree found that there were few important differences in the commissions and instructions handed down to governors in the 1770s and those issued to the governors of Virginia, Jamaica, Barbados and the Leeward Islands a century earlier.[22]

The commissions and instructions stipulated the powers and responsibilities of the governor and how the colonial administration was to look. The governor's commission was the more formal of the two documents. It revoked the authority of the old governor and appointed the new, and granted the latter the broad powers necessary to execute his office.[23] The manner in which the governor was expected to execute these powers was laid out in his instructions. The document consisted of three major parts. The general instructions were the longest and were concerned with civil government of the colony; the trade instructions outlined the governor's responsibilities in relation to the acts of trade and navigation; the additional instructions amended or added to the other instructions and were usually prepared after the other two.[24]

In addition to the governor's commission and instructions, there were other instruments through which the British government communicated with the colonial governor. Warrants and royal letters directed the governor to, for example, assume a certain attitude or policy toward a political matter, or to secure the passage of a piece of legislation through the colonial assembly; the commission declaring the governor the vice admiral of the province gave him power over admiralty or maritime affairs in the colony. On a less formal level, British officials corresponded regularly with the governor. It was in the letters between the governor and the Secretary of State for the Southern Department and the Board of Trade in particular where specific matters of concern on both sides were dealt with and, as Labaree notes, were the best indication of how the system worked in practice.[25]

It is the governor's commission and instructions that are most important for the current study because, although the terms they stipulated had no formal or legal backing, British officials and colonials alike came to consider these documents the "constitution" of the colony. The commission especially was significant because it was on this public instrument that the formal powers of the governor and the executive was based. The instructions as well, although most of the sections were the concern of the governor alone, contained directives of a constitutional nature, including those that dealt with the powers and procedures of the provincial assembly. If the representatives in the legislature did not follow these directives, the governor could veto their bills and even dissolve the assembly.[26]

The Board of Trade was responsible for drawing up the commissions and instructions to new governors. By the mid-eighteenth century, commissions seldom changed from governor to governor so they typically took at the most two weeks to prepare. In 1759, the Board completed the commission to the new governor of Virginia, Lord Amherst, on the same day its preparation was ordered.[27] The commission was then forwarded to the Privy Council, usually through the Secretary of State for the Southern Department, and from there proceeded through the final stages of approval. The instructions took longer to draw up, about two or three months. It was this document that would serve as the governor's guide to administering the province and so the Lords Commissioners were careful in its preparation. Any changes that had occurred since the last instructions were issued, such as modifications in policies concerning metropolis-colony relations or changes in the conditions of the province, were incorporated; former colonial governors and officials in other areas of government, law officers and merchants, virtually anyone of any consequence with an interest in the colonies, were consulted.[28] The completed document, along with a representation explaining the changes made, were submitted to the Privy Councillors, who in most cases approved the document. The Secretary of State's office then prepared the final copy, which was signed by the monarch and given, along with the commission and other papers, to the new governor at his departure.[29]

The stability of the commissions prepared during the eighteenth century is perhaps understandable, given their generality. But the uniformity of the instructions, across time and across colonies, is, as all researchers who have studied these documents note, quite remarkable. Differences did appear in sections that dealt with specific local conditions, but those parts concerning political, judicial and religious affairs remained virtually the same. After the late seventeenth century and the Board of Trade's failure to institute the Poynings procedure in Jamaica and Virginia, every province was granted a local assembly that had the right to initiate legislation. The instructions may have become more protracted, as the Board strove to delimit the actions of the colonial legislatures relative to the Crown and to the British government.[30] But for the greater part of the eighteenth century, "British officials showed no inclination to change the constitutional system of a single royal province."[31] English law extended to the colonies, a principle that was expressed in the earliest colonial grants and in most provisions thereafter.[32] The commissions and instructions, although they gave the colonial assemblies some jurisdiction over how the judiciary might be administered in each province, specified that legal matters remained within the control of the Crown and should be regulated by royal rather than colonial officials. Hence it was the governor, with the consent of his council, that created the Courts of Justice in the colony as per the governor's commission; the instructions required that changes in the judicial system be approved by the Crown and that new legislation be in conformity with English legal doctrines. British officials took these principles seriously and kept a watchful eye on all colonial judicial affairs to insure they did not stray from these standards.[33]

The commission and instructions also identified the governor as the head of the established church in the colony. The documents directed him, in association with the Bishop of London, to oversee the operation of churches in the area, insure that the Book of Common Prayer be read every Sunday, that maintenance was provided for the clergy, etc. He was also to encourage religious and moral behavior among the colonists by setting up schools to instruct youth in the principles of the Church of England and punishing those who broke laws prohibiting blasphemy, sabbath-breaking and other conduct contrary to religious teachings.[34] As for the place of other religions in the colonies, it had never been formally established that English legislation respecting recusants extended to the provinces. Nevertheless, the principles contained in these measures were generally accepted. There was some tolerance shown toward Protestant nonconformists in the colonies in accord with the English Toleration Act.[35] Roman Catholics, however, were subject to penal measures of some sort in every province, measures that were imposed by both the provincial and British governments. In Maryland, for example, Catholics were disenfranchised in 1718, had to pay double taxation and could not inherit land; in 1705, the English attorney general declared that a British decision that sanctioned the perpetual imprisonment of any bishop or priest discovered saying mass applied to the colonies. In addition to grievances such as these, Catholics were barred from holding public office. The commission and instructions issued to governors of royal provinces required that the governor, his council and any other office holders, including assembly men, take a number of oaths, including the oath against transubstantiation and a declaration of fidelity to the Protestant succession, pledges offensive to Catholics.[36] But oaths and declarations were not the only way that Catholics were prevented from participating in politics. In Rhode Island, where there were no religious tests, Catholics were simply denied political rights.[37]

It is important to emphasize how established this method of "government by instruction" was by the mid-eighteenth century and how routine the preparation of the governors' commissions and instructions had become. Indeed, it seems that the Board of Trade and the Privy Council made special effort to keep these documents as consistent as possible across time and across colonies. In the instructions to a new governor, changes from the old instructions were only introduced when absolutely necessary, and even then, both bodies appear to have tried to keep as close to the former phraseology as possible. The instructions also tended to match those issued to governors in other provinces around the same time. Whatever changes the Board of Trade decided to include in one set of documents were usually included in subsequent documents prepared for other governors.[38] As Labaree writes, the adherence of British officials to this method of colonial rule and their reverence for the conditions contained in the documents on which the system was based, was "almost fanatical,"[39] resulting in a system that "was fixed, static, and unchanging."[40]

Even though there were few *formal* institutions applicable to royal policymaking in Quebec, there was a well-established system of *informal* institutions associated with royal government in other colonies overseas. As routine as these procedures had become, however, as taken for granted as were the powers, rights and freedoms embodied in the documents and practices that comprised this system, none were constitutionally entrenched. Officials in the metropolis had always understood that the "rules" associated with colonial governance were very different, more pliant, than those associated with, for example, Irish rule. In 1670, during a debate about the rights of the English Parliament to tax Ireland, the distinction was made between "the distinct kingdome" of Ireland and the colonial "plantacions." Whereas the existence of the Irish Parliament made it questionable whether Ireland could be taxed by the English Parliament, it was noted "That we do not yet offer to tax our plantacions which is in kindnesse to them."[41] The notion that the institutions, powers and privileges extended to the colonies were granted by the British government out of "kindnesse" and did not constitute immutable colonial rights was held by British officials throughout the eighteenth century, a fact that was to have important implications for the negotiation of policy in Quebec.

Informal Institutions Governing Relations between the British Executive and the British Parliament

In the era of the Treaty of Limerick, the influence of the English Parliament and English party politics on the process surrounding the negotiation and passage of the ratification bill were, although not inconsequential, not as significant as they were to later become. There were no formal institutions defining the relationship between the English Parliament and the Irish Parliament. And, although the revolution settlement conveyed that the English Parliament would henceforth have greater control over English politics, the *informal* institutions, those operational norms and procedures that were required for this power to be exercised actually, had not yet developed to the point where that control was real. The monarch continued to wield considerable power over the choice of his executive. Since these were the men who determined Anglo-Irish policy, the policymaking process remained, to a large extent, in the hands of the sovereign and his chosen ministers.

The situation was much the same in the colonies in the seventeenth and early part of the eighteenth centuries. The relationship between the English/British Parliament and the colonial assemblies was nowhere formally subscribed, and in the relative absence of any informal institutions allowing MPs control over the monarch's choice of ministers, the officials in charge of colonial affairs were to a large degree the servants of the monarch. This was certainly true of the Lords of Trade (the body that was later to become the Board of Trade) under the later Stuarts. The lords were the creation of advisers to Charles II and essentially an instrument of the Crown, a truth that was evident in their "energetic" support of James II's authoritarian policy in the American colonies.[42] With the accession of William III, the name of the body changed but its character did not. As had traditionally been the case, it was the monarch who set up the new board responsible for overseeing trade and plantations in 1696. Granted, William's decision to establish the Board of Trade was in response to attempts by MPs to institute an analogous body under the control of the English Parliament that would have weakened the power of the Crown over the empire's trade and plantations. Nevertheless, William's actions insured that colonial administration and commerce remained the domain of the royal prerogative, where it more or less stayed until the Board's dissolution in 1782.[43]

By 1774, however, the role of the British Parliament in British politics, and so on the making of colonial policy, had changed considerably. The Declaratory Act of 1766 established formally the subordination of the colonies to the British Parliament. Perhaps more importantly, however, informal institutions enabling British MPs to determine who would constitute the sovereign's ministry were more firmly in place. Recall that William III, like his Stuart predecessors, made use of a group or "cabinet" of high office holders, who were part of his ministry but were essentially separate from the English Privy Council, to assist him in rule. At the time, the cabinet was considered unconstitutional and dangerous because Charles II and James II, and to a lesser extent, William III, used it to maintain the power of the Crown relative to the legally recognized Privy Council and the English Parliament.[44] So concerned was the English Parliament about the effect of the cabinet on its ability to enforce Crown responsibility that two provisions were included in the Act of Settlement to do away with the cabinet all together. Fortunately for future MPs, the provisions were later repealed, because it was by means of the cabinet system that the British House of Commons eventually acquired control of the British government.[45]

Anne continued William's practice of using her prerogative of appointment and dismissal to choose her ministries and cabinets without any acknowledged recourse to Parliament. Like William, Anne was a proponent of "mixed" government and strove to avoid rule by party. During her reign, however, it became increasingly clear that a successful cabinet and ministry depended on Parliament, and that an administration based on party was much more stable than a coalition government. It also became apparent that the cabinet was a useful piece of government machinery. By Anne's death, it was primarily the cabinet and not the Privy Council that provided advice to the monarch and directed state business. Although there was still some concern over how responsibility could be enforced upon its members, the cabinet was no longer considered dangerous.[46]

It was during the reigns of the first two kings of the House of Hanover that the British Parliament, or more accurately the British House of Commons, began to acquire some real control over the cabinet and the ministry, and by extension, the British government. A number of elements came together to precipitate this change. First, there was the tendency of the first two Hanoverian kings to acquiesce to British politicians. George I had trouble understanding British ways and, because he spoke little English, had great difficulty communicating with his ministers. Traditionally, the monarch attended all cabinet meetings, voicing his or her opinions on government matters. Soon after his accession George I stopped this practice, finding the task of trying to understand discussions conducted in a language not his own too tiresome to endure.[47] He was more than happy to leave government business to his chosen ministers. George II, although he knew more about government matters than his father, did not involve himself much in British politics either. When he did, he generally (although not always cheerfully) supported his executive.[48] Under the first two Georges, British politicians operated relatively free of Crown influence for almost fifty years. The process of transferring control of government business to a now independent cabinet progressed greatly during this period.

The cabinet may have been capable of fixing policy relatively independently of the monarch, but it required the approval of the British House of Commons to carry it out. A second and related development was the emergence of the notion that the cabinet and ministry were responsible not to the Crown but to the lower house. Although the government executive continued to be appointed by the monarch, during the reign of the first two Georges, the real power of the monarch to select and maintain ministers of his own choosing diminished considerably. By the middle of the century, it was very difficult for men who did not have the confidence of the House of Commons to form an administration.[49]

Finally was the refinement of the party system. For the cabinet to be successful in promulgating government policy it was necessary that its membership be unified and that a majority of the House of Commons be agreeable to their position. Although the British Parliament had been divided into two factions – Tory and Whig – at least since the Restoration,[50] it was not until the eighteenth century that party government became more established that these conditions were met.[51]

It is important to remember that the cabinet system of government as it developed during the eighteenth century did not suddenly appear, nor was it in any way planned. As George Adams writes, "the progress made had to be progress with no definite aim, with no conception, even by the most far-sighted statesmen who were leading the advance, of the result towards which they were reaching."[52] The idea that the cabinet and ministry were an "Executive Committee of the two Houses of Parliament, practically chosen by the majority of the House of Commons"[53] was slow to take hold and exert itself. For all the advances this form of government made during the first half of the century, by 1760 it had not, as Richard Pares puts it, "formally passed over from the position of a check on the executive government and become, in effect, the executive government itself."[54] So when George III acceded to the throne in that year, determined to restore responsibility for ministers to the monarch and to reestablish the sovereign's command over the initiation and direction of state business, the cabinet system of government was in no way so firmly established or even understood to prevent him from doing so.

The extent to which George III actually changed, or even wanted to change, existing procedures, however, has been the subject of some debate. The standard explanation, the one that has been most popular with American and British Whig historians in particular depicts George III as "the villain *par excellence*, a would-be autocrat seeking to turn back the constitutional clock."[55] According to this account the king was a calculating despot who, together with his "secret cabal" of councillors, connived throughout his reign to override the authority of the cabinet and the British Parliament to put in place his own tyrannical policies. More recent research has determined that this picture of George III is inaccurate. It is true that the king involved himself in politics much more than either of the first two Georges, and kept himself informed on virtually all aspects of government business. It is also true that the king wanted to take back from the cabinet the power of appointing ministers. But it is now known that, although George III certainly influenced government policy, he was no dictator. "[H]aving chosen his ministers," writes P. D. G. Thomas, "he let them govern."[56] The first colonial Secretary, Lord Hillsborough, described in February 1775 the king's usual practice:

> [The King] always will leave his own sentiments, and conform to his Ministers, though he will argue with them, and very sensibly; but if they adhere to their own opinion, he will say, "Well. Do you choose it should be so? Then let it be."[57]

Furthermore, George III evidently thought it unconstitutional to influence policy by declaring his personal stand on government matters; he only ever made public his views at the urging of his ministers. Mostly, he would keep his opinion secret and supported his cabinet even when he disagreed with them. In 1766, American opposition to the Stamp Act forced the British government to take another look at the legislation George III was against the repeal of the Act but refused to make his opinions known in case his ministers decided to revoke it. When the prime minister informed him that the cabinet had resolved to reverse the Act, George told him to make his support of its decision public. Even when the opponents of the repeal approached the king and offered to press for his preferred solution, modification of the Act, George held firm: "I do not think it constitutional for the Crown personally to interfere in measures which it has thought proper to refer to the advice of Parliament."[58] The king apparently acted in much the same way – concurring with the policy of his cabinet and only involving himself in its formulation at his ministers' request – during the American crisis.[59] George III evidently understood and respected the British constitution; there is little evidence, either in his writings before he took the throne or in his actions during his reign, that he wished to subvert or abolish representative government.[60]

What this means with regard to the development of the cabinet system and the power of the British Parliament over government business is that it did not take the giant strides backward during George III's reign that is often claimed. It is possible that the role of cabinet would have established itself more quickly had George III been as apolitical as his two Hanoverian predecessors. But there is no question that the cabinet, its procedures and powers relative to the Crown, were much better defined by the end of George III's reign than they had been at the start. At some time during his rule, for example, the cabinet began to consider government business without any reference from the king. In the past, the monarch had to give his or her permission for the cabinet to discuss government matters; by the early nineteenth century, it was becoming established procedure that any cabinet member could call a session on any subject within his department without recourse to the Crown.[61] And whereas it was unclear in 1760 whether or not the monarch was constitutionally bound to take the advice of his or her cabinet ministers, by 1809 at least, the idea that the monarch was obliged to follow the ministers' recommendations if they insisted upon it was becoming an accepted belief.[62]

Even what is considered to be George III's main accomplishment, that of returning greater control over ministerial appointments to the Crown, did not introduce as significant a modification to the institutions of government as is sometimes claimed. Since it was impossible to rule effectively without a ministry that could secure a majority in both houses of the Parliament, he still had to consider party allegiances when deciding on the composition of his ministries. Granted, George III did, at the start of his reign, try to supercede this reality by appointing a politically inexperienced personal favorite, Lord Bute, to the post of prime minister. Bute failed to win over the politicians, however, and the king was forced to abandon the idea of governing through a friend and accept that ministries could not be formed without negotiation.[63] Even Lord North, who served as prime minister from 1770-1782 and who is often characterized as George III's "lackey," weak-willed and ready to defer to the king, was only able to head the government as long as he did because he held the confidence of the majority of MPs. Once he lost their support, he lost his power, and no amount of political maneuvring on the part of George III could maintain North's ministry.

By the end of the eighteenth century, the British Parliament was well on its way to establishing most of the procedures that were to serve as the basis for responsible government in the nineteenth century. Even though many of Parliament's claims were still only dimly perceived and even less suredly argued, a good number of the *informal* institutions, the norms and operational procedures that were to allow MPs in the British Parliament the control over government that had been presented them by the revolutionary settlement, were in place.

Implications for Quebec

Changes in the informal institutions surrounding relations between the British executive and the British Parliament affected colonial policymaking and so had repercussions for Anglo-Quebec policymaking. As the British Parliament came to have more influence over the Crown's choice of ministers and government policy in general, the relatively "closed" process of policymaking for the colonies became subject to the more "open" and turbulent world of Parliamentary politics. The colonies, their economy, their governance, their social conditions, were more readily and openly discussed by MPs, a change that affected how British ministers, whose positions of power were becoming more and more dependent on maintaining the support and regard of the British Parliament, responded to colonial matters. The British Parliament also began passing more legislation respecting the colonies. Until the mid-eighteenth century, the British Parliament had not involved itself much in colonial affairs. It is true that British MPs had never been reticent in passing legislation concerning colonial trade. From the Navigation Acts of the late seventeenth century and into the next century, the British Parliament passed measures restricting the way in which colonial commerce was conducted. But aside from these (albeit numerous) measures, little colonial legislation had issued from Westminster. In the 1760s this began to change. In 1765, the British Parliament voted overwhelmingly to impose stamp duties on legal documents and other printed materials in the colonies. The revenues raised from this tax were to go toward maintaining imperial forces stationed in the colonies since the close of the Seven Years' War. Although the Stamp Act was eventually revoked in 1766, the repeal was accompanied by the Declaratory Act, and was soon followed by the Townshend Acts. The latter were a series of measures that sanctioned the right of the Crown to tax certain items in the colonies without recourse to the provincial assemblies for the purpose of helping to finance the colonial administration. Any surplus was to be paid to the Royal Exchequer and distributed by the British Parliament.[64] After years of relative neglect, the British Parliament began legislating for the colonies in earnest.

Whereas the monarch and his or her servants had once held a virtual monopoly on the formulation of colonial policy, colonial legislation was now being shaped by a much wider array of opinions and interests. This, of course, could work to the benefit or detriment of actors involved in the process. The support of MPs in the British Parliament of measures desired by colonials was an obvious advantage to the colonial interests, whereas Parliamentary opposition could sabotage their efforts to secure approval or repeal of favored legislation. Similarly, the disposition of the British Parliament toward government initiatives could help or hinder their cause. With the addition of so many new voices to the colonial policymaking process, the entire procedure became much more unwieldy, less predictable and more difficult for political actors to manipulate and control.

Informal Institutions Governing the Policymaking Process

It was not only British MPs who became more involved in the policymaking process during the eighteenth century. The 1700s also saw an increase in the participation and influence of "the public" – organized lobby groups as well as less structured "popular" assemblies – in and on political decisionmaking. Individuals who had once existed "outside" the corridors of power, both physically and effectually, became politicized to the extent that MPs and administrators had little choice but to consider their demands and protestations when formulating policy recommendations. Like the "rise of Parliament," the "rise of public opinion" was at once encouraged by and contributed to changes in the informal institutions surrounding British policymaking that permitted the inclusion of many more groups and individuals in the process.

Lobby groups were not new to the political process. In London, individuals with common interests had been coming together since the early seventeenth century to persuade government officials to adopt, modify or repeal policies that concerned them. In the eighteenth century, however, the character of these groups, their composition, the arguments to which they appealed, and their general disposition, went through a number of changes. As Alison Olson explains, the early interests tended to be "ascriptive" or "institutional" in nature. They represented either kinship groups (in the former case) or legally chartered institutions such as guilds, town corporations, universities and trading companies (in the latter case). Rather than pressure administrators to concede to their demands, these groups worked in cooperation with ministers to insure that their interests were respected, rendering loans and gifts and the politically responsible behavior of their membership in exchange for political considerations.[65] Although there were some colonial groups that could be described as either ascriptive or institutional – associates, neighbors and families of colonial proprietors were an ascriptive interest, for example, the provincial assemblies could be considered an institutional group – colonial interests in general did not engage in this type of lobbying, primarily because their members lacked the formal organizational structure required.[66]

By the middle of the eighteenth century, however, the older groups had been superceded by what Olson calls "associational" or "voluntary" groups. These groups – which included mercantile and labor associations, dissenting churches, independent craftsmen and the like – had less control over membership and so could not provide the government the same guarantees than could the older groups. They were, however, able to supply officials with information concerning their various areas of expertise. This, in addition to their growing electoral influence, helped persuade government administrators, if not to abide by their demands, at least to allow them to participate in the policymaking process.[67] It was through these kinds of associations that colonial interests had the greatest impact on royal policy in the colonies. In cooperation with groups with similar concerns overseas, colonial interests pressed British officials for adoption, modification or repeal of measures important to them. The information they provided administrators concerning conditions in the colonies was vital to decisionmakers with little direct knowledge of colonial realities. Most officials were quite willing to listen and concede to the demands of these groups. Olson argues that these trans-Atlantic groups played a crucial role in helping to unite the empire, especially during their "heyday" from 1721 to 1754.[68]

It was in the latter half of the eighteenth century that a kind of group emerged that was very unlike those that had come before it. Almost everything about the public-opinion lobby was different from earlier groups. The membership of earlier associations was relatively homogeneous; the membership of public-opinion lobbies was diverse and claimed to speak for large sections of the public. Earlier groups pushed for policies that were of specific concern to their membership; public-opinion lobbies sought changes in major policy areas, including constitutional ones. Whereas early interests tended to be relatively conciliatory towards government and administrators, public-interest lobbies were more disputatious and often openly hostile to government.[69]

In Britain, particularly in London, the emergence of these more "radical" groups was accompanied and facilitated by a number of events. According to John Brewer, although there were demonstrations of popular protest and "political" activity and agitation before the mid-eighteenth century, it was not until the 1760s that these occurrences developed a real focus or began to have a significant impact on the decisions emanating from Westminster. Government instability, a poor economy and the rise of a political press provided the ideal circumstances for the popularization of the type of politics fostered by John Wilkes.[70] Wilkes was an MP who first garnered the wrath of the British administration and Parliament in 1762 for attacking the government in his newsletter, the *North Briton*. Wilkes accused the government of exercising arbitrary power and undermining the liberties of those he affectionately called "the middling and inferior class of the people," the "ordinary people." Arrested on a warrant for seditious libel, imprisoned in the Tower, released, expelled from Parliament and outlawed, he returned to London from Paris in 1768 and was elected MP for Middlesex. He was again imprisoned, released and again expelled from the House of Commons in 1769. Although he was twice reelected, Parliament prevented him from taking his seat in the House by declaring void his victories.

It was around Wilkes and the issues that he raised and reiterated in his speeches and numerous publications that London's "radical" political community came together.[71] Wilkes appealed to "the people." He painted his struggle with the administration as the struggle of all Englishmen, that of the common man against the growing powers of the government. He emphasized his role as the guide rather than the leader of the movement, and stressed the responsibility of "everyman" to check arbitrary rule. Like no one else before him, Wilkes actively recruited public support, then "thrust the initiative into his supporters' hands."[72] By the time of his election as MP for Middlesex, they were ready to take up the cause. "Wilkites" across the nation expressed their support for the MP-become-martyr, sending petitions demanding his release from the King's Bench prison and holding public demonstrations on his birthday and celebrations on the day of his release in 1770.[73] In addition to these and other more spontaneous exhibitions of popular protest, Wilkes helped spawn more organized lobbying efforts. The pro-Wilkite Society of Supporters of the Bill of Rights (SSBR) was the first out-of-doors group formed to campaign for Parliamentary reform.[74] Here was a group that epitomized the new "radical" type of organization that Olson argues emerged during the later eighteenth century: a loose-knit assemblage of individuals come together to lobby for a political cause who were unconcerned about encouraging the wrath of the administration.

Radicalism and popular protest were on the rise in the colonies as well, particularly in the American provinces. There was a public outcry there when the British Parliament passed the Stamp Act in 1765. Its enactment incited riots in Boston and other towns and prompted American merchants to boycott English trade goods. There were more organized efforts as well, such as the Sons of Liberty, groups of radicals who harassed stampmasters and otherwise obstructed attempts to implement the Act, and the Stamp Act Congress, a group comprised of representatives from nine American colonies who came together to petition British officials for repeal of the Act.[75] The Townshend Duties provoked another collaborative boycott of British trade goods. The acts also contributed to tensions that led to a group of radicals dumping English tea into Boston Harbor in December 1773 and demonstrations in Annapolis, Maryland, Greenwich, New Jersey and Charleston, South Carolina.[76] True to the "radical" school, the colonists justified their actions in terms of a "larger" political issue, the constitutional right of the metropolis to tax the colonies for revenue without recourse to the provincial assemblies. Membership was varied and their methods were antagonistic rather than conciliatory.

The American radicals found sympathy among the radical community in Britain, and in London especially. The drive to repeal the Stamp Act was a trans-Atlantic enterprise, involving proponents of "Wilkite" methods and appeals on both sides of the ocean. They cooperated to protest the Townshend Duties as well. In May 1769, the SSBR included in their petition complaining of the government's treatment of Wilkes and its general abuse of English liberties an attack on the ministry's handling of American affairs. The colonial cause they linked to their own; as Olson explains, "[t]hey applied the American demand for 'no taxation without representation' to the plight of the unenfranchised in England, using it as the rationale for demanding an expansion of the English electorate."[77] These and other efforts caused considerable consternation among British officials and helped bring about the repeal of the offending measures. The embryonic political culture of the beginning of the century had become, by the 1770s, a focused and comparatively powerful force in politics.[78]

The "rise of public opinion" in Britain and colonies during the eighteenth century influenced the informal institutions surrounding the formulation of government policy, including colonial policy. Just as the increasing power of the British Parliament over British politics expanded the number of politicians who could now legitimately participate in government decisionmaking, the growing influence of public sentiment on policy negotiations helped alter the informal institutions that had once inhibited the influence of out-of-doors groups and opinion on policy outcomes to include these voices. Again, this could work to the benefit or detriment of those traditionally involved in colonial policymaking. On balance, it made policy negotiations, already becoming unwieldy with the addition of more politicians to the process, even more difficult to manage.

In addition to essentially forcing the British policymaking process to be more open to other views and interests, the rise in popular protest, the "radical" sort in particular, changed the way in which out-of-doors groups were permitted to approach government on policy issues. No longer did government lobbying involve only groups and government officials negotiating mutually-satisfying policy arrangements. Now organized and openly hostile attacks on government were possible. This was to have an important effect on the way in which other actors responded to these groups as well as on the character of the groups themselves and their power to influence royal policy in the colonies.

The preceding has specified three informal institutions that would influence policymaking in Quebec and shape the institutional context in which the Quebec Act was to emerge: the procedures associated with "government by instruction," the routine system of colonial governance that had emerged out of Britain's long experience with colonial rule; the norms and procedures structuring the power of the British Parliament relative to the British executive that allowed British MPs influence over government policymaking, and made the process more open, more volatile, more affected by the vissitudes of self-interest and party politics; and the norms that concerned the role of "the public" in government decisionmaking, informal institutions that prescribed that officials need now consider not only the disposition of MPs with regard to legislation, but also of the increasingly well-organized and radical public as well.

It should be emphasized again that, although no formal changes had been made to the British constitution establishing formally these procedures, these behaviors had, by 1774, become relatively routinized in government operations. Individuals and groups engaged in activities related to any of these areas were therefore bound to abide by, or at least take into account, these informal institutions.

Political Actors

The well-established and *formal* institutions that characterized Anglo-Irish relations at the end of the seventeenth century specified clearly the individuals and/or groups that were authorized to take part in Anglo-Irish government affairs. The *informal* institutions surrounding Anglo-Quebec politics did not delineate the significant actors as explicitly, but they did provide some indication of the participants typically involved in colonial policymaking. On the British side, the monarch and the British Parliament played important roles, as did the British Privy Council and the Board of Trade, as well as the Secretary of State for the Southern Department and, after 1768, the Secretary of State for the Colonial Department. On the Quebec side, the colonial executive, the governor in particular, played crucial roles. Further, with the entrance of "the masses" into the policymaking process, it is necessary to consider the character of the politicized "publics" on both sides of the Atlantic, the inhabitants of London and in particular Quebec who chose to become involved in the process via organized interest groups.

As in the case of the Treaty of Limerick negotiations, the array of pro- and anti-toleration sentiment amongst the actors involved in the formulation of the Quebec Act had important implications for the policy outcome. Following is a description of each along with an assessment of their sentiments and intentions concerning Quebec policy.

The British Monarch

According to John Brooke, during the years leading up to the Quebec Act, George III did not concern himself with colonial affairs to any great degree.[79] Much of his time during this period was taken up managing the John Wilkes affair, finding a stable ministry, and the day-to-day business of court functions. Like most Britons, he wished to maintain supremacy over Britain's colonial possessions. But beyond this general desire, he apparently had no clear plan or strategy concerning colonial policy. George dealt with each colonial matter as it arose and endeavored to be fair to both sides. If he preferred one over the other, he tended to favor the colonies. It was his vote that decided that the Stamp Act was to be repealed rather than enforced militarily.[80] Although he had wished to see the Act modified, he chose to support his ministers and revoke the measure rather than force the legislation on the colonists. With respect to religion, there are some who characterize George as a relatively tolerant monarch. His coronation oath bound him to uphold the privileged position of the Church of England in the empire. He was also apparently quite devout himself. But he had no desire to aggrieve Dissenters or Catholics.[81] He was quite accepting of the various Protestant nonconformist religions. Of Quakers he was particularly fond, and once declared that if it were not for his coronation oath he might have become a Quaker.[82] According to these authors, George's charitable views of Protestant recusants extended to the Catholic variety, especially French Catholics who George saw as "a breed apart" from their coreligionists, "who had their own peculiar ways."[83] Indeed, at one point he wished to give public honor to certain French-Catholic Candians for distinguished service in the administration of Quebec.[84]

Not all of George's actions conform with this characterization, however. Philip Lawson mentions that George's personal prejudices against Catholics "ran very deep," and notes his reaction to a proposal by Lord Radnor in 1766 to require all bishops in Britain to report to British officials the number of "papists" in each diocese. George III told Grafton, First Lord of the Treasury at the time, that "I wish to know who have most distinguished themselves in support" of this proposal, and added "Lord Radnor's zeal on this occasion is very meritorious and I shall certainly when I see him thank him."[85] His later actions also seem to confirm this view. His adamant opposition to concessions to Catholics in the 1790s and after the Anglo-Irish union in 1801 helped to delay Irish Catholic emancipation until almost a decade after his death.[86] George expressed openly his hostility and "invincible repugnance" to concessions to Irish Catholics,[87] and even demanded from his ministry in 1807 a written guarantee "that they would never, under any circumstances, propose to him further concessions to the Roman Catholics, *or even offer him any advice upon the subject.*"[88] This hardly corresponds with J. C. Long's portrayal of a monarch who had at all times "stood for liberty of conscience" and who had "protected the Quakers, the Methodists, the Moravians, and all other sects in their freedom of worship."[89]

If George's attitudes toward Catholics at the time of the passage of the Quebec Act are unclear, what is certain is that, prior to 1774, the king had made no effort to change any of the laws affecting British recusants. In fact, he was adamant that existing laws be upheld, and said it was the duty of ministers to "prevent alteration in so essential a part of the constitution as everything that relates to religion."[90]

Personal attitudes would not have been the only factors influencing George III's views on Catholic relief. Just as it was necessary for William III to consider the international consequences of his treatment of Catholics, particularly how his Catholic policy would affect his relations with his Catholic allies, George had to be mindful of the bigger issues. There were, for example, the matters of military security and the loyalty of subjects, in particular Catholic subjects, living under the British Crown to consider. The Treaty of Paris left Britain in possession of territories with large populations of French Roman Catholics whose allegiance was still uncertain and whose future in the British empire had still to be determined.

That the loyalty of Britain's new subjects might be secured by means of tolerant treatment did not, however, enter into the king's calculations. George was more concerned that French Catholics might unite in opposition to their conquerors. At the announcement of James Murray's appointment to the top post in Quebec in 1763, the new governor was told that "the king suspected that the Canadians would use the liberty granted of professing their religion to hold on to the French connexion and to combine for the recovery of their country." Murray was ordered to watch the priests closely and punish "the slightest suspicion of interference by them in civil affairs" by removing them from the province.[91] While George was clearly aware of the larger issues, prejudice and distrust colored his reading of the Quebec situation.

The Board of Trade

The Board of Trade began its life as the Lords of Trade in 1675, a committee of the Privy Council created by Charles II and his advisors to oversee colonial matters. The Board of Trade was established by William III in 1696 in response to attempts by English MPs to set up a similar body that would be answerable to Parliament. By instituting the Board himself, William managed to keep colonial affairs within the jurisdiction of the Crown.

The Board of Trade was comprised of seven chief officers of the state and eight members who were not otherwise employed by the government. The eight represented the "real" membership of the Board. They attended meetings regularly and ordinarily did most of the work. The "official" members were excused from attending all Board gatherings, although some or all of the principal Secretaries of State – those of the Northern, Southern, and after 1768 the Colonial Departments – would often be present, whether or not their attendance was specially requested.[92] According to its commission, the Board's main tasks were to oversee England's trade, England's poor and England's colonies. To fulfill these responsibilities the Lords Commissioners were given authority over the commissions and instructions to the provincial governors, colonial appointments, and provincial legislation. They were also to keep strict accounts of all funds raised by the colonial assemblies, and adjudicate complaints about colonial administration and other concerns. This they were to accomplish by maintaining frequent contact with colonial officials, especially the governor, and other individuals and groups connected to the colonies.[93]

These were wide-ranging responsibilities, yet the Board was an advisory body only. It was not given the authority to act on its own, only to provide information requested by other government officials and departments. The king in council had final say on all colonial matters. The Board's president was not a Secretary of State. He could not initiate legislation, nor could he personally approach the king or council. Effectively, the Board was a division of the Secretary of State for the Southern Department's office. Although the Lords Commissioners handled most colonial business, it was the latter official who was responsible officially for colonial matters.[94] After 1768, colonial responsibilities were transferred from the Southern Secretary to the new office of the Secretary of State for the Colonies and the Board of Trade was subsumed by the new department. While the colonial Secretary became the president of the Board, the Board itself remained an advisory body. Until its abolition in 1782, it never occupied any more important a position in the administration.

Initially, issues relating to trade took up most of the Lords Commissioners' time. Although matters dealing with the administration of the colonies were to take on greater importance as the century progressed, commercial matters remained a priority. Consistent with this focus, the Board of Trade from its inception paid special attention to the disposition of Britain's merchant community. The merchants never failed to be consulted on colonial matters and it was on information provided by them and their demands that the Board most often acted.[95] Predictably the merchants were most concerned with legislation that violated their interests in some way, measures that required they pay duties on British goods imported into the colonies for example. The Board of Trade kept special eye on colonial legislation that might affect the merchants' interests and invariably rejected any measure that might hurt them. The Board was even known to incorporate restrictions against similar legislation being proposed in the colonies in subsequent instructions to the governors.[96]

The British merchants were interested in more than trade legislation, however. They, like others, had become accustomed to seeing the institutions traditionally associated with the "old representative system" – a representative assembly, English law, and established Protestantism – granted to British colonies. Whether, as David Milobar suggests, the merchant community was more committed to these institutions than were others, whether they subscribed more strongly to the "country" ideology that held these were factors on which the wealth of the British empire was based, is not so important here as is how the Board of Trade responded to these sentiments.[97]

With respect to colonial governance, the Board seems to have worked at contradictory purposes. Throughout the colonial period, the Board was bothered by the growing power of the provincial assemblies and sought to reduce it. The Lords Commissioners were instrumental in transforming most of the colonies in America into royal provinces by the early eighteenth century, and persisted in their attempts to pressure the remaining colonies to conform to this system of rule. Control over the provincial executive was only one aim of the Board during this period, however. Control over colonial legislation was another. After failing to secure the imposition of a Poynings' Law-type of procedure on the legislatures of Jamaica and Virginia, the Lords Commissioners undertook to diminish the powers of the assemblies through their instructions to the colonial governors. As the century progressed the instructions became longer as the Board tacked more restrictions on the methods of framing legislation.[98] The commitment of the Lords Commissioners to strengthening royal authority in the colonies was remarkably consistent, unaffected by changes in ministry or personnel.

Given the energy spent by successive Boards on trying to restrict the powers of the colonial assemblies, it would seem to follow that the Lords Commissioners would have been opposed to granting representative institutions of any sort to the colonies. But the Board was resolute in its support of the "old representative system" of colonial governance, even under circumstances that would be considered less than ideal, even dangerous, to modern observers. It was the Board of Trade that framed the Proclamation of 1763 that recommended that the newly ceded territories, including Quebec and Grenada with their large populations of French Catholics, be granted the same British institutions as all other royal provinces. And as late as 1772, in the face of the growing acrimony of the American assemblies, the Lords Commissioners advised that the traditional form of governance be established in Vandalia, a new colony being planned for the American west.

It is likely that the Board was influenced by British merchants on these matters. Lord Hillsborough was president of the Board of Trade when the Proclamation was framed and was good friends with the Southern Secretary at the time, Lord Halifax. Halifax had served as Board president from 1748 to 1761. Adhering to precedent, Halifax would have asked the merchant community their thoughts on how the new territories should be governed, or at least advised Hillsborough to do the same. Lord Dartmouth was Colonial Secretary and Chief Lord Commissioner of the Board when the Vandalia project was being considered. He too had been president of the Board before (in 1765) and perhaps carried some sympathy for the merchants from his past experience. Although it may be difficult to find direct evidence of merchant influence on the Board of Trade, it is clear that the Lords Commissioners were committed to establishing government in the colonies that was in accord with merchant interests.

If the Board was consistent in its support of the "old representative system" in the colonies, it seems to have experienced a shift in its attitudes toward Catholics and the rights of Catholics in the new world. "Tolerant" is not a word that could have been used to describe the Lords Commissioners under Halifax in 1755. In that year, some 10,000 Catholic Acadians were removed from their lands by the governor of the province of Nova Scotia, Charles Lawrence. Although the Lords of Trade did not order the expulsion they "did nothing to make such an outrage, which had been often suggested, impossible or to punish those responsible for it."[99] Quite the contrary: after the expulsion was completed they recommended that Lawrence be promoted to the post of governor of the province.[100] Compare these actions to those of the Board some thirteen years later. In 1768 the Lords Commissioners admonished the new governor of Grenada, Robert Melville, for passing a constituent act in the province that stipulated all assembly representatives had to conform to the requirements of the Test Act on the grounds that it gave "disgust and dissatisfaction" to French Catholics in the province. To correct this perceived wrong, they submitted to the Privy Council a report that recommended that French Catholics in Grenada be allowed to vote in elections, sit in the assembly and be appointed to the provincial council. The report was duly approved.[101] Obviously the Board no longer held firm to that aspect of merchant "ideology" that said Protestantism should be ascendant in the colonies.

Thus, in 1774, the Board of Trade had a long history of supporting the "old representative system" in Britain's colonies. While expressions of tolerance had not been characteristic of the Board in the past, however, the anti-Catholicism inherent to their directives appears to have waned somewhat, at least with respect to Grenada.

Secretaries of State Southern and Colonial

Colonial matters were the responsibility of the Secretary of State for the Southern Department until 1768 when they were transferred to the newly created office of the Secretary of State for the Colonies. In the period 1763 to 1768 there were five different Southern Secretaries. Lord Hillsborough was the first Colonial Secretary. He was succeeded by Lord Dartmouth in 1772, a close friend of Lord North's, who was Secretary for the colonies in 1774.

It has already been suggested that Darmouth, having served as president of the Board of Trade in 1765, may have had some sympathy for the merchant community given the promerchant stance of that body. He certainly seemed to be supportive of the "radical" faction of the commercial community. In 1766, Dartmouth allied himself with these merchants and voted in cabinet for repeal of the Stamp Act. He also opposed other similiar sorts of taxation measures for the colonies. Even as the American situation worsened, Dartmouth's support of the "radical" stance did not waver. He was one of only two members of the cabinet that opposed the authoritative measures proposed by North to punish the Bostonians after the Boston Tea Party. Finding himself outvoted, Dartmouth took the liberty, as president of the Board of Trade, to insert directions in the instructions to the new governor of Massachusetts to use "gentle means" to quiet the people, and to call in troops "only if absolutely necessary." He continued to push for conciliation with the colonists until the revolution.[102] Dartmouth's abiding support of causes consistent with merchant ideals shows an affiliation with the views of the merchant community, implying that he would have advocated the traditional form of governance in Quebec. It is significant that he promoted the Vandalia project and supported the establishment of traditional institutions in the planned province as late as 1772.

Dartmouth's position on Catholics and Catholicism is more difficult to ascertain. What is known is that he was a very religious man, a devout Methodist, who could never shake rumors that he was considering taking orders in the Church of England. Although he always denied it, his religiosity still affected his relations with other politicians: the Southern Secretary, Lord Weymouth, apparently called him the "psalm-singer."[103] While this says nothing concrete about Dartmouth's sentiments concerning Catholics, it suggests that he likely would not have been anxious to promote Catholicism in Quebec for its own sake.

The British Parliament

The position of the British Parliament toward Quebec policy before passage of the Quebec Act is difficult to assess since MPs were little involved in Quebec affairs between the passage of the Proclamation in 1763 and the Quebec Act eleven years later. They did, however, take an interest in the American colonies after 1760, and in policy toward Catholics at various times, so it is possible to glean from their judgments on these matters how they might have approached the Quebec question in 1774.

The English/British Parliament had a long tradition of passing anti-Catholic legislation. Roman Catholics were subject, like Protestant recusants, to the fines under the Acts of Uniformity enacted during the first half of the sixteenth century. A series of penal laws restricting Catholics and Catholicism specifically were put in place between 1571 and 1593, laws that were extended in 1606 and 1610. A reprieve from serious persecution during Charles I's reign and the interregnum was followed by the passage of a fresh assortment of anti-Catholic measures after the Restoration. The first Test Act in 1673 barred Catholics from civil and military positions, while the second in 1678 prevented them from sitting in Parliament. In December 1691, less than three months after the signing of the Treaty of Limerick, the English Parliament decided that Catholics had no place in the Irish Parliament either, and so passed legislation that required that all high office holders there take an oath offensive to Catholics. During the 1699-1700 session, English MPs approved an act to restrain "the growth of popery" in England to counter, its supporters claimed, the executive's excessive lenience towards Catholic subjects.[104] In 1705, to show that English MPs were not above extending penal legislation to the colonies, Parliament raised no objections to the attorney general's decision to extend to the colonies an English decision sanctioning the perpetual imprisonment of any bishop or priest discovered saying mass.

Although enforcement of the penal laws was erratic, the British Parliament made no serious attempt to repeal or alter any of them as the century progressed. Nor did it feel it necessary after the Seven Years' War to rethink how Catholics should be treated in the colonies. The debate on whether Britain should retain Canada or Guadeloupe raged in the press and at Westminster. But MPs were quiet about the articles of the Treaty of Paris that stipulated that Catholics in the ceded territories could practice their religion only "as far as the laws of Great Britain permit." They were unconcerned, apparently, that these terms implied that Britain's penal laws would apply in the new regions. Up until the 1760s British MPs had given little or no indication via legislation that they as a body would be agreeable to a policy tolerant of Catholics in Quebec.

The silence of British MPs on the Catholic question was in contrast to their zeal to involve themselves in matters of colonial taxation and governance after 1760. The approval of the Stamp Act in 1765 ended a long spell of Parliamentary neglect of the colonies and the start of a period that saw the passage of a number of measures binding on the colonies. The Declaratory Act, the Townshend Duties and the so-called "intolerable acts" were all attempts by British MPs to press colonists, especially in the American provinces, to comply with their vision of the metropolis-colony relationship. The American colonies and their assemblies were ultimately subordinate to the British Parliament when it came to not only trade but any sort of legislation. When the colonists took issue with this treatment and began to oppose Parliamentary legislation openly and actively, British politicians including MPs were surprised and somewhat confused. When American belligerence continued to grow – the Boston "Massacre" of 1770, the burning of the *Gaspee*, an English schooner sent to enforce the Navigation Acts and revenue laws in Rhode Island, in Providence Harbor in 1772 – they became annoyed and then angry. The Boston Tea Party was a watershed. When word of its occurrence finally reached Britain in January 1774, nearly a month after it happened, it "shocked Englishmen, who compared its importance to Bonnie Prince Charlie's rebellion of 1745"[105] and galvanized public and government support against the colonists. The measures that were framed by the British Prime Minister Lord North and his ministers to punish the colonists – the "intolerable acts" – were supported by large majorities in the British Parliament in the spring. Some MPs thought they were not severe enough.[106]

The British Parliament was a body with a long history of supporting and preserving anti-Catholic legislation. MPs, however, had only recently begun to take an interest in colonial matters, especially those American. By 1774 American reactions to the colonial legislation passed by the British Parliament had generated a good degree of anti-American feeling among MPs. Although the colonists had some support in London, the majority of MPs were not sympathetic to their cause.

The British Privy Council

By 1763, most of the real work of the British Privy Council was being done by the cabinet. Since the Restoration, the membership of the council had grown steadily, while its ability to handle normal administrative duties had decreased. More and more, the business of advising the king on colonial matters fell to a committee of the Privy Council that was referred to by a variety of names: the committee on "Appeals from the Plantations," of the "whole Council," for the "Affairs of the Plantations," and others. The membership of the committee confirms, however, that it was essentially the cabinet making the decisions. Meetings were usually attended by one or both of the Secretaries of State for the Northern and Southern Departments and after 1768 the Colonial Secretary, the First Lord of the Treasury, the Lord President of the council, one or both of the chief justices and the president of the Board of Trade, and occasionally other important officials, including the Chancellor of the Exchequer, the heads of the Admiralty and the War and Navy departments.[107]

Two factors need to be considered when assessing the position of the cabinet and by extension the Privy Council on the Quebec Act. Of course the opinions of the individual members of the cabinet mattered. As important, however, were the views of the people to whom the cabinet was responsible. The power of the cabinet to dictate government policy had increased since the days of William and Mary. Although the notion that the cabinet was the "executive committee" of the British Parliament had not yet taken firm hold, the cabinet required the support of MPs to maintain its authority. Members, however, were still required to answer to the king, who appointed them and who could force them to give up their positions if he wished. In the case of Quebec, it was necessary that the cabinet consider the traditionally anti-Catholic stance of the British Parliament and the relatively recent rise in anti-American sentiment among MPs, as well as the views of George III, which are implied in his support of anti-Catholic MPs and the benign disposition he had heretofore shown toward colonial matters.

With respect to individual members of the cabinet, judging from his position on other colonial matters and his religious nature, the Colonial Secretary and the president of the Board of Trade, Lord Dartmouth, would likely have backed the traditional form of governance for Quebec, the "old representative system" and an ascendant Protestant church. But what of the head of the ministry, Lord North?

North was appointed by George III to the position of First Lord of the Treasury in 1770. He remained prime minister for twelve years, heading the most stable ministry since the king's accession to the throne. North enjoyed the unshakable confidence of the monarch, to whom the prime minister remained steadfastly loyal, in spite of George's refusal to accept any of North's periodic requests to resign. North also had strong support in the British Parliament, which was by the late eighteenth century at least as necessary as the backing of the king to insure a ministry's survival.

"Preposterous" was what North called the Townshend Duties as Chancellor of the Exchequer under the Grafton ministry (1767-1768). North was not, however, particularly sympathetic to colonial concerns. Although he had supported repeal of most of the measures, he had disagreed with Grafton that all the duties should be thrown out. North felt that one exaction, that on tea, should remain as a reminder to the colonists of the supremacy of the British Parliament. On his appointment as prime minister in 1770, North managed to convince the cabinet of the same and the Townshend Duties were revoked, save one.[108]

North remained committed to the principle of Britain's Parliamentary supremacy throughout the years leading up to the revolution. He, like other Britons, was confounded by the actions of the American colonists in the early 1770s, first in Rhode Island, then in Boston and elsewhere. By 1773 his disenchantment with colonials was obvious. He did not, however, respond to American belligerence with as heavy a hand as some of his contemporaries might have wanted him to. North received news of the Boston Tea Party with more bewilderment than indignation. He ignored cries for "bloody reprisals," concerned that such a response would just foster dissent in the colonies.[109] Although he himself endorsed a more forceful approach in the colonies, he allowed the Colonial Secretary, Lord Dartmouth, every opportunity to persuade more vehement cabinet ministers to adopt a more conciliatory stance toward the Bostonians.[110] The measures that North finally presented to the British Parliament in March 1774 – the Boston Port Bill, the Massachusetts Government Act, the Quartering Act and the Justice Act – although roundly condemned by the American colonists and their proponents, reflected the sentiments of the majority of British MPs and the public as well as the king. Dependent as he was on the support of the monarch and the British Parliament, North could hardly have done otherwise.

Notwithstanding the criticism he has endured for helping to lose the American colonies, North seems to have behaved, at least in the period leading up to the passage of the Quebec Act, like the consummate British politician, dedicated to maintaining the supremacy of the British Parliament while being careful to consider the views of the king and other officials and the tone of public sentiment.

The Colonial Governor

Quebec had two governors between 1764 and 1774, James Murray, who served from the establishment of civil government in the province until 1766, and Guy Carleton, governor from 1766 to 1777.[111] Both Murray and Carleton were military men first, administrators second, a fact that affected their approach to the Quebec situation in important ways.

Murray joined the British army when he was not yet twenty years old and saw a good deal of active service in Europe and in North America. In October 1760, Murray, along with Ralph Burton and Thomas Gage, were chosen by the commander-in-chief, Jeffrey Amherst, to administer the newly conquered regions of Quebec, Trois-Rivières and Montreal. For the next three years Murray's main task was to retain Quebec. Although the British had defeated the French on the Plains of Abraham, the Seven Years' War was not over, and there was always the chance that France would try to retake the area, or that the French Catholic inhabitants would rise up against their British conquerors. There were also the Americans to watch. Murray was already worried about them in 1759. In a letter to the Secretary of State, William Pitt, Murray expressed his concern that if the British succeeded in driving the French from New France, there would be nothing to secure the continued dependence of the American colonies on Great Britain and so little to stop them from leaving the empire.

The commission issued to Murray on 21 November 1763 declared him the "Captain General and Governor in Chief" of Quebec. The commission gave him the authority, on the advice of his council, to call assemblies and create law courts in the colony. Once an assembly was called he could also make laws for the colony. Until then he was restricted "to make such rules and regulations, by the advice of our said council, as shall appear to be necessary for the peace, order and good government of our said province." These "rules and regulations" were to be sent to London for approval.[112] Contrary to Murray's own expectations the commission did not make him commander of the troops in the province. This apparent omission was only in accord with American precedent. Governorships in the colonies to the south were civilian appointments only; British troops were detachments of the British army serving abroad.[113] Precedent did not impress Murray, who took the decision of British ministers to give responsibility of the colony's troops to Ralph Burton as a personal affront. Murray argued to officials that Quebec was not like other colonies, that given its small population of Britons it could only be governed by "military force," and that military government in the province had up to now been the norm.[114] Unfortunately for the governor, his pleas had little effect on government officials, and his quarrels with Burton concerning the proper defense of Quebec only contributed to his and the brigadier's recall to England two years later.

Like Murray, Guy Carleton had joined the army young, at seventeen, and had distinguished himself in the military service in Europe, North America and the West Indies. He was named Lieutenant Governor and Administrator of Quebec on 7 April 1766 on Murray's recall, but had to wait for his commission as Captain General and Governor in Chief until 12 April 1768. Carleton's commission mirrored Murray's, except that the new governor was made commander-in-chief of the provincial troops and so was granted the military authority Murray had wanted so desperately. While Hilda Neatby[115] says that it would be "grossly unjust" to suggest, as William Kennedy[116] does, that military security "appeared to him the only vital issue as far as Quebec was concerned," it was certainly a fundamental consideration of the governor's. As commander of the troops, Carleton was responsible for evaluating the state of Quebec's defenses, a task that apparently caused him great anxiety. The French threat had not disappeared, and, like Murray, Carleton was troubled by what would happen to the province if American belligerence, which had already exhibited itself in the furor surrounding the Stamp Act, were to increase. On 15 February 1767, the governor wrote a letter to General Gage in which he worried about the strategic role Quebec would play if this happened.[117]

Murray and Carleton's dispositions toward the American colonies were affected by more than concerns about defense, however. Like the majority of Britons in the metropolis, they were disturbed and frankly disgusted with the behavior of the American colonists, an attitude that was enhanced by the aristocratic-military nature of their upbringing. Carleton was especially averse to the growing republicanism of the colonists. His fears of "mobocracy" underlay his repeated warnings to British officials that Quebec had to be prepared for an American attack. In contrast, the governors "felt . . . some affinity with traditional French Canadian society which reminded them of a certain European way of looking at social life," one dominated by social hierarchy, political structure and clerical control.[118] Their "admiration for the legacy of the past"[119] only contributed to their aversion to things American, including popular assemblies which, Carleton maintained, "the better sort of Canadians fear" as they "render the People refractory and insolent."[120]

Whereas their army experience insured that the two governors of Quebec would place an inordinate amount of importance on the military security of the province, there is nothing that would suggest that they would be especially supportive of a policy of toleration in Quebec. Rather, their backgrounds suggest the opposite. Carleton was born in Ireland; his family had lived there since the beginning of the seventeenth century and was now part of the mostly anti-Catholic Protestant Ascendancy in that kingdom. And if John Brebner[121] believed that Murray was more "enlightened" than the governor who ordered the Acadians expelled from Nova Scotia, that there was "little reason to doubt that Murray's stay in Halifax" around the time of the expulsion "had impressed him deeply with the unhappy fate of the Acadians" and predisposed him to the charitable treatment of Quebec Catholics, he forgot that in 1765 Murray recommended the Acadians remaining in Bonaventure be removed in the same "illiberal and ill-considered" way.[122]

So the two governors had much in common. It is true that Carleton was much better connected politically than Murray. Carleton's friends in government listed like a who's who of officials responsible for colonial policy: Shelburne, Hillsborough, Dartmouth, North. George III himself was an admirer and ally of Carleton's, calling him at his appointment to the Quebec governorship a "galant & Sensible Man." Murray's place among the politicians was not nearly as impressive. He did have the backing of the ministries in power while he was in Quebec, those of Newcastle, Bute and Grenville, as well as the support of Lord Egremont. Halifax, Shelburne and Dartmouth, however, were indifferent toward him, as were other important officials. But otherwise, Murray and Carleton shared many of the same concerns about Quebec and colonial governance and likely held some of the same attitudes toward Catholicism.

The Anglo-Quebec Merchants

By 1760, Anglo-Protestant merchants had begun to arrive in the colony; by 1765 there were fifty established in Montreal alone. They were from Scotland, England, Ireland and the American colonies primarily, come to the province to take advantage of new business opportunities.[123] The fur trade interested most – furs comprised almost 80 percent of the colony's total exports in 1760 – although some invested in other industries such as wheat, flour, lumber, potash and iron production. The occasional merchant arrived as an independent, but most had connections with larger firms in London.[124]

The circumstances facing these men striving to acquire a commercial foothold in the province were not ideal. Hostile country, hostile Amerindians, and a hostile climate all conspired against them. Bankruptcies were common and many returned to their homelands, or were compelled to look for other ways to make a living in the province, having failed to survive the competition and conditions in the new colony.[125] These were not easy or particularly cultured times and the men who succeeded in business in such a harsh environment were not particularly cultured people.[126] James Murray called them "cruel, ignorant, rapacious fanatics," "the most immoral collection of individuals I have ever known."[127] Carleton was less disparaging but still called them fortune hunters. Philip Lawson quotes a traveler to the colony in 1765 who remarked that "the British inhabitants as yet settled in Canada, are the scum of the earth."[128] But the Anglo-Quebec merchants were not in the colony to impress administrators or tourists with their civility; they were there to make money. Although their characters may have offended the more genteel, their attributes were consistent with their motives.

The position of the British merchants on matters of colonial governance and administration and religion has already been touched upon. David Milobar emphasizes the effect of "British intellectual traditions" on the merchants' claims about what was the proper system of rule for Quebec. According to Milobar, they were firm supporters of the "country ideology," a system of beliefs that upheld "the virtues of the rule of law, property rights, mixed government, the balanced constitution, and the Protestant ascendancy."[129] These were the factors on which the wealth of the British empire was based; one had only to look at the failure of New France to duplicate the golden experience of the American colonies to see how a despotic government and the practice of "popery" killed entrepreneurial spirit and commercial success. But it was more than ideology that influenced the merchants' notions about how Quebec should be ruled. Britain's long legacy of participatory governance was certainly a factor in the merchants' claims.[130] That most every other colony in the British empire had, since the seventeenth century, been granted English institutions as a matter of course contributed to the merchants' expectations about what would happen in Quebec as well. Although strongly held convictions concerning "the rights of Englishmen" informed their position, simple precedent played as important a role. It is likely that these structural constants were responsible for promoting the formulation of such a set of beliefs in the first place.

The Anglo-Quebec merchants were a collection of competitive, commercially-minded individuals who held strong opinions about how Quebec government and administration should look. An "old representative system" of rule, English law and property rights and an ascendant Protestant church were the institutions that they wanted, indeed expected, established in the province.

The French Canadians

A major school in the French Canadian nationalist tradition maintains that French Canada was "decapitated" by the British conquest, that the British victory resulted in the wholesale departure of the "better classes" of Canadians and deprived those inhabitants left behind of their natural leaders.[131] This view has been somewhat exaggerated. It is true the conquest prompted some of those who made up the upper crust of society in New France to quit the colony. But the vast majority of the inhabitants, including most of the "better sort," landholding *seigneurs* and officers of the *troupe de la marine* for example, stayed behind.[132] There were a number of reasons why this may have happened. Hilda Neatby contends that it was a matter of money, that only the Canadians who could afford passage removed to France; the remainder stayed.[133] Lawrence Gipson adds that most Canadians had been born and raised in the colony and may have been reticent to "return" to a homeland they had never seen.[134] Also, he says there was a feeling amongst Canadians after France ceded the province to Britain in the peace treaty that they had been "forsaken" by the French king. Whatever their reasons, only 300 of the 60,000 or so inhabitants quit the colony.[135]

Enough of the wealthier merchants and seigneurs withdrew, however, to permit smaller traders and landholders to anticipate taking their places in commerce and in the social life of the province. For the Quebec merchants this was not to be. The arrival of the British and American merchants to the colony after the conquest introduced a climate of competition to which the Quebec merchants were unaccustomed. They had some advantages over the British which at first allowed them to hold their own against the newcomers. The Quebec merchants had more experience and established contacts in the fur trade, for example, having spent years in the business. For a while, some worked as partners with the British merchants, combining Canadian skill and their connections with British money. It did not take long, however, before the British, with their capital and their "unsavory" trade practices, managed to overcome whatever advantages the Canadians had and take over trade and industry in the province. The Britons' very different approach to business helped them to establish their predominance. Whereas French traders were more likely to act individually and confine themselves to one sector of trade, British merchants formed partnerships and diversified, using gains in one industry to invest in others.[136] By 1770, Britons controlled 75 percent of the colony's business. That the Quebec administration tended to favor British merchants over Canadian when distributing lucrative military supply contracts and other sorts of patronage only hurt the Canadians more, as did the suspicions and outright prejudice that Canadian merchants had to endure at the hands of the British military in particular. But for a few notable exceptions (the Baby family, for example), the dreams Canadian merchants had at the conquest of taking over where the larger French traders had left off evaporated with the coming of the British.[137] While some were to join their voices to those of the British merchants demanding English institutions be established in the colony, the Canadian merchants were too weak to affect colonial policy on their own.

This was less so in the case of the remaining traditional power holders in Quebec, the clergy and landholding *seigneurs*. Very early, these men were to establish themselves as allies of their new British masters. This was thanks, to some extent, to the benign treatment of the colony before the peace. The institutions that operated in New France under French rule have already been described.[138] A British presence did not automatically bring a change in these conditions. During the three years following the conquest it was uncertain whether Canada would remain under British rule come the end of the war. General Amherst told the three military governors he left in charge to administer the colony as fairly and charitably as possible, to maintain many of the existing institutions in the province and to insure generous treatment of the French Catholic inhabitants. Murray followed his orders closely. He and his immediates continued to work through the same French Canadian militia captains who had served as Canadian "justices of the peace" under the French regime. He appointed Canadians to his ruling council and to other administrative offices, and insured that all legal cases involving French-speaking inhabitants would be tried in the French language and according to French law.[139] The inhabitants were allowed to continue to practice their religion unmolested.

In the years following the peace, traditional French Canadian power holders endeavored to maintain their social position and prestige in the colony. Certainly they were in no position to begin demanding concessions from their conquerors. Neither were they accustomed to presenting their interests in this manner. Collective political representations were rare under French rule; if they had ever expressed their shared opinions to officials it was usually only at the request of the governor or the *intendant*.[140] Declarations of loyalty to their new masters were, however, frequent. The Catholic clergy, well aware of the precarious position of the Catholic church in the colony, were more than cooperative with Murray and his executive during the military regime. They encouraged their flocks to obey their new leaders and readily offered up prayers for the king on Murray's request.[141] On the appointment of Murray to the post of governor in 1763, a number of Canadians signed an address to George III stating that "[Murray's appointment] conformed fully to their wishes" and "stressed the new Governor's worthiness to occupy the post by reason of his 'paternal care' and his efforts to counteract the misfortunes that the war had brought."[142]

Governors Murray and Carleton both appreciated the deference and aristocratic character of these men and became their champions in the colony and in London. The Canadians' military tradition and aversion to English institutions such as the parliamentary system aligned with the governors' sentiments.[143] The clergy and *seigneurs* would of course have wished to maintain their status and the free exercise of their religion, and given their situation vis-à-vis the Quebec administration, were in a position to affect the complexion of colonial rule.

The various actors involved directly and indirectly in Quebec policymaking may be classified as holding pro- or anti-Catholic dispositions. There is some debate on this but it appears that George III was generally intolerant of Catholics, although his views of French Catholics in Quebec was somewhat more charitable, perhaps derived from his paternalistic stance toward Britain's colonies. He tended to side with his ministers, North in particular, when it came to colonial policy, although he was known to overrule ministerial recommendations that seriously offended his sensibilities. Taken together, the king was somewhat of a wild card concerning Quebec policy, suspicious of Catholicism and the French for personal reasons and reasons of imperial security, but usually supportive of his ministers even when their counsel was contrary to his own views.

History shows that British MPs were no champions of Catholic toleration. Further, by 1774 they had developed a keen interest in colonial policy. It is true that Quebec was not high on their list of priorities – the American colonies received much more, and increasingly unsympathetic, attention – but it did suggest that the new province had the potential to become a concern. The British Privy Council, although headed by ministers chosen by the Crown, were now largely responsible to Parliament, and so reflected that responsibility independent of the personal view of its members. Given Parliament's history of anti-Catholicism, it is likely the British Privy Council would have been intolerant as well.

The Lords Commissioners of the Board of Trade, as well as the Secretaries of State responsible for colonial policy, belonged to the "old school" of colonial administration. Although they had begun to take a more tolerant stance toward Roman Catholics in the empire, they continued to advocate the old representative system of governance in the colonies. In contrast, the governors of Quebec, Murray and Carleton, were less concerned about administrative precedent when it came to the government of Quebec than with insuring the province's military security. Although by no means advocates of toleration, the governors' views of French Catholics were tempered by the latter's deference and apparent support of British authority and of British rule. For their part, Quebec's *Canadien* inhabitants, officially powerless but potentially influential in terms of their numbers, were not anxious to rock the boat, although were hopeful that their new rulers would treat them charitably. The comparatively few Protestant Britons in the province, on the other hand, chafed under military rule and were outspoken in their opposition to a Quebec administration that did not conform to the old representative system of governance in effect in most other British colonies.

The positions of the major actors involved in Quebec policymaking were a mixed bag, and thus reflective of the complexity of the situation. The Quebec question encompassed many contemporary debates – the position of Catholics relative to Protestants in the empire, of France relative to Britain, of the metropolis over the colony, the right of representative government against the paternalism (or authoritarianism) of the mother country – and so the lack of consensus, even within the same body or group, is perhaps not surprising.

Before moving to the actual events surrounding the passage of the Quebec Act, it is necessary to discuss one more area in which informal institutions were operating, namely those governing the relations between the major actors involved in the policymaking process. There were informal institutions in place that structured the way in which colonial policy was typically handled and helped define the major players that participated in the negotiations. These factors did not, however, specify what the capacity of each of these players was to influence the actual policy outcome, how much importance was placed on the views of each actor, and what their prospects were for influencing the resulting legislation. The relative power of the actors involved is of obvious importance. The Treaty of Limerick case demonstrated how, even though the power relations between the actors participating in the policymaking process may be well defined (by Poynings' Law and the tradition of English governance in Ireland), informal institutions (such as Henry Capel's bargaining strategy) can dictate to a large degree how much authority these actors really have over policy outcomes.

Informal Institutions Shaping Relations between Actors Involved in the Policy Process

Aside from the king and the Privy Council who had final say on all important colonial matters it was the Board of Trade that had the greatest potential to affect policy in the provinces. Almost all colonial business came under the scrutiny of the Lords Commissioners at some point, and each new Board had access to the records of previous Boards. Whereas the Secretaries of State "owned" their papers, and took them away with them upon leaving office, Board of Trade documents stayed at the Plantation Office. Over the years the office had assembled a massive archive of colonial orders, reports, minutes and correspondence along with maps, books and other materials about the colonies. With such access to desired information the Board had the capacity to exercise a great deal of power over colonial affairs. At the same time, however, the Board was only an advisory body. It is true that its commission was inexact. The Lords Commissioners were granted the power to nominate colonial officials including governors and councillors but it was unclear whether this authority amounted to control of provincial patronage; and, although the nature of their duties suggested that the Board had jurisdiction over colonial correspondence, there were no definite instructions specifying that authority. The commission was unambiguous, however, when it came to the Board's role in relation to the king and council and other state departments. The Board's primary task was to collect and present information; the actual initiation and execution of policy remained outside the scope of its powers.[144] The power of the Board over colonial affairs was indirect. Its capacity to affect colonial policy depended on how closely other government departments followed its counsel, which in turn depended on how the Board was viewed by these other offices.

As contingent as its powers were it would be expected that the Board experienced periods of considerable influence as well as times when its control over colonial business was eroded severely. After an initial period of "settling in" during which their responsibilities and the extent of their powers were better defined, the Lords Commissioners under William III were active and influential. The Board experienced a blow to its stature in 1702 with the appointment of the earl of Nottingham to the position of Secretary of State for the Southern Department. Nottingham deprived the Board of many of its most important tasks, taking over colonial correspondence and what little control the Lords Commissioners had over colonial appointments.[145] Although the amount of colonial business handled by the Board continued to keep them busy, their power and prestige relative to other government departments suffered. The status of the Board of Trade continued to decline until the earl of Halifax took up the post of president in 1748. By 1752, he had managed to boost the Board's authority over colonial affairs. He obtained an order in council that assured the Lords Commissioners the powers granted them in their commission. He reestablished the Board of Trade's position as the primary body with whom colonial officials corresponded and its control over provincial nominations, "which, under Halifax, meant an almost complete direction of colonial patronage."[146] It remained an advisory body, but now it was able to launch colonial projects on its own and choose the matters to which it wanted higher officials to pay attention.[147]

Halifax was replaced as president by Lord Sandys in 1761. On 15 May, an order in council stripped the Board of Trade of its power over colonial nominations, diminishing the power and prestige of the Board considerably. Although the Lords Commissioners did retain control over correspondence with the colonies, provincial patronage was from then on the prerogative of the Secretary of State for the Southern Department.[148] Sandys was succeeded by Charles Townshend on 2 March 1763, who was soon replaced by the earl of Shelburne a little over a month later. Shelburne had been reluctant to take up the presidency because the Board's powers were so restricted. Although he finally gave in and accepted the post he had no intention of relinquishing any of the Board's existing authority and wasted no time writing to the Southern Secretary, Lord Egremont, and telling him so.[149] He was very protective of his and the Board's responsibilities, and tried to conceal Board business from Egremont's office as much as possible. This created a rift between the offices that was reflected in the correspondence of May to July 1763 concerning how the new territories acquired by Britain by the Treaty of Paris should be administered.[150]

Egremont died suddenly on 21 August and Shelburne resigned his post. Halifax became the new Southern Secretary and convinced officials to appoint his friend, the earl of Hillsborough, to the Board presidency. Whereas relations between the Board and the office of the Southern Secretary had been tense during Shelburne's term, they were now more congenial. Halifax knew firsthand how knowledgeable the Lords Commissioners were about colonial issues and asked for their opinions and recommendations regularly. Their importance was also acknowledged by other government officials, as when the First Lord of the Treasury, George Grenville, made funds available to increase the number of Board staff and their salaries.[151]

Hillsborough was replaced as Board president by Lord Dartmouth in 1765. There was increasing talk of making the head of the Board a Secretary of State to consolidate colonial business in one powerful office headed by a new colonial Secretary of State but nothing came of the matter during Dartmouth's term. He and the Board continued dealing with colonial affairs with the same powers as the previous Board, albeit with less zeal than did Hillsborough and his officials. In fact, the Board had little to do with the most important issue of the day, the Stamp Act. Aside from collecting and copying documents related to the matter for the British Parliament to use, it stayed out of the matter.[152]

In August 1766, the Rockingham ministry fell and Hillsborough was back as Board president. Changes came almost immediately. The Secretary of State for the Southern Department was made responsible for all colonial matters, and the Board of Trade was reduced to a board of report only. It is unclear whose decision it was to emasculate the Board. The new Prime Minister, William Pitt, was anxious that his ideas concerning the colonies hold sway. By transferring authority over the colonies to the Southern Department, he had more control over colonial policy, given that his personal adherent, Lord Shelburne, was now ensconced in that office. On the other hand, it appears Lord Hillsborough only agreed to return to the Board on the condition that the Board's powers be formally (read: by order in council) reduced. What is certain is that the already waning influence of the Board of Trade on colonial affairs was diminished further.[153]

In 1768, colonial affairs were transferred from the Southern Secretary to the newly created office of the Secretary of State for the colonies and the Board of Trade came under his direct supervision. After that the Board was "little more than an adjunct to the secretary's office."[154] a situation that "weaken[ed] the board as a body with a distinct individuality separate from and independent of the secretary."[155] Although now headed by a Secretary of State, the Board's duties did not change much; they certainly did not increase. It continued reviewing colonial legislation, providing information on the request of other departments and considering and adjudicating petitions and complaints as before. But it had little to do with any of the important legislation affecting the colonies during the following years. In fact, in 1774, when so many unprecedented decisions were taken concerning the colonies, the Board held fewer meetings and dealt with less business than ever before.[156]

Historically, the power of the Board to affect colonial policy depended on its relations with other state officials, particularly with the Secretary of State for the Southern Department and later the Colonial Secretary. If the Secretaries of State were willing to allow the Board the authority to act in accord with its commission, as in William III's day and when Halifax was president, the Lords Commissioners could be quite influential. If, on the other hand, the Secretary was unmindful of the Board's rights with regard to colonial affairs, the Board's powers and influence could be undermined significantly.

There is another aspect to this, however, and that concerns the nature of the business over which the Board exercised control. It is true that Halifax raised the stature of the Board during his term and restored to the Board a number of its traditional prerogatives. But these prerogatives pertained more to routine administrative business, the "everyday" running of individual colonies, than to the "bigger" aspects of colonial policy.[157] The review of colonial legislation, the nomination of provincial officials, the preparation of governors' commissions and instructions and the adjudication of grievances were crucial to the smooth operation of royal governance in the colonies. None of it, however, confronted seriously the larger issues related to royal government in the colonies, such as the constitutional relationship between the colonies and the mother country, or the powers of the provincial assemblies relative to the British Parliament. This was acceptable during the first half of the eighteenth century, during which British officials, the ministry and the British Parliament in particular, were not much interested in colonial policy. Provided everything was operating relatively smoothly on the provincial front, British officials were happy to let conditions remain as they were. But after 1760, the "bigger" issues started to gain importance and engage the attentions of ministers and MPs. The Board's influence on these matters had never been great and once they took center stage the relative power of the Board to affect colonial policy was naturally reduced. This, combined with the reduction of its authority in 1766 to a board of report only, meant that whatever capacity the Lords Commissioners had once had to influence and initiate colonial policy independent of other government departments was effectively erased. By 1774 informal institutions were in place that restricted the capacity of the Board of Trade to impact on policy outcomes. They were still consulted on colonial affairs, but their role in and consequently their power over the policymaking process was marginal.

Quebec policy was affected by changes in the power relations between British officials responsible for colonial affairs and out-of-doors interest groups as well. Trans-Atlantic interest groups, merchant groups especially, had for some time been carrying on a mutually-beneficial relationship with government officials in which merchants, in exchange for information about the colonies, would acquire some assurance from policymakers that their demands would be considered. By the latter half of the eighteenth century informal institutions had developed that established that these out-of-doors interests would almost always be consulted on colonial matters, by the Board of Trade certainly, but by other officials responsible for colonial affairs as well. In the 1760s, however, the relationship began to change. Except for the Board of Trade, British administrators gradually stopped asking trans-Atlantic groups for advice on colonial business and began to rely increasingly on "in-house" informants – politicians, clerks and military men with experience in or with the colonies, for example – and agents of their own choosing. It is true that there were four years, 1765 to 1769, when the Anglo-colonial merchants again enjoyed close relations with government ministers.[158] But with the fall of the Grafton ministry, their influence evaporated. Coming to talk to Lord North in 1773 about the American situation, theLondon merchants trading to North America were bluntly told to "return and set quietly in their counting houses."[159]

What prompted such changes to policymaking procedures? Alison Olson draws on traditional interpretations of the period when she says that the political instability of British politics during the 1760s and 1770s prevented out-of-doors groups and their agents from developing the lasting associations with ministers that were necessary to continue to affect policy outcomes. Nancy Koehn takes a different approach.[160] She challenges the old view that political instability resulted in confusion and legislative inconsistency and argues that, despite all the changes in government during this period, British officials were constant in their commitment to the government's major concern, to manage the debt accumulated during the Seven Years' War. With British MPs complaining about their personal tax burdens, and colonists refusing to comply with taxes legislated by the British Parliament, British officials turned to the excise to help pay for the costs of the war. This meant, however, that the British government had to keep domestic interests happy so that protests about the levies on their manufactures might be kept to a minimum. Whereas Olson's explanation implies that all out-of-doors interests lost leverage with the British government during this period because of political instability, Koehn argues it was only the colonial and Anglo-colonial groups that suffered as the focus of ministers shifted from foreign to domestic concerns.

Whatever the cause, by 1774 the informal institutions surrounding the relationship between trans-Atlantic groups and government officials responsible for colonial policy had changed to the detriment of colonial and Anglo-colonial interests. Once regular participants in the colonial policymaking process they now played a secondary role in negotiations.

The manner in which institutions arrayed pro- and anti-Catholic forces in the Quebec case was quite different than what was observed in Ireland during the Treaty of Limerick ratification bill negotiations. In the latter case, the formal institutions structuring the Anglo-Irish relationship suggested that tolerant interests would prevail over intolerant ones. Informal institutions, however, developed over the course of negotiations to undermine the formal powers held by William III and his supporters and resulted in anti-Catholic forces in the Irish Parliament and administration succeeding in diluting the tolerant spirit of the Treaty of Limerick. In the case of Quebec, no comparable formal institutions existed to regulate Anglo-Quebec relations. However, there were present informal institutions that stipulated the individuals and groups authorized to participate in colonial policymaking and their relative powers. Precedent had established that the Board of Trade, in negotiation with Anglo-colonial merchants, prescribed the terms of governance in British colonies. These terms, which place severe restrictions on the activities of Catholics as well as on the practice of Catholicism, had become exceedingly routine by the 1760s; they were applied automatically to any and all colonial possessions as a matter of course. This, together with indications that many of the officials in charge of promoting colonial policy, including the king, George III, were intolerant of Catholics, suggests that the British government would not implement a tolerant policy in Quebec. Unsurprisingly, the Proclamation of 1763 established the "standard" colonial form of governance in Quebec.

Over the course of the eleven years of negotiations that preceded the passage of the Quebec Act, however, a number of changes occurred in the informal institutions governing the Anglo-colonial policymaking process. The British Parliament began to involve itself more and more in colonial matters, opening up what had once been a relatively "closed" procedure to the vicissitudes of party politics and reducing the authority of the monarch to act unilaterally on colonial business. The "public" had also found its voice, and was expressing its stand on broader, constitutional issues by means of lobby groups much less conciliatory to government interests than in the past. Accompanying these changes was a reduction in the powers of the Board of Trade relative to other interests involved in the process. Government officials no longer turned to the Anglo-colonial merchants for information on the colonies, preferring instead to consult their own representatives and emissaries. Further, Britain's relations with the American colonies was becoming increasingly acrimonious, throwing a pall over any discussions concerning North American territory. The institutional context was in a state of flux, providing little guidance to officials attempting to establish the conditions of Quebec rule. How this situation came to affect the progress and outcome of Quebec policy is the subject of the next chapter.

Notes

1. Lawrence Henry Gipson, *The British Empire Before the American Revolution, Volume IX: The Triumphant Empire: New Responsibilities Within the Enlarged Empire, 1763-1766* (New York: Alfred A. Knopf, 1956), 162-64; W. P. M. Kennedy, *The Constitution of Canada 1534-1937: An Introduction to its Development Law and Custom* (New York: Russell & Russell, 1973), 39-41; A. Shortt and A. G. Doughty, eds., *Documents Relating to the Constitutional History of Canada, 1759-1791, Volume I* (Ottawa: J. de L. Tache, 1918).

2. Shortt and Doughty, *Documents Relating to the Constitutional History of Canada.*

3. K. A. Stanbridge, "England, France and their North American Colonies: An Analysis of Absolutist State Power in Europe and in the New World," *Journal of Historical Sociology* 10, no. 1 (1997): 27-55.

4. W. J. Eccles, *Essays on New France* (Toronto: Oxford University Press, 1987), 137.

5. A. Berriedale Keith, *Constitutional History of the First British Empire* (Oxford: Clarendon Press, 1930), 9-10; Martin Wight, *The Development of the Legislative Council 1606-1945* (London: Faber & Faber Ltd., 1946), 28.

6. For more on the Irish Declaratory Act see below, 143-45.

7. Keith, *Constitutional History of the First British Empire*, 350-51.

8. Leonard Woods Labaree, *Royal Government in America: A Study of the British Colonial System Before 1783* (New Haven: Yale University Press, 1930), 8. Labaree writes that a letters patent was "the highest expression of the prerogative in all the royal provinces." It granted special powers to the colonial governor or lesser officials for various

purposes.

9. Keith, *Constitutional History of the First British Empire*, 14-17; Wight, *The Development of the Legislative Council*, 37.

10. Virginia was the first permanent English settlement in North America and was founded in 1607.

11. Lawrence H. Leder, *America – 1603-1789: Prelude to a Nation* (Minneapolis: Burgess Publishing Co., 1978), 37.

12. Leder, *America – 1603-1789*, 37-44; Darrett B. Rutman, *The Morning of America* (Boston: Houghton Mifflin Company, 1971), 109.

13. Leder, *America – 1603-1789*, 44.

14. Ibid., 63, 65.

15. Wight, *The Development of the Legislative Council*, 28.

16. Keith, *Constitutional History of the First British Empire*, 12-13; Labaree, *Royal Government in America*, 219-22.

17. Evarts Boutell Greene, *The Provincial Governor in the English Colonies of North America* (New York: Russell & Russell, 1966), 15-22; Keith, *Constitutional History of the First British Empire*, chapters 4 & 5, 167-70.

18. Wight, *The Development of the Legislative Council*, 28.

19. Labaree, *Royal Government in America*, 224-25.

20. Oliver Morton Dickerson, *American Colonial Government, 1696- 1765: A Study of the British Board of Trade in its Relation to the American Colonies, Political, Industrial, Administrative* (New York: Russell & Russell, 1962), 226; Keith, *Constitutional History of the First British Empire*, 243.

21. Dickerson, *American Colonial Government*, 227-28; Keith, *Constitutional History of the First British Empire*, 270.

22. Labaree, *Royal Government in America*, 420-23.

23. Greene, *The Provincial Governor in the English Colonies*, 93; Labaree, *Royal Government in America*, 9-11.

24. Keith, *Constitutional History of the First British Empire*, 179-82; Labaree, *Royal Government in America*, 14-18.

25. Labaree, *Royal Government in America*, 23-30.

26. Greene, *The Provincial Governor in the English Colonies*, 95-96; Keith, *Constitutional History of the First British Empire*, 180-81; Labaree, *Royal Government in America*, 30-32.

27. Labaree, *Royal Government in America*, 51-53.

28. Ibid., 52-62.

29. Ibid., 67-68.

30. Ibid., 222-23.

31. Ibid., 443.

32. Keith, *Constitutional History of the First British Empire*, 3.

33. Ibid., 255; Labaree, *Royal Government in America*, 373, 376.

34. Keith, *Constitutional History of the First British Empire*, 222-23; Labaree, *Royal Government in America*, 115-18.

35. Keith, *Constitutional History of the First British Empire*, 226-27. The Toleration Act of 1689 allowed Protestant nonconformists in England freedom of worship and education.

36. John Garner, "The Enfranchisement of Roman Catholics in the Maritimes," *Canadian Historical Review*, 34, no. 3 (1953): 203-204; Greene, *The Provincial Governor*

in the English Colonies, 54-55; Labaree, *Royal Government in America*, 76-87.

37. Keith, *Constitutional History of the First British Empire*, 228.

38. Labaree, *Royal Government in America*, 425-26.

39. Ibid., 444.

40. Ibid., 426.

41. Quoted in Ian K. Steele, "The British Parliament and the Atlantic Colonies to 1760: New Approaches to Enduring Questions," in *Parliament and the Atlantic Empire*, ed. P. Lawson (Edinburgh: Edinburgh University Press, 1995), 38.

42. Dickerson, *American Colonial Government*, 18-20; I. K. Steele, *Politics of Colonial Policy: The Board of Trade in Colonial Administration "1696-1720"* (Oxford: Clarendon Press, 1968), 9.

43. Arthur Herbert Basye, *The Lord Commissioners of Trade and Plantations Commonly Known as the Board of Trade 1748-1782* (New Haven: Yale University Press, 1925), 1-2; Steele, *Politics of Colonial Policy*, 10-18.

44. Thomas Pitt Taswell-Langmead, *English Constitutional History* (London: Stevens & Haynes, 1890), 699-701.

45. George Burton Adams, *Constitutional History of England* (New York: Henry Holt and Co., 1956), 374-76.

46. Adams, *Constitutional History of England*, 377-82; Taswell-Langmead, *English Constitutional History*, 704.

47. Adams, *Constitutional History of England*, 384-90.

48. Richard Pares, *King George III and the Politicians* (London: Oxford University Press, 1967), 61-64; Taswell-Langmead, *English Constitutional History*, 721. It is generally maintained that George II's political inadequacy had more to do with personal weakness than uninterest. Richard Pares says that George II simply did not know how to deal with the politicians. As a result, he rarely succeeded in controlling his ministers, or exercising influence in areas outside those that the politicians did not mind leaving to him. There have been challenges to this portrayal, however. See Ian R. Christi, "George III and the Historians – Thirty Years On," *History* 71, no. 232 (1986): 215-16. Christi notes evidence offered by Richard Lodge and J. B. Owen that shows that George II had more power over his ministers than previously thought. In these accounts, George II is represented as a comparatively powerful king, dictating policy, overriding the recommendations of his officials, playing off ministers against each other to get his way, fending off their attempts to meddle in army and court appointments and overseeing general elections.

49. Adams, *Constitutional History of England*, 393-95.

50. Taswell-Langmead, *English Constitutional History*, 660-62.

51. Adams, *Constitutional History of England*, 388. See Pares, *King George III*, 70-92, for a sketch of what party politics looked like during the latter half of the eighteenth century.

52. Adams, *Constitutional History of England*, 383.

53. Taswell-Langmead, *English Constitutional History*, 701.

54. Pares, *King George III*, 94.

55. P. D. G. Thomas, "George III and the American Revolution," *History* 70, no. 228 (1985): 16.

56. Ibid., 17.

57. Quoted in Thomas, "George III and the American Revolution," 17.

58. Quoted in Thomas, "George III and the American Revolution," 23.

59. Thomas, "George III and the American Revolution," 25-31.

60. John Brooke, *King George III* (New York: McGraw-Hill, 1972), 55-58; Pares, *King George III*, 94.

61. Pares, *King George III*, 154-57.

62. Ibid., 163.

63. Ibid., chapter 4.

64. Keith, *Constitutional History of the First British Empire*, 344-66.

65. Alison Olson, *Making the Empire Work: London and American Interest Groups 1690-1790* (Cambridge: Harvard University Press, 1992) 2.

66. Ibid., 2-3.

67. Ibid., 2-4.

68. Ibid., chapters 7 & 8.

69. Ibid., 4.

70. John Brewer, *Party Ideology and Popular Politics at the Accession of George III* (Cambridge: Cambridge University Press, 1976) 146.

71. Olson, *Making the Empire Work*, 146.

72. Brewer, *Party Ideology and Popular Politics*, 171.

73. Brewer, *Party Ideology and Popular Politics*, 177-79.

74. Brewer, *Party Ideology and Popular Politics*, 21; Olson, *Making the Empire Work*, 146. Brewer notes that the SSBR's other mandate was to pay off debts incurred by Wilkes, debts that Brewer says were "incurred more through riotous living than political commitment."

75. Lawrence H. Leder, *America – 1603-1789: Prelude to a Nation* (Minneapolis: Burgess Publishing Co., 1978), 169-71.

76. Ibid., 86.

77. Olson, *Making the Empire Work*, 146.

78. The preceding discussion only touches upon a number of issues that have been covered more thoroughly in other sources. For more on the "rise of public opinion" in England see, in addition to Brewer, *Party Ideology and Popular Politics*, 1976, and Olson, *Making the Empire Work*, 1992, see James E. Bradley, *Popular Politics and the American Revolution in England: Petitions, the Crown and Public Opinion* (Macon, Ga.: Mercer, 1986); and John Sainsbury, *Disaffected Patriots: London Supporters of Revolutionary America, 1769-1782* (Kingston: McGill-Queen's University Press, 1987). See also Charles Tilly, *Popular Contention in Great Britain 1758-1834* (Cambridge, Mass.: Harvard, 1995) for his interpretation of why and how spontaneous and disorderly demonstrations of public ire gradually gave way to more politically acceptable methods of agitation.

79. John Brooke, *King George III* (New York: McGraw-Hill, 1972), 174.

80. Leder, *America – 1603-1789*, 171.

81. Brooke, *King George III*, 260-61.

82. J. C. Long, *George III* (London: Macdonald & Company Ltd., 1962) 45-46, 181.

83. Ibid., 296.

84. Colin Haydon, *Anti-Catholicism in Eighteenth-Century England, c. 1714-1780: A Political and Social Study* (Manchester: Manchester University Press, 1993), 171.

85. Philip Lawson, *The Imperial Challenge: Quebec and Britain in the Age of the American Revolution* (Montreal & Kingston: McGill-Queen's University Press, 1994), 98, 100.

86. Thomas Bartlett, *The Fall and Rise of the Irish Nation: The Catholic Question 1690-1830* (Dublin: Gill and Macmillan, 1992), 203-204, 271, 288.

87. Ibid., 271.

88. Taswell-Langmead, *English Constitutional History*, 733, emphasis in original.

89. Long, *George III*, 242.

90. Brooke, *King George III*, 261.

91. W. P. M. Kennedy, *The Constitution of Canada 1534-1937: An Introduction to its Development Law and Custom* (New York: Russell & Russell, 1973), 40.

92. Basye, *The Lord Commissioners of Trade and Plantations*, 2-3; Dickerson, *American Colonial Government*, 22-24.

93. Dickerson, *American Colonial Government*, 25-26.

94. Ibid., 107.

95. Labaree, *Royal Government in America*, 60-61.

96. Ibid., 61.

97. David Milobar, "The Origins of British-Quebec Merchant Ideology: New France, the British Atlantic and the Constitutional Periphery, 1720-70," *The Journal of Imperial and Commonwealth History* 24, no. 3 (1996): 364-90.

98. Labaree, *Royal Government in America*, 222.

99. Basye, *The Lord Commissioners of Trade and Plantations*, 44.

100. Ibid., 45.

101. C. S. S. Higham, "The General Assembly of the LeeWard Islands, Part II," *English Historical Review* 41, no. 163 (1926): 373-74.

102. Alan Valentine, *Lord North* (Norman: University of Oklahoma Press, 1967), 259, 312-15, 323.

103. Ibid., 77-78.

104. Henry Horwitz, *Parliament, Policy and Politics in the Reign of William III* (Newark: University of Delaware Press, 1977), 268.

105. Leder, *America – 1603-1789*, 186-87.

106. Valentine, *Lord North*, 313-22.

107. Dickerson, *American Colonial Government*, 81-100; Lawrence Henry Gipson, *The British Empire Before the American Revolution, Volume IX: The Triumphant Empire: New Responsibilities Within the Enlarged Empire, 1763-1766* (New York: Alfred A. Knopf, 1956), 7-9, 11.

108. Leder, *America – 1603-1789*, 178.

109. Ibid., 187.

110. Valentine, *Lord North*, 314.

111. The following relies on the biographies of Murray and Carleton found in the *Dictionary of Canadian Biography, Volumes IV and V.*

112. Alfred Leroy Burt, *The Old Province of Quebec* (Toronto: The Ryerson Press, 1933), 80-81.

113. Hilda Neatby, *Quebec: The Revolutionary Age, 1760-1791* (Toronto: McClelland and Stewart Limited, 1966), 31.

114. Ibid., 32.

115. Ibid., 103.

116. Kennedy, *The Constitution of Canada 1534-1937*, 59.

117. Burt, *The Old Province of Quebec*, 154-55; Kennedy, *The Constitution of Canada 1534-1937*, 59.

118. Fernand Ouellet, *Economic and Social History of Quebec, 1760-1850* (Ottawa: Gage Publishing/Institute of Canadian Studies, Carleton University, 1980), 97.

119. Ibid.

120. Quoted in Ouellet, *Economic and Social History of Quebec*, 100. See also Donald Creighton, *The Empire of the St. Lawrence* (Toronto: The MacMillan Company of Canada Ltd., 1956), 38-39.

121. John Bartlet Brebner, *New England's Outpost: Acadia Before the Conquest of Canada* (Hamden, Conn.: Archon Books, 1965), 274.

122. G. P. Browne, "James Murray," in *Dictionary of Canadian Biography, Vol. IV, 1771-1800* (Toronto: University of Toronto Press, 1979), 571.

123. Creighton, *The Empire of the St. Lawrence*, 22-27; Allan Greer, *Peasant, Lord, and Merchant: Rural Society in Three Quebec Parishes 1740-1840* (Toronto: University of Toronto Press, 1985), 142; Susan Mann Trofimenkoff, *The Dream of Nation: A Social and Intellectual History of Quebec* (Toronto: Gage Publishing Ltd., 1983), 28.

124. Creighton, *The Empire of the St. Lawrence*, 30.

125. Jose Iguarta, "A Change in Climate: the Conquest and the Marchands of Montreal," in *Readings in Canadian History: Pre-Confederation*, ed. F. Douglas and D. B. Smith (Toronto: Holt, Rinehart & Winston of Canada Ltd., 1990), 262.

126. Creighton, *The Empire of the St. Lawrence*, 27.

127. Quoted in Kennedy, *The Constitution of Canada 1534-1937*, 43.

128. Philip Lawson, *The Imperial Challenge: Quebec and Britain in the Age of the American Revolution* (Montreal & Kingston: McGill-Queen's University Press, 1994), 55.

129. David Milobar, "The Origins of British-Quebec Merchant Ideology: New France, the British Atlantic and the Constitutional Periphery, 1720-70," *The Journal of Imperial and Commonwealth History* 24, no. 3 (1996): 366. See also Creighton, *The Empire of the St. Lawrence*, 32; Ouellet, *Economic and Social History of Quebec*, 94-97.

130. Stanbridge, "England, France and their North American Colonies."

131. The "decapitation thesis" was first put forth in the mid-nineteenth century by two French-Canadian historians, Michel Bibaud and F. X. Garneau. The thesis was picked up and expanded in the 1950s and 1960s by Maurice Séguin and Michel Brunet. For an overview of this thesis and its critics see Dale Miquelon, ed., *Society and Conquest: The Debate on the Bourgeoisie and Social Change in French Canada 1700-1850* (Toronto: Copp Clark Publishing, 1977); and Karen Stanbridge, "The French-Canadian Bourgeois Debate: History and the Ideology of Colonialism," *International Journal of Comparative Race and Ethnic Studies* 1, no. 1 (1994): 127-33.

132. Burt, *The Old Province of Quebec*, 12; Trofimenkoff, *The Dream of Nation*, 26.

133. Neatby, *Quebec: The Revolutionary Age*, 23.

134. Gipson, *The British Empire Before the American Revolution*, 159.

135. Pierre Tousignant, "The Integration of the Province of Quebec into the British Empire, 1763-91, Part I: from the Royal Proclamation to the Quebec Act," in *Dictionary of Canadian Biography, Volume IV: 1700-1800* (Toronto: University of Toronto Press, 1979), xxxiv.

136. Greer, *Peasant, Lord, and Merchant*, 147-49; Ouellet, *Economic and Social History of Quebec*, 93.

137. Iguarta, "A Change in Climate"; Ouellet, *Economic and Social History of Quebec*, 79, 93-94; Trofimenkoff, *The Dream of Nation*, 28-29.

138. See above, 71.

139. Gipson, *The British Empire Before the American Revolution*, 156-59.

140. Allana Reid, "Representative Assemblies in New France," *Canadian Historical Review* 27, no. 1 (1946): 19-26.

141. Neatby, *Quebec: The Revolutionary Age*, 25-27; Trofimenkoff, *The Dream of Nation*, 29-30.

142. Gipson, *The British Empire Before the American Revolution*, 163.

143. Ouellet, *Economic and Social History of Quebec*, 99-100.

144. Basye, *The Lord Commissioners of Trade and Plantations*, 3-5.

145. Ibid., 25-31.

146. Dickerson, *American Colonial Government*, 108.

147. Basye, *The Lord Commissioners of Trade and Plantations*, chapter 2.

148. Labaree, *Royal Government in America*, 44.

149. Dickerson, *American Colonial Government*, 124-29.

150. Ibid., 128-32.

151. Basye, *The Lord Commissioners of Trade and Plantations*, 133, 140, 142.

152. Ibid., 143-52.

153. Ibid., 154-66.

154. Ibid., 171.

155. Ibid., 181.

156. Ibid., 190.

157. Ibid., 73n.

158. Olson, *Making the Empire Work*, 144-45.

159. Ibid., 134.

160. Nancy F. Koehn, *The Power of Commerce: Economy and Governance in the First British Empire* (Ithaca: Cornell University Press, 1994).

Chapter 5

The Quebec Act, Part II

The previous chapter identified the fundamental institutions, formal and informal, in operation at the time of the Quebec Act's passage, as well as the actors sanctioned by those institutions to participate in Anglo-Quebec policymaking. This chapter will now examine the process leading up to the Quebec Act to show how recognition of these institutions and their role in negotiations can help in understanding how and why such unprecedented legislation came to be promulgated.[1]

The Proclamation of 1763, the Merchants and James Murray

After the signing of the Treaty of Paris in February 1763, the Secretary of State for the Southern Department, Lord Egremont, requested the Board of Trade make some suggestions about how Britain's new territories should be administered. The information Egremont provided the Board concerning Canada included copies of the treaty and three reports prepared in 1762 by James Murray, Ralph Burton and Thomas Gage, the military governors who had been administering Quebec, Trois Rivières and Montreal, respectively, since the conquest. Murray's report was the longest. In it he stated that the allegiance of French Catholics in Quebec could be secured by assuring them that their religion would be protected. He also reported that the French Catholics in the province were not "ripe for such a government as prevails in our other colonies." The then president of the Board of Trade, Lord Shelburne, and the Lords Commissioners seem to have taken Murray's remarks to heart. In their report dated 8 June 1763 they advised that Quebec should be governed by "a Governor and Council under Your Majesty's immediate commission and instructions," a recommendation that went against the British precedent of establishing Protestantism and Protestant institutions in colonial territories. They suggested, however, that the boundaries of the province be drawn closely so that the concessions could be confined to as immediate an area as possible. This was crucial as French Catholics, they believed, were a population that would "greatly exceed for a very long period of time" all other settlers in the colony.[2]

Egremont disagreed with the Board's recommendation that the West should not be included within the bounds of Quebec, a point of difference that caused a rift between him and Shelburne. He was, however, comfortable with most of the rest of the Board's counsel, including the implication that Britain's "new French subjects" should, and would, be granted some special privileges. The Southern Secretary was anxious to keep the new subjects in the colony, a desire he had expressed already three years earlier at the capitulation of Montreal.[3] The Board's report was consistent with these concerns. Notwithstanding disagreements on the boundary issue, the Board of Trade was directed to begin drafting the commissions and instructions for the new governments of the ceded territories.

However, it was not Shelburne and Egremont who framed the Proclamation. The Southern Secretary died suddenly in August and his post was taken up by Lord Halifax. Shelburne quit the Board presidency and was replaced by Lord Hillsborough in September. The Proclamation that was submitted by the Board to Halifax on 4 October and approved by the Privy Council the next day incorporated some of the Board's recommendations of the 8 June report, including its suggestion that the West remain free from any civil jurisdiction. With respect to the province's form of governance, however, the system proposed in the Proclamation differed markedly from the sort that the Lords Commissioners under Shelburne had advised. Hillsborough and the Board decided that, in addition to a governor and council, Quebec should be granted an elected assembly "as in the other North American colonies." Also different was the Board's stance on other institutions in the province. French law was to be abolished, and there was no suggestion that any concessions to French Catholics would be made beyond the vague assurance that their religion would be protected "as far as the laws of Britain permit."

The Proclamation put in place the conditions necessary to convert the colony into a royal province. That this objective was in the minds of officials who framed its terms, and was to happen sooner rather than later, was confirmed in the new governor's commission and instructions. The documents were filled with particulars concerning how Quebec's assembly would be regulated, including all oaths that its Protestant representatives had to take; precious little detail was provided about the jurisdiction and powers of the governor and council that was to rule in the meantime. English law was to be instituted in Quebec; how exactly that was to be done was unclear, except that Murray should look to other colonies, especially Nova Scotia, for guidance.[4] And the process of Anglicization was to begin immediately. A long and detailed section was also included that outlined how settlement was scheduled to proceed in the province, including how townships were to be laid out and how land grants were to be administered. It also directed the governor to prepare a proclamation advertising these grants and extolling the virtues of the new province, and to arrange for its publication in the American colonies. Clearly British officials intended on populating the province with Protestant Britons and Americans.[5]

Not surprisingly, the Proclamation was well received by British merchants in Quebec. They had become restless under military rule, and frustrated with having to abide by the French institutions that had remained in operation since the conquest. They were anxious that civil government be established so that they could proceed with administering and legislating for the colony through a representative assembly. To suggest that they were disappointed with the manner in which Murray chose to interpret his instructions is an understatement. Having waited three years for Quebec to become a British province, the merchants were incensed by the governor's actions. Murray believed most of the recommendations in the Proclamation were unsuited to conditions in Quebec. He ignored instructions to adopt wholesale British law in the colony, and continued to allow French law in the civil courts, eventually permitting Catholics to sit on juries and practice law in the colony. The old seigneurial land laws were maintained. Murray also decided to "postpone" the election of an assembly indefinitely and legislate by appointed council only.

Why did Murray stray so far from the terms of the Proclamation and his instructions? He had already, in his report of 1762, made clear his position concerning Quebec governance, particularly his opinion that the province was not "ripe" for an elected assembly along the lines of those in America. First, there was the problem of submitting the vast majority of Catholic inhabitants to the rule of only a handful of Protestants. It was not that this method of governance was unprecedented. Ireland, of course, had been ruled by a Protestant minority for nearly a century. But the system was preserved in Ireland with the help of British troops. British MPs were averse to the presence and maintenance of a standing army in England during peacetime, so British officials kept most of the country's troops in reserve in Ireland. At least 12,000 men were accommodated in – and paid for by – Ireland most of the time.[6] Although the number of troops in North America was raised after the end of the Seven Years' War, this only amounted to about 7,500 men to secure all of Britain's possessions on the vast continent. As far as Murray was concerned, to prohibit almost 95 percent of the population from participating in any way in the administration of the province, particularly when there were not enough troops in the colony to maintain order if France did try to retake the colony, was not only unfair but dangerous.

Finally, Murray was loath to hand over rule of the province to men whom he personally detested. Perhaps it was, as some have said, aristocratic bigotry that made Murray hate the British merchants to such a degree. Cultured and obedient the traders were not. In contrast, Quebec's French inhabitants, who Murray called in 1764 "perhaps the bravest and the best race upon the globe,"[7] had been respectful and complaisant since the conquest. The British merchants were coarse and demanding in comparison, and their nature offended Murray. "In a late-eighteenth century setting of commercial pushiness and pretensions," writes Susan Trofimenkoff, "there was something soothing about the aristocratic, military values harboured in certain sectors of Canadian society," values to which Murray himself subscribed.[8]

The reaction of the British merchants on both sides of the ocean was swift.

Already in December 1763, several months before Murray officially became governor,[9] the Board of Trade received its first indictment of Murray. Asserting that they were responding on behalf of complaints from Britons overseas, the "merchants in London trading to Quebec" submitted a petition claiming that Murray's activities in the province were harming the colony's economic interests. In Quebec, merchants from around the province sent petitions and agents to air their grievances before Murray and administrators in London. On 16 October 1764 the grand jury of Quebec produced a presentment highly critical of Murray and his government. The document declared that all public accounts should be laid before the grand jury as it was the only "representative body" in the province.[10] It also condemned Murray's decision to let Catholics serve on juries in judgment of Britons, claiming that it was contrary to English law. These last comments were added to the presentment as an appendix unbeknownst to the few Canadians who sat on the grand jury and was signed only by the British members. Later, the Canadians who had included their signatures on the document apologized to an indignant Murray saying that they had not really understood what they were signing. The British merchants, however, were unrepentant and continued their tirade against the governor and his policies.[11]

The removal of Murray from the province now became the merchants' main goal. In April 1765, they hired a London lawyer, Fowler Walker, to make their case to government officials and other notables.[12] Walker immediately launched a slander campaign against Murray in London, bombarding the British government with letters and remonstrations accusing Murray of all manner of atrocities in the province.[13] That same month, another petition from the merchants in London trading to Quebec was presented to the Board of Trade. Again they admonished Murray for the manner in which he was administering the province and urged that a representative assembly be called in Quebec immediately. This petition differed from the first, however. Not all who signed it were merchants. The petition included the signatures of the mayor and four aldermen of the city of London, as well as four British MPs. Their inclusion underlined that the merchants' demands amounted to more than just self-interest; they were a matter of principle.[14]

Also notable about this petition was that it included the names of most of the leading North American merchants in London, a group of about fifteen or twenty who were emerging as the driving force behind most of the commercial lobbies in London. These men, such as Barlow Trecothick and Brook Watson, were powerful and well connected with government. Watson was a leading member of the Canada Committee, a group of merchants called upon by the British government to settle the Canada Bills issue after the conquest. They were to head the public agitation in London protesting the Stamp Act the following year, a campaign that was organized very much like the drive to have Murray recalled. Philip Lawson goes so far as to suggest that the Murray campaign was a "dress rehearsal" for the movement against the Stamp Act. It taught the leaders of the merchant community in London the effectiveness of petitions and public appeals to constitutional principles in lobbying government.[15]

Walker continued his assault on Murray's character and competence, appearing in front of the Board of Trade to complain of a billeting ordinance passed in the province by Murray, while two more petitions from Quebec and London, this time addressed to the king, both demanded that Murray be dismissed and the province be granted a representative assembly. The merchants' campaign had the desired effect on government administrators. In June 1765, the Board of Trade reported to the Privy Council "that the Governor Murray, and Lieutenant Governor Burton, did not upon this occasion conduct themselves according to the duty of their several situations."[16] Although the Privy Council did not automatically endorse the Board's report, they did express their "surprise" at some of Murray's actions. Finally, Murray lost whatever ministerial support he had when the Grenville ministry fell on 9 July 1765. Three months later, Murray and Burton were recalled from the province.

In the end, the charges against Murray were dropped for lack of evidence. This occurred partly because the merchants in Quebec, having succeeded in getting Murray removed from the province, lost interest in the matter, leaving Fowler Walker and the London merchants to face Privy Councillor investigators without their help, and partly because evidence actually was lacking. Many of the indictments against Murray had been exaggerated or fabricated outright. Walker admitted as much to the Privy Council when he told them "that the papers sent over from Canada were never intended to come before the Council in a judicial way and that he had no witnesses to support any of the charges." In early April 1767, the council dismissed the charges against Murray, calling them "groundless, scandalous and derogatory to the said governor."[17] Nevertheless, the merchants had scored a major victory, and they looked forward to the appointment of a new governor who they were confident would see matters their way.

The Government's Response

Whereas the merchants responded quickly to the Proclamation, or more precisely James Murray's interpretation of the Proclamation and his instructions, there was little immediate reaction from most British officials. It is significant that those few who did express an early opinion on the terms of the documents, however, did so on grounds very different from the merchants. In December 1764, Lord Chief Justice William Mansfield, having learned through a representative of James Murray's in London of conditions in the province, wrote to the First Lord of the Treasury, George Grenville, expressing his disappointment and disbelief at how the Quebec situation had been handled by British administrators. "Is it possible," Mansfield wrote, "that we have abolished their laws, and customs, and forms of judicature all at once? – a thing never to be attempted or wished. The history of the world don't furnish an instance of so rash and unjust an act by any conqueror whatsoever: much less by the crown of England, which has always left to the conquered their own laws and usages with a change only so far as the sovereignty was concerned."[18] Mansfield did not follow the merchants and condemn Murray for failing to abide by the terms of the Proclamation. Rather, he implied that the document itself was legally flawed because it specified terms that were contrary to the decision taken in *Calvin's Case* in 1609.

Another law officer was concerned about the Proclamation with regard to legal precedent. After 1760 a number of British "land sharks" appeared in the province with the aim of augmenting their property holdings. In 1764 they approached the government complaining of Canadians who had refused to take the oath of allegiance to the new king, and charged that, in accord with English penal legislation, these Catholics should be considered aliens without the right to inherit or transfer property under the new administration. The British attorney general, Fletcher Norton, decided against the speculators. "I conceive that the definitive treaty which has had the sanction and been approved by both Houses of Parliament meant to give, and that it has in fact and in law given to the inhabitants of those ceded countries a permanent and transmissible interest in their land there; and that to put a different construction upon the treaty would dishonour the Crown and the truth, and it would be saying that by the treaty they were promised the quiet enjoyment of their property but by the laws were to be immediately stripped of their estates."[19] Fletcher decided that the toleration granted to Quebec Catholics in the Treaty of Paris was more binding legally than the Proclamation's implication that England's penal laws extended to the colonies. This was because the Treaty had been approved by the British Parliament, whereas the other document had been instituted by an order in council only. Fletcher's statements were in accord with the principles that were later legally confirmed in the decision taken by Lord Mansfield in the case of *Campbell v. Hall*.

This attention to legal precedent seems to have fallen down in 1765, however. On 10 June, Fletcher and Solicitor General William De Grey ruled that Catholics in Quebec were "not subject, to the incapacities, disabilities, and penalties to which Roman Catholics in this kingdom are subject by the Laws thereof."[20] In other words, they decided that the British penal laws did not extend to Quebec. In the liberal tradition, the ruling is generally hailed as groundbreaking, an enlightened decision, a watershed, a judgment that traced "the way to the eventual abolition of the oath under the Test Act."[21]

But the ruling raises many questions, not the least important being why the law officers ignore precedent in this case? There was, after all, a legal precedent in place: the 1705 decision of then Attorney General Sir Edward Northey that stated the colonies *were* subject to English penal legislation.[22] Their ruling was clearly contrary to this judgment. Philip Lawson suggests that they may not have understood the precedent.[23] Alfred Burt implies they simply ignored precedent. They "gave no reason for this opinion, perhaps because their only reason was common sense and not law."[24] There is some evidence, however, that they simply missed the precedent. Their decision came only three days after the Board of Trade requested their opinion on the matter. Burt notes that in the papers of Lord Dartmouth, who became president of the Board shortly after the decision, the law officers' decision is immediately followed by Northey's ruling of 1705, "with exact references to statutes."[25] Presumably it was the law officers and not Dartmouth who unearthed this ruling and forwarded it to the Board. If this is the case it means that Fletcher and De Grey were both aware of and understood the legal precedents on this issue and were concerned that they be brought to light. It appears that their actions in this case were not so inconsistent with their previous behavior after all.

Although the law officers may have been contemplating Quebec issues, it was not until 1765 that the merchant-led furor surrounding Murray's administering of the province compelled other British administrators to take a closer look at the Quebec situation. A number of reports were produced that year that exemplified the disagreement existing amongst British officials concerning Quebec policy. Whether or not the government should institute an assembly in the province depended on who one talked to and when. In May 1765, a report of the Board of Trade (still under Lord Hillsborough) warned that Quebec could and should not be made into a royal province for some time.[26] In August, the law officers agreed. In a draft of a bill aimed at settling the revenue problems of the province they rejected outright the government's option of instituting a provincial assembly in the colony to levy taxes.[27] By September, however, the Board (now under Lord Dartmouth) had reversed itself. In a report submitted to the king in September, the Lords Commissioners recommended that an assembly be called in the province as soon as possible.

Similar inconsistencies existed on the matter of religion. The Board's May report detailed myriad regulations that should be put in place in the province to regulate the practice of Catholicism. These recommendations were in contrast to the decision of the law officers in June that the penal laws against Catholics did not extend to the colonies. On 2 September the Board again changed its mind. Now instead of restrictions on their behavior, the Lords Commissioners counseled that Quebec Catholics should be allowed to vote for representatives in the assembly they were recommending. They also harshly criticized Murray's attempt at combining systems of justice in the province, not because he had combined English and French law, but because they thought the concessions Murray extended to French Catholics did not go far enough.

Some order did arise out of all this confusion. In response to the Board's admonishment of Murray's system of justice, the Privy Council looked into the matter in the early months of 1766 and with the help of the attorney general Charles Yorke and the Lords Commissioners devised a plan to overhaul the Quebec justice system. They intended to include the new reforms in the instructions to the governor of Quebec. But when the plan came before the council in June the lord chancellor, Lord Northington, refused to endorse it. It is true the reforms proposed went beyond those suggested by the Board of Trade. They included a provision that stated that all cases involving property would be adjudicated using French laws, and another that allowed for the appointment of Catholic judges. But the chancellor did not reject the reforms because he thought they were too generous. Northington was more concerned about protocol. He questioned the right of the king and council to make policy for Quebec at all. He argued that only the British Parliament could alter the postconquest settlement. As far as Northington was concerned, "the old Canadian laws" were still in effect legally in the province and would remain that way until the British Parliament decided otherwise. Again, the principles of the *Campbell v. Hall* case, although they were not legally established until 1774, had entered into discussions concerning Quebec. That the principles were still "informal" enough to be overcome, accounts for Philip Lawson's statement that "[i]n different circumstances, supported by the king, the government probably could have pulled off the policy by order in council."[28] Nevertheless, they were enough of an obstruction to delay approval of the reforms until the ministry that conceived of them was dissolved. The program was shelved.

Guy Carleton and Quebec

Meanwhile, with Murray removed, the British merchants in Quebec looked forward to the arrival of the new governor, Guy Carleton, who they were confident would be more sympathetic to their demands. Carleton, along with the new chief justice and attorney general for the province, William Hey and Francis Maseres, arrived in the province in September 1766 with a bias against Murray and a high regard for the British merchants. The traders had insured, through their representatives in London, that Carleton was familiar with their sentiments concerning Quebec before he left England. Hey and Maseres were friends with Fowler Walker and were no doubt also briefed on the merchants' views before their departure. On top of this, Maseres was a French-born Huguenot and an anti-Catholic. From all indications, circumstances favored the British merchants in Quebec.

Carleton's first years as governor were far from trouble free. He immediately became involved in a political imbroglio with Murray's adherents in the provincial council. British and Canadian merchants complained of oppressive restrictions on the western fur trade and a dispute arose between the traders and the governor of Newfoundland concerning the seal fishery in the east. And there were other distractions. A struggle between merchants and government officials, begun during Murray's term concerning the legality of certain duties imposed in the province, came to a head under Carleton. A protracted court battle ended with the administration finally giving up trying to collect the duties. Another conflict arose when law officers in the province decided that British bankruptcy laws applied to Quebec, a ruling to which merchants in the province were adamantly opposed. The British merchants in Quebec had obviously not lost their taste for political agitation. Yet the merchants were taciturn about provincial governance during this period. Early in his tenure, Carleton was approached by some British merchants and asked if he would mind if they submitted a petition for an assembly. Carleton said he objected to petitions of any sort, but told them he was in favor of assemblies in general and asked that they conceive a plan for a representative body that might fit the conditions of the province. When the merchants returned a few weeks later, the tenor of Carleton's response evidently cowed them and the matter was dropped for awhile. Later, a few British merchants tried to resurrect the campaign but failed to stimulate enough interest in the project and gave up. Until 1770, the issue that had helped to bring down James Murray was ignored by the British merchants in Quebec.

While Carleton managed to avoid or defuse any major confrontations with the British merchants over the colony's administration during this period, this does not mean that he did not have strong opinions on how the province should be governed. Although Carleton may have come to Quebec on the side of the merchants, it was not long before he adopted many of the same ideas as his predecessor. The commissions and instructions prepared for him by the Board of Trade were almost identical to the papers given to Murray. But, like Murray, Carleton made little effort to follow any of the directions contained in them. No representative assembly was called. He could not fathom how such a body could work in Quebec. He told British officials the "better sort" of Canadians were against an assembly. Carleton said they observed events occurring in the American colonies and wanted nothing to do with institutions that appeared to them to breed only insolent behavior. Carleton agreed with the seigneurs arguing that in a province like Quebec, "where all men appear nearly on a level," a representative assembly "must give a strong bias to republican principles," a situation Carleton evidently wanted to avoid.[29] So he, like Murray, continued to govern the colony with his council only. English law was not instituted in the province either. It is true that Carleton was critical of Murray's handling of Quebec justice. This was not, however, because Murray had failed to abolish French law, but because Carleton disagreed with the way in which Murray had chosen to combine English and French systems. The new governor continued to advocate an integrated system, but a different one. And although initially suspicious of the French Catholic population in the province, within a few months of his arrival it was obvious that Carleton's attitude towards the Canadians was changing. Already in November 1766, Carleton was writing to England begging for redress for the "poverty-stricken" French seigneurs, asking that the government sanction the application of the proceeds from liquor licences toward grants for relief of the Canadian *noblesse*.[30] The softening of Carleton's attitudes toward Quebec French Catholics, the seigneurs and the senior clergy in particular, was to affect profoundly the governor's vision for Quebec's future when combined with his concerns over the military security of the province.

The Search for Solutions

Northington quashed plans for Quebec legal reform in 1766 and the Rockingham ministry fell. Quebec issues then took a back seat to the events in the American colonies. It was not until May 1767, when rumors that the opposition in the British Parliament was ready to mount an offensive against the government accusing them of dragging their feet on Quebec, that the administration began again to look seriously at the Quebec situation. Of course little had happened in the meantime to make the situation any clearer, and this was reflected in the views espoused by the new administration. The Advocate General, James Marriot, was asked by the new Southern Secretary, Lord Shelburne, to review a rewrite of the Archbishop of

York's report of 1764 that recommended that the practice of Catholicism be strictly regulated in the province. Marriot supported the Archbishop's suggestions wholeheartedly, a clear indication that the notion that Catholicism could be eradicated in Quebec was still held by at least some high-ranking officials.[31] The Southern Secretary saw things somewhat differently as evinced by a letter he wrote to Board of Trade outlining his views on the situation. He expressed his disappointment that the plan to overhaul Quebec's legal system had not been implemented the previous year, as well as his regret that an assembly had not been called in the province and stated his conviction that "as perfect tranquillity would be established in Quebec as in any of the other American colonies, could an assembly be called."[32] He went beyond the Board's report of 2 September and proposed that Catholics be allowed to sit in the assembly and be nominated to the provincial council. This he believed could be done without the approval of the British Parliament, through simple alteration of the governor's commission and instructions.[33]

These differences were exacerbated in 2 June when the rumors proved true and the opposition in Parliament launched its attack.[34] This changed circumstances dramatically. Administrators were now not only compelled to decide on a course of action in Quebec, they would be required to convince a majority of British MPs that the course was an appropriate one. Ministers decided they needed more information. An order in council was issued on 28 August directing the governor, council and law officers in Quebec to report on the system and make recommendations. Shelburne instructed his secretary, Maurice Morgann, to deliver the order to Quebec and to return with the reports. Shelburne also wrote to Guy Carleton advising him that the government was considering treatment of Quebec and asking for his comments.

Carleton provided yet another perspective on a situation already overburdened by conflicting opinions. In his response to Shelburne's letter and his subsequent correspondence Carleton stressed that Quebec must be prepared in case of attack, from France certainly, but from the American colonies as well. To that end, Carleton recommended that forts be constructed in various parts of the colony, especially at the two "entrances" to Quebec, the inland waterways (to help protect the colony from invading Americans) and the St. Lawrence (to block a French invasion). But beyond the need for fortifications, the governor spoke of the importance of securing the French Catholics in the province, especially the seigneurs and the clergy, the men who Carleton believed held the most influence over the rest of the population. But Carleton eschewed strong-arm tactics; instead he argued that these men – and hence the rest of the French population – could be won over to the British side by less aggressive means, through the proper system of rule and administration. He denounced the terms of the Proclamation, calling them too severe, and wrote that all should be repealed and Canadian laws be restored. He counseled that seigneurial tenure as it existed in New France be resurrected in the province. In light of the seigneurs' opinions on representative assemblies, Carleton said such a body should not be established, but official positions, including some on the provincial council, should be made open to Canadians. Carleton went as far as to recommend that a French Catholic regiment be raised, vowing that "no doubt but these gentlemen would prepare to serve where duty and interest require them."[35] He even suggested that some Canadians should be placed in British battalions in the American colonies to "make them turn their eyes from France" and "preserve an interest here for future events."[36] Carleton made sure to praise the courage of the Canadians and emphasized their experience with the conditions in the province. Of the 18,000 men he estimated were available for duty, "above one half have already served, with as much Valor, with more Zeal, and more military knowledge for America, than the regular Troops of France, that were joined with them."[37] Carleton thus linked civil responsibility with defense, a connection that he was to continue to promote during the years leading up to the Quebec Act's passage.[38]

To add to the confusion, the Quebec traders in London decided to revive the cause of an assembly in the province. In 1768, two letters were presented to the British Privy Council, one signed by the Canada Committee and the other by "Sundry Merchants Trading to and deeply interested in the Province of Quebec," asking that an assembly be established in Quebec. Nothing new was expressed, except that, for the first time, the merchants recommended that Catholics be admitted to the council and the assembly. The efforts of the London merchants were not matched by their counterparts in Quebec. There was little forthcoming from the Quebec traders until 1770. It was only then that they forwarded their own demands for a representative body. It is significant, however, that this petition said nothing about permitting French Catholics to participate in Quebec governance. Neither did another petition from the Quebec merchants in 1773 mention that Catholics should be allowed in the assembly. Indeed, it was not until 1774, after the Quebec Act was passed, that the British merchants in Quebec made any concessions on this point.[39] The Anglo-Quebec merchant lobby was clearly not unified in their position on the assembly.

How did British ministers respond to these varied opinions? In the end the merchants' demands were given short shrift. The council forwarded the letters from the Quebec traders in London to the Board of Trade (again under Lord Hillsborough, now the Colonial Secretary) for review. The result was a report issued in July 1769 endorsing the merchants' suggestions. In addition to reviving the 1766 plan for judicial reform, the Lords Commissioners counseled that oaths offensive to Catholics be waived in Quebec and French Catholics – seigneurs specifically – be admitted to the province's council, its proposed assembly, and all other important posts.[40] Unfortunately for the merchants, the Board's recommendations were shelved by the Privy Council primarily because ministers wished to wait to consider Quebec until Maurice Morgann returned from the province with the reports of the colonial officials. Whereas the London merchants' letters may have convinced the Board of Trade to issue an official report in support of their proposals, the representations from the Quebec merchants had little effect on anyone. Ministers had already let it be known that they were more interested in the opinions of Morgann and colonial officials than Protestant merchants. The Quebec merchants' appeals fell on deaf ears.

It is interesting to note that the difference between Quebec and London merchants on the Catholic question was only one of a number of issues that they disagreed on after 1765. Once James Murray was recalled from the province, many of the London merchants who participated in the campaign against the erstwhile governor, flung themselves into efforts to repeal the Stamp Act. In contrast, the British merchants in Quebec appear to have submitted to the stamp duties without much complaint. Certainly they did not protest the tax with the same vehemence as their London and American counterparts, although there is evidence that suggests that at least some Quebec merchants had opposed the Act.[41] Around 1769 the Quebec merchants dropped Fowler Walker as their agent in London and hired in his place Frances Maseres, the former Quebec attorney general. Walker continued, however, to keep in close contact with the Quebec traders in England and to represent them on occasion. It is possible that the Quebec merchants had come to believe that Walker's London experience impeded his capacity to represent properly their interests and then decided to employ an agent who had suffered the province first hand. It seems that the merchants who had once joined in common cause against Murray no longer felt it was possible or to their benefit to combine forces to agitate for an assembly.

In contrast to the experiences of the Board of Trade and the Anglo-Quebec merchants, Carleton's recommendations were well received in Britain. In 1768, the Colonial Secretary, Lord Hillsborough, wrote to Carleton saying that George III approved of "his every sentiment," including his recommendations concerning the treatment of the Canadians, and that once a new constitution was drawn up for Quebec, tolerance of Roman Catholics would be considered seriously. In the meantime, he was told to make sure that the Canadians be allowed to practice their religion undisturbed.[42] Carleton's suggestions that seigneurs be allowed to serve in the army and other positions of trust were commended, although administrators said they would have to move cautiously on these points. Hillsborough expressed less enthusiasm for Carleton's opinions on Quebec's governance. As was mentioned, Carleton's instructions – prepared by the Board under Hillsborough's direction – specified that an assembly be called in the province as soon as possible. Aside from the Colonial Secretary's personal views on this matter, however, the cabinet supported most of Carleton's ideas about Quebec. Anxious to drive home his points more forcefully, the governor requested leave to come to London to meet and discuss Quebec matters with ministers in person. It took two years, but leave was finally granted in December 1769. The governor was assured by Hillsborough that the Privy Council would do nothing about Quebec until they had a chance to talk to him.[43]

Thus it stood at the end of 1769: so many opinions, so little apparent progress. Nor did the long-anticipated return of Maurice Morgann in January 1770 help matters. Although all in the province agreed that Quebec's justice system was in desperate need of an overhaul, each proposed a different solution to the problem. Chief Justice William Hey believed that the system should be based on English law; Francis Maseres recommended an amalgam of French and English laws in a written code, and offered four different scenarios from which British ministers could choose. Carleton, having read the reports of his law officers and found them wanting, outlined his own plan, which counseled that the old French laws should be restored almost in their entirety. All that the reports made clear was that a solution was far from imminent.

Four years later, however, a solution had been found. How the British government produced the solution, how officials finally managed to overcome the diversity of opinions and conceive of the terms of the Quebec Act, let alone have the act passed by the British Parliament, has been the topic of wide debate. This is in part because much of the formulating and negotiating of Quebec policy after 1770 happened behind the closed doors of the British executive.

The Quebec Act

Guy Carleton made a conscious effort to convince British officials that his assessment of the Quebec situation was the prudent one. He had already received some favorable responses to his recommendations before he was granted leave from the province in December 1769. On his arrival in London the following August, he continued to push his policy with cabinet ministers with all the adroitness of a twentieth-century salesman.[44] He repeatedly drove home the importance of securing Quebec in case of attack from France or the American colonies, fostering the notion among ministers that defense had to play a crucial role in any decisions made about the province. He stressed that French Catholics would continue to outnumber Protestants in the province for some time, and painted a picture of mass depopulation and emigration from the province and economic disaster if the king's new subjects were not given some incentive to stay. He then offered his recommendations.

By 1771, Carleton's campaign was having some impact on cabinet ministers. At a meeting on 7 June, all the officials present agreed that an assembly should not be implemented in the province, everyone but Lord Hillsborough, who was "entirely of opinion to agree with the report of the Board of Trade (10 July 1769) for immediately convening a full legislature in the said province for the settling their laws, revenues, etc."[45] At the same meeting the ministers requested that the law officers consider "the several reports and papers relative to the laws and courts of judicature of Quebec, and the present defective mode of government in that province" and "prepare a general plan of civil and criminal law for the said province."[46] In their request they specified that the law officers consult "Governor Carleton and such others as they should think fit."[47] The officers took their time preparing their reports. The last was not received until the spring of 1773. In the end, two of the three reports[48] – those prepared by Attorney General Edward Thurlow and Solicitor General Alexander Wedderburn – were in agreement with Carleton's recommendations.[49]

Lord North passed all three reports to the Privy Council for review. By July 1773, the prime minister had decided to act on the matter and introduce a Quebec bill in the next session of Parliament. By November, orders had been given to the

Board of Trade to prepare a Parliamentary bill. "[A]fter so many years of neglect of the business of Quebec from the first establishment of it," complained John Pownall, undersecretary to Lord Dartmouth and the clerk ordered to put the measure together, "everything now is to be done in a hurry."[50]

Word of the Boston Tea Party reached London a few days after Parliament opened in January 1774. If North had intended to present the Quebec legislation early in the session, he had to change his plans; the American situation took precedence. In the spring, the British Parliament passed by large majorities the acts labeled "intolerable" by the American colonists, measures that closed the port of Boston, suspended the Massachusetts assembly, permitted the governor to quarter British troops in colonists' homes and allowed British officials to go back to England to face trial for capital offenses. It was not until these measures had been approved, in late May at the tail end of the Parliamentary session, when many members were already preparing to retire to their country estates for the summer, that North introduced the Quebec bill in the British House of Commons.

Opposition MPs were immediately suspicious of North's actions, and accused him of trying to force the legislation through a thinning house to circumvent criticism. They demanded to see the evidence supporting such a policy. North refused, telling them there was not enough time to produce and examine all the relevant reports. They insisted that Governor Murray be called to give testimony. North refused again, saying "if every person is to be called who has happened to have resided in the province, we may go on for ever and ever . . . his [Murray's] attendance is not to give necessary information, but to create unnecessary delay."[51] They did, however, hear from strong proponents of the bill, Alexander Wedderburn, Edward Thurlow, and of course Guy Carleton, whose able performance prompted one MP to extol "He is the most valuable witness I ever heard in my life."[52] Lord North himself campaigned vigorously for the Act, rising to his feet seventy-two times during the seven days over which the Act was debated. And there was debate, over the articles concerning Quebec law and justice, over the Western boundary, over the issue of government and in particular over the matter of religion. There were many MPs who just could not bring themselves to accept the degree of toleration toward Catholics that was being proposed by the government. The legislation was deemed "popish from the beginning to the end" and would open the gates to despotism. Virtually everyone in government was accused by these MPs of being a "papist"; only the king was spared. Yet the government prevailed. The Quebec Act was passed in the House of Commons on 7 June 1774 by a vote of 56 to 20. It passed the Lords ten days later, 26 to 7.

In a last ditch effort to stop the bill from becoming law, the mayor of London and a group of merchants went to the king's residence to request that he not sign the legislation. The merchants' complaints concerning the articles of the Act that stipulated all disagreements over property would be adjudicated according to Canadian law had been heard during the Commons debates but had obviously not had much impact on the final vote. Perhaps they could convince George III that the legislation should not be implemented. They could not. The king denied that the bill was even before him, then rushed off to sign it and immediately prorogued

Parliament. An inauspicious end, it seems, to the long process that established in Quebec a form of governance that was to be called "the greatest departure from tradition ever made, and the chief model upon which the crown colony system was constructed a generation earlier."[53]

Discussion

Recognition of the formal and informal institutions affecting Anglo-Quebec policymaking in the late eighteenth century contributes to the understanding of events leading up to the passage of the Quebec Act and their outcome. Institutions helped to array the factors and forces surrounding the process in such a way as to encourage the individuals and groups propounding ideas that were eventually to be included in the legislation to triumph over those with more traditional views on the Quebec question. This was accomplished not in any rigid way, for by no means was the Quebec legislation inevitable or predictable. Rather, they provided limits on some actions and ideas, and helped to foster others, and as a result shaped (rather than dictated) the policy outcome.

What separated the process as it applied to Quebec from the process in Ireland was the *nature* of the institutions; most of the institutions were informal rather than formal. Consequently, the institutions surrounding the Quebec case were comparatively pliant, which was to have a significant affect on how the process unfolded. Formal institutions defined the bounds of Anglo-Irish policymaking. There was a long Parliamentary tradition in Ireland that assured Irish MPs a say in policy promulgated in their kingdom. This power was restricted, however, by the presence of a Crown-appointed executive and the legislative process dictated by Poynings' Law. These factors together, although they could not determine policy, did much to shape the Anglo-Irish policymaking process in advance of negotiations by specifying the actors who could legitimately take part in the process, the relative powers of those actors, and so forth. In contrast, there were very few formal "rules" that applied to relations between London and Quebec. It is true that there were well-established *informal* procedures governing the relationship between the metropolis and other colonies overseas, but they did not apply to Quebec specifically. Moreover, they were informal and so were inherently more vulnerable to change. The institutional framework surrounding Quebec policymaking was hence more flexible, better able to accommodate new or unconventional ways of negotiating and formulating policy than was the Anglo-Irish system. In such an environment, the powers of the actors involved, indeed the identity of the players themselves, was much less predictable than in the Irish case.

This flexibility was not immediately evident, however. The informal institutions which had emerged and endured around policymaking for the American colonies were established well enough that, once it was determined that Britain would retain Quebec, individuals involved with Quebec policy conformed to those procedures almost automatically. Given how routine the governance of royal provinces had become by 1763, it is hardly surprising that the Proclamation and the commission and instructions to governor Murray read the way they did. In hindsight, the documents may seem shortsighted, considering how little recognition they gave to the special circumstances surrounding Quebec governance. At the time, however, the intention was to transform Quebec into a British colony, complete with British institutions and a privileged Protestant church. The settlers that British administrators had hoped would stream into the new province from Britain and the American colonies would not have accepted an administration different from that common in other royal provinces, so institutionalized had this form of governance become. Halifax and Hillsborough may be criticized now for ignoring Shelburne's more "thoughtful" analysis of Quebec governance and deciding to institute English institutions and a full-blown Protestant assembly in the province, but their approach was entirely consistent with past procedures. So embedded were these institutions in colonial policymaking that "it would have been only by rare good fortune" that even Shelburne, as able and astute as he has been made out to be, could have produced a document much different from the Proclamation.[54] Presuming that Shelburne was even interested in forging new political ground in Quebec – and there is some evidence that this was not the case at all[55] – it would have been much more difficult for him in 1763 to counter the institutionalized procedures surrounding metropolis-colony relations and establish an entirely new form of governance in Quebec than is generally recognized.

The same institutions that helped to conceal from ministers the problems inherent to the Proclamation, help to explain why officials were for so long hesitant to consider and implement alternatives to the "old representative system." The changes to the established method of administration that were bandied about for Quebec were substantial: an appointed council as opposed to a representative assembly, Catholic toleration rather than penal legislation. It would take time for such ideas to reach the policy stage, time for administrators to become comfortable with the notion that such terms were better suited to the Quebec situation than the old established ways.

Given these circumstances, the contemporary argument that the Quebec Act was written in haste for the purpose of intimidating the American colonies into submission is unlikely. As alien as the terms of the Quebec Act were to the usual method of British governance, British officials would not have been able to conceive of, let alone convince a majority of British MPs to pass, such a novel arrangement in such a short period of time. Long-practiced procedures have considerable inertia, and can help to perpetuate certain ideas and actions on the part of individuals involved in the policy process, even if they no longer make sense in the immediate context. Note the tenacity with which many present and past members of the Board of Trade clung to tradition. It was the Lords Commissioners who had been central to maintaining the informal institutions that upheld the "old representative system" for the better part of a century.

It was not only British government officials who were affected by these institutions. British merchants in Quebec and London were as accustomed and committed to the "old representative system" as were British politicians. The governor's commission and instructions were looked upon by most as the "constitution" of the colonies. The Quebec administration's refusal to abide by the conditions contained in these documents appeared to the merchants a felonious attempt to undermine what they saw as established constitutional principles. That these "principles" were nowhere formally specified did not concern the merchants. That the only formal institution which made direct reference to royal governance in the colonies, *Calvin's Case*, actually validated the actions of the governors was not important to them. The informal institutions that had developed around the metropolis-colony relationship stipulated that Quebec receive the system of governance and administration specified in the Proclamation and in the governors' commissions and instructions, the same systems that were in operation in all other British provinces in the empire. It was on these precedents and procedural norms that the Anglo-Quebec merchants based their rejoinders.

Given the extent to which government administrators, merchants, and others on both sides of the Atlantic viewed, in 1763, the procedural precedents associated with the metropolis-colony relationship as established, secure, indeed *entrenched*, it has been argued that these "rules" were more "formal" than informal, as the preceding has claimed. J. P. Greene contends that the procedures characterizing relations between London and the colonies in the eighteenth century composed an "imperial constitution" that, while it was based on very different ideas about the rights of Britons in the colonies and the power of the British Parliament over representative assemblies in the rest of the empire, was just as valid and lawful as were the written legal directives to which British officials turned for guidance and grounds in legislating for Britain's overseas possessions.[56] This "new legal history" maintains "that constitutional power was ultimately whatever was both asserted and accepted, however much all parties insisted that their position was grounded in eternal verities."[57]

Of course by the midcentury, these informal institutions, what Greene refers to as the "imperial constitution," comprised accepted procedures. But the fact remains that they were *not* written, they were *not* legally constituted and ultimately did not coincide with the formal institutions to which British administrators came to adhere. This is more than an arbitrary categorization, because it was the written rules that would take precedence in the end. When the actions of British administrators are observed during this period, one is left with the impression that, once they had accepted that the old colonial system was not appropriate for Quebec, they proceeded as if they could do more or less as they pleased in the new province, as long as they were true to the few written rules that applied to the colony. This is not to say that it was inevitable that British administrators would prevail because they based their actions on institutions that were formally and legally grounded. One need only to look to the experiences of William III and his proponents during the Treaty of Limerick ratification bill negotiations to witness how formal institutions do not guarantee mastery over legislative outcomes. Rather, British administrators, having "the law" behind them, would have had an institutional advantage over colonials, merchants, and others who based their positions on institutions that were not formally recognized. Whether that advantage translated into an actual policy victory depended on the coming together of a number of other factors, institutional and contingent.

Crucial in this regard were changes to a number of the informal institutions governing the distribution of power amongst actors involved in the policy process. These changes wrought a general reduction in the power over policy of individuals and groups who remained steadfast in their desire to see the old representative system, or some variation of it, implemented in Quebec.

The Anglo-colonial merchants were one group promoting traditional governance in Quebec that became a casualty of modifications to the informal institutions surrounding colonial policymaking. The "opening" of the British policymaking process that accompanied the rise of the English/British Parliament and the increasing influence of out-of-doors groups on the actions of ministers, helped the merchant community acquire access to policy negotiations that had at the beginning of the century been closed to all but the government executive and select individuals and groups. This benefited the merchants in the first half of the eighteenth century when British officials consulted them on virtually all colonial matters. After 1760, however, circumstances arose that led to changes in the informal procedures governing this relationship. Political instability and the decision on the part of ministers to favor domestic over colonial interests meant that government officials began to neglect merchant interests. Changes in merchant lobbying techniques also contributed to the erosion of their powers when traders on both sides of the Atlantic began to involve themselves in the new public-opinion lobbies and adopt the more "radical" techniques typical of these associations. Openly hostile to government and unafraid to criticize publicly government policy, colonial and Anglo-colonial merchant groups began to be viewed by officials in a more negative light. As a result, their access to policymakers became more restricted. The informal institutions governing colonial policymaking, having once favored merchant interests, underwent changes that reduced the capacity of the Anglo-Quebec merchants to affect legislation in the colonies, indeed removed their right to participate in the policy process at all.

Merchant influence suffered further from changes to informal institutions that reduced the power of the Board of Trade relative to other actors involved in the policymaking process. The Board of Trade had long been merchant-friendly, essentially the government broker of commercial interests. This worked to the advantage of colonial and Anglo-colonial traders during the first half of the eighteenth century when most decisions concerning the colonies were merely a rubber stamp of the Lords Commissioners' recommendations. As the century progressed, however, the British government, especially Parliament, began to involve itself more in colonial affairs and focus on the larger issues of colonial rule beyond the Board's historical jurisdiction. The informal institutions that had once affirmed that colonial policy would comply with the Lords Commissioners' recommendations changed so that the Board, although it was still consulted on colonial affairs, no longer had as important a role to play in colonial policymaking. Its deliberate reduction in 1766 to a board of report only devalued the recommendations of the Lords Commissioners even further. Whatever power the lords

Commissioners, and by extension the merchants, had with ministers largely disappeared.[58]

Changes in informal institutions helped to undermine the position and power of colonial and Anglo-colonial merchants and the Lords Commissioners of the Board of Trade in the policymaking process, individuals who hitherto had provided most of the information on which British officials based their decisions concerning colonial policy. British administrators began receiving most of their information from other sources, mostly "in-house," and the views of the most ardent supporters of the traditional form of governance in Quebec were depreciated. The way was open for a new solution and James Murray, and in particular Guy Carleton, were there to provide British officials with one. Military men themselves, military considerations affected their views concerning how Quebec should be administered. The French and American threats, along with considerations surrounding the loyalty of Quebec's French Catholic subjects on a continent lacking for British troops, were matters that dominated their opinions on Quebec policy. With the powers of the Board of Trade and merchant communities over colonial policy deteriorating, the governors' interpretation of the situation in the province had greater impact on policymakers than it would have in the past. By undermining those with views different from Carleton and his adherents, informal institutions helped to shape the nature of royal policy in Quebec. Most of Carleton's suggestions concerning religion and the administration of the colony were adopted wholesale into the Quebec Act; the articles that were not entirely in accord with his views, such as those related to the justice system, at least reflected the spirit of his solutions.

While the institutional context surrounding colonial policymaking changed over the course of negotiations to favor Carleton and his proponents and reduce the influence of actors promoting a traditional approach in Quebec, institutions by no means dictated the triumph of Carleton's program. Factors and forces outside the institutional context combined with institutions to lead to this result. That the Quebec governor held the confidence of important officials, as well as the king, helped his cause. In the end, however, his success lay in his being able, out of a mixture of skill and not a little luck, to cast the problems of the province in terms of issues that only became more pressing as time went on, namely defense and the threat of American and French attack. He then went on to convince officials that his were the only logical solutions to the problems that he himself had framed. American resistance to the Stamp Act and the Townshend Acts were followed by the Boston Massacre in 1770 and events in Rhode Island, Boston and elsewhere. Ministers may have agreed in principle with Carleton's recommendations but it took the growing recalcitrance of the American provinces and the possibility of French complicity to push them to finally act on those recommendations.

Of key importance was colonial security. The British government decided to leave some 7,500 troops in North America after 1763. The British Parliament had authorized the money required to support these regiments, but only on the condition that the American colonies be required to pay taxes.[59] American opposition to the Stamp Act and later the Townshend Acts, however, forced British officials to rethink whatever plans they may have had concerning colonial defense. With no new tax revenues coming in from the American colonies, and British MPs refusing to contribute further supplies for North American defense, there was little money to spend on more troops or fortifications overseas. Furthermore, with American belligerence on the rise, many of the troops that were already there were forced to move away from their assigned posts to contain the unruly masses on the Atlantic coast.[60] This left areas already undermanned without any military supervision.[61] The British government did not have the money or the men to secure Quebec or the Canadians by repressive means. Concessions were a cheaper and, if Carleton was to be believed, a foolproof way of securing the neutrality of the Canadians in case of war with France or the thirteen colonies, if not their allegiance and possibly even their military assistance. It was by combining concessions with colonial defense, a matter about which ministers were already fretting and could readily understand, that Carleton succeeded in getting British officials to begin thinking seriously of instituting a more liberal policy in the province.

Although North had decided that the Quebec question was to be resolved in the next session of Parliament, before difficulties arose in the American colonies, incidents in Boston only amplified an already pressing need to settle matters in the province. Not only this, but they seemed to provide proof to British officials that the foundations on which the terms of the Act had been formulated, that the French Catholic population had to be secured in case of American and French recalcitrance, were accurate. The Quebec Act was a policy that had been framed in preparation for precisely such developments. Events in Boston made its authors that much more confident that the Quebec Act was necessary and British officials that much more anxious to implement its terms.

All this might go some way toward explaining how ministers were convinced of the viability of the Quebec Act, but what of the MPs in the British Parliament? Carleton's "brilliant" presentation in the House of Commons of his recommendations for Quebec convinced at least some MPs that the Quebec bill was a desired measure. As well, North's decision to wait and introduce the act to a thinning house at the end of the session perhaps increased the likelihood of its passage. But there appear to have been other forces encouraging the majority of British MPs to approve the policy. If Philip Lawson is to be believed, there was no connection between the Quebec Act and the "intolerable acts" passed that spring to punish the rebellious colonists. Even though contemporary Americans immediately drew connections between the measures, even though the popular press had picked up on and was promulgating the view that the acts were linked, Lawson insists that "the connection escaped most MPs and informed observers at the time."[62] According to William Kennedy, however, Lord North himself, upon presenting the Quebec bill, made it plain to British MPs that the legislation was indeed connected to the American troubles.[63] North declared that the Act was brought in because "His Majesty's message recommended Parliament to take up the subject." The king's message to which North referred, dated 7 March 1774, urged the commons "to enable [the king] effectually to take such measures as might be most likely to put an immediate stop to the present disorders in North America, and also to take into their most serious consideration what regulations and permanent provisions might be necessary to be established for better securing the just dependence of the colonies on the crown and Parliament of Great Britain." Although the king had mentioned nothing specific about Quebec, North made a point of associating the Quebec bill with the "intolerable acts."

This does not mean, as contemporary critics of the Quebec Act and some later historians maintained, that the Quebec measure was a hastily written ruling tacked on to the other measures to warn the colonists to the south that they would be subject to a similar sort of "despotic" governance if they did not start behaving themselves. Given the unprecedented nature of the Quebec Act's terms, that would have been impossible. It does not preclude the possibility, however, that North may have decided to use the anti-American sentiment already coursing through the commons to help legitimate and gain approval of the Quebec Act.

Finally, what can be made of the actions of the king? Comparing the processes surrounding the passage of the Treaty of Limerick ratification bill and the Quebec Act, what is immediately evident is the reduced role of the monarch in the policy proceedings. Whereas William III occupied a major role in the process leading up to the ratification of the Treaty of Limerick, it is difficult to find any mention of George III in accounts describing the events surrounding the Quebec Act. It is the British ministry, Lord North in particular, who was the driving force behind the legislation. The change in focus, from the monarch to the ministry, is reflective of the transformations in the informal institutions that had occurred in British politics since the Glorious Revolution. The more modern idea that cabinet ministers were the "executive committee of the British Parliament" rather than the personal representatives of the monarch, and were answerable to MPs first, was in no way firmly established. But there is little question that their independent role in government decisionmaking relative to the sovereign had broadened considerably, to the point where, at least in the case of the Quebec Act, they more or less dictated the legislation emanating from London.

Of course the monarch may have raised objections to the measure given his apparent repugnance toward Catholics and Catholicism; it was likely not easy for the North ministry to win the king's approval of the legislation. Lawson more or less concedes his bewilderment on this last point, admitting "it is not known how this was done" but calls it "the great achievement of North's ministry in 1774."[64] It is true that no one knows how North managed to convince George III to come to his side. But given the king's respect for the views of his ministers, North's in particular, and that North presumably presented the Quebec measure to him as the best way in which to secure the continued dependence of the province on the Crown as well as its defense, perhaps George's support of the Act is not so difficult to understand. As will become clear in the next chapter, it is likely that North and his advisors used many of the same arguments, especially those which linked concessions to Catholics with imperial defense, to convince the king, as well as MPs in the British Parliament, to support Catholic relief in England and Ireland four years later. Carleton's legacy was to be felt well beyond the boundaries of the former French province.

Hence the Quebec Act can be understood as the outcome of a number of significant and contingent historical events unfolding within an institutional context characterized by an absence of formal institutions and a collection of informal institutions that underwent changes that reduced the power of actors supportive of traditional policy in Quebec relative to those who propounded a more tolerant approach. That the institutions surrounding this process were largely informal helps to account for the capacity of ministers and groups promoting tolerance to promulgate such unprecedented policy. While colonial history had a long tradition of anti-Catholicism, and while this tradition certainly discouraged novel approaches to the Quebec situation for some time, once the decision had been made to extend concessions to Catholics in the province there were no significant institutional barriers to their implementation.

Notes

1. The events leading up to the Act's passage have been recounted many times. The following relies especially on the following sources: Alfred Leroy Burt, *The Old Province of Quebec* (Toronto: The Ryerson Press, 1933); Donald Creighton, *The Empire of the St. Lawrence* (Toronto: The MacMillan Company of Canada Ltd., 1956); W. P. M. Kennedy, *The Constitution of Canada 1534-1937: An Introduction to its Development Law and Custom* (New York: Russell & Russell, 1973); Philip Lawson, *The Imperial Challenge: Quebec and Britain in the Age of the American Revolution* (Montreal & Kingston: McGill-Queen's University Press, 1994); Peter Marshall, "The Incorporation of Quebec in the British Empire, 1763-1774," in *Of Mother Country and Plantations: Proceedings of the Twenty-Seventh Conference in Early American History*, ed. V. B. Platt and D. C. Skaggs (Bowling Green, Ohio: Bowling Green State University Press, 1971); Hilda Neatby, *Quebec: The Revolutionary Age, 1760-1791* (Toronto: McClelland and Stewart Limited, 1966); Pierre Tousignant, "The Integration of the Province of Quebec into the British Empire, 1763-91, Part I: from the Royal Proclamation to the Quebec Act," in *Dictionary of Canadian Biography, Volume IV: 1700-1800* (Toronto: University of Toronto Press, 1979). Most of the important documents associated with this period, including merchant petitions, have been reproduced in A. Shortt and A. G. Doughty, eds., *Documents Relating to the Constitutional History of Canada, 1759-1791, Volume I* (Ottawa: J. de L. Tache, 1918).
2. Burt, *The Old Province of Quebec*, 76, 82-83; Tousignant, "The Integration of the Province of Quebec," xxxv.
3. Tousignant, "The Integration of the Province of Quebec," xxxiii.
4. Kennedy, *The Constitution of Canada 1534-1937*, 36.
5. Burt, *The Old Province of Quebec*, 82.
6. S. J. Connolly, *Religion, Law and Power: The Making of Protestant Ireland, 1660-1760* (Oxford: Clarendon Press, 1992). Connolly notes that an English Act of 1699 determined that the regular army would number 12,000 in Ireland and 7,000 in England.
7. Quoted in Kennedy, *The Constitution of Canada 1534-1937*, 41.
8. Susan Mann Trofimenkoff, *The Dream of Nation: A Social and Intellectual History of Quebec* (Toronto: Gage Publishing Ltd., 1983), 35.
9. The Proclamation was approved by the British Privy Council on 5 October 1763. It and Murray's commission and instructions did not go into effect until nearly a year later, on 10 August 1764.

10. Members of the Grand Jury were appointed, not elected. Presumably, merchants called it "representative" only because it had merchant, including *Canadien*, representation.

11. Creighton, *The Empire of the St. Lawrence*, 41-42.

12. Ibid., 42-45.

13. Burt, *The Old Province of Quebec*, 123-24.

14. Lawson, *The Imperial Challenge*, 54.

15. Ibid., 62-63.

16. Quoted in Lawson, *The Imperial Challenge*, 59.

17. Burt, *The Old Province of Quebec*, 126.

18. Quoted in Lawson, *The Imperial Challenge*, 58.

19. Quoted in Lawson, *The Imperial Challenge*, 57.

20. Quoted in Lawson, *The Imperial Challenge*, 45.

21. Tousignant, "The Integration of the Province of Quebec," xli.

22. See above, 78.

23. Lawson, *The Imperial Challenge*, 45.

24. Burt, *The Old Province of Quebec*, 94.

25. Ibid., 509, n34.

26. Lawson, *The Imperial Challenge*, 68-69.

27. Ibid., 70.

28. Ibid., 83.

29. Quoted in Kennedy, *The Constitution of Canada 1534-1937*, 45.

30. Burt, *The Old Province of Quebec*, 153.

31. Lawson, *The Imperial Challenge*, 96.

32. Quoted in Burt, *The Old Province of Quebec*, 151.

33. Ibid., 151-52.

34. Marshall, "The Incorporation of Quebec," 55-57.

35. Quoted in Burt, *The Old Province of Quebec*, 155.

36. Ibid., 155-56.

37. Shortt and Doughty, *Documents Relating to the Constitutional History of Canada*, 282.

38. Kennedy, *The Constitution of Canada 1534-1937*, 59-60; Neatby, *Quebec: The Revolutionary Age*, 100.

39. The merchants asked the King to "call a General Assembly in such Manner, and of such Constitution and Form as to your Majesty, in your Royal Wisdom, shall seem best adapted to secure its Peace Welfare and good Government." Francis Maseres took this passage to mean that the British merchants in Quebec would now allow Catholics on the assembly if the King felt that it was proper. See Francis Maseres, *An Account of the Proceedings of the British and Other Protestant Inhabitants of the Province of Quebec in North America in Order to Obtain an House of Assembly in That Province* (London, 1775). The merchants' petition to the king of 1773 is reproduced in Shortt and Doughty, *Documents Relating to the Constitutional History of Canada*.

40. Burt, *The Old Province of Quebec*, 165-66.

41. William Kerr, "The Stamp Act in Quebec," *English Historical Review* 47 (1932): 648-51. On Guy Carleton's arrival in the province, a group of merchants presented him with a representation welcoming the new governor that proclaimed proudly their happy submission to the Stamp Act duties. Another smaller group of merchants presented a separate petition of welcome. This one said nothing about the Stamp Act.

42. Kennedy, *The Constitution of Canada 1534-1937*, 59-60; Neatby, *Quebec: The Revolutionary Age*, 60-61.

43. Ibid., 62.

44. Lawson, *The Imperial Challenge*, 111.

45. Quoted in Lawson, *The Imperial Challenge*, 116.

46. Quoted in Burt, *The Old Province of Quebec*, 182.

47. Lawson, *The Imperial Challenge*, 115.

48. Lawson, *The Imperial Challenge*, 117-19. Lawson notes that the third report was prepared by advocate general James Marriott, the same officer who recommended in 1767 that Catholicism essentially be eradicated from Quebec. Marriott's views had changed little in six years. He recommended strict regulations be placed on the practice of Catholicism in the province – he did not agree with the 1765 decision that British penal laws did not extend to the colonies – and although he counseled that the "ancient laws and usages" be restored in Quebec, it was on the understanding that it only be temporary, and that English laws and ways would eventually be implemented.

49. Burt, *The Old Province of Quebec*, 182-84.

50. Lawson, *The Imperial Challenge*, 124.

51. Quoted in Lawson, *The Imperial Challenge*, 134.

52. Martin Wight, *The Development of the Legislative Council 1606-1945* (London: Faber & Faber Ltd., 1946), 38.

53. Arthur Herbert Basye, *The Lord Commissioners of Trade and Plantations Commonly Known as the Board of Trade 1748-1782* (New Haven: Yale University Press, 1925).

54. R. A. Humphreys, "Lord Shelburne and the Proclamation of 1763," *English Historical Review* 49, no. 194 (1934): 241-64.

55. Ibid.

56. J. P. Greene, *Peripheries and Centre: Constitutional Development in the Extended Polities of the British Empire and the United States, 1607-1788* (Athens: University of Georgia Press, 1986); J. P. Greene, *Negotiated Authorities: Essays in Colonial Political and Constitutional History* (Charlottesville: University Press of Virginia, 1994).

57. Ian K. Steele, "The British Parliament and the Atlantic Colonies to 1760: New Approaches to Enduring Questions," in *Parliament and the Atlantic Empire*, ed. P. Lawson (Edinburgh: Edinburgh University Press, 1995), 33.

58. Alison Olson, *Making the Empire Work: London and American Interest Groups 1690-1790* (Cambridge: Harvard University Press, 1992). Olson also maintains that the reduction in the power and influence of the Board of Trade on colonial policy was one of the major factors that diminished the political potency of merchant groups.

59. John L. Bullion, "Security and Economy: The Bute Administration's Plans for the American Army and Revenue, 1762-1763," *William and Mary Quarterly* 45, no. 3 (1988): 499-509; P. D. G. Thomas, "The Cost of the British Army in North American, 1763-1775," *William and Mary Quarterly*, 45, no. 3 (1988): 510-16.

60. The removal of troops from the west was actually a relief to Quebec traders who for years had been complaining of the arbitrary duties and generally oppressive treatment meted out by officers in charge of these posts.

61. Tousignant, "The Integration of the Province of Quebec," xxxvii.

62. Lawson, *The Imperial Challenge*, 141.

63. Kennedy, *The Constitution of Canada 1534-1937*, 63.

64. Lawson, *The Imperial Challenge*, 98.

Chapter 6

The Irish Catholic Relief Act, 1778

By the end of the 1770s, Irish penal laws had restricted legally the rights and activities of Irish Catholics for eight decades. It is true that the actual enforcement of the laws during the eighteenth century was patchy. Although measures against Irish ecclesiastics were ardently enforced during the early years of Protestant rule – over 400 regular clergy were transported out of Ireland after the 1697 passing of the Bishops' Banishment Act, and attempts were made to track down the hundreds more clergymen who defied the legislation and remained in the kingdom[1] – the laws against the Catholic clergy gradually fell into disuse as the century progressed. Priest-hunters determined to collect the rewards offered by the Irish government for seizing and convicting unregistered clergymen were active in the first two decades of the eighteenth century, then disappeared.[2] Laws were more rigidly enforced when Britain was perceived to be under a Catholic threat, as during the Stuart rebellion in Scotland in 1715 and the outbreak of war with Spain in 1718, but then loosened once the danger had passed.[3]

Irish Protestants were more vigilant in their enforcement of laws against Catholic property owners. Protestant contemporaries were well aware that the possession of land was closely linked to social and political power in Ireland. Laws circumscribing the rights of Catholics to inherit and purchase land were deemed necessary to maintain the Protestant Ascendancy in Ireland. Of special significance were the "popery acts" of 1704 and 1709 passed by the Irish Parliament during the reign of Queen Anne that put into place all manner of restrictions on Catholics' land rights. While the ambiguity of the acts gave rise to myriad legal complications,[4] they nevertheless had considerable impact on eighteenth-century Catholic Ireland. The Act of 1709, for example, established that any Protestant who reported a Catholic who had taken part in a transaction in violation of the penal laws was entitled to a share of that transaction. The legislation gave rise to the figure of the

Protestant "discoverer," an independent enforcer of the penal laws, who helped overcome some of the difficulties associated with upholding anti-Catholic legislation in a kingdom wanting of Protestant state officials. Even so, there were a number of Catholic landowners who managed to evade the property laws and preserve their landholdings in various ways.[5] Catholics participated in illegal property dealings, some with the cooperation of Protestant discoverers: out of the more than 2,000 "discoveries" reported between 1708 and 1778, over 90 percent were collusive, arranged to protect Catholic landholdings.[6]

Despite the inconsistency in their enforcement, the penal laws aggrieved and inhibited Irish Catholics. Laws against the Irish clergy may have been evaded by many churchmen and mainly overlooked by ruling Protestants, but they still "hung like the sword of Damocles" over the heads of Catholics, "who were thus reminded that they must tread warily."[7] Although Sean Connolly and others have maintained that the penal laws did not have so great an impact on the structure of Irish society as has been claimed,[8] Connolly concedes that the Catholic community would have experienced the laws that forbade Catholics to vote, to hold positions of power, to buy land, to carry arms, and otherwise live and act freely, as grievous and oppressive.[9] "Out of all proportion to their actual effect," writes R. F. Foster, "the Penal Laws reflected Protestant fears and affected Irish mentality, creating a tension of resentment born of enforced deference as well as necessitating the elaborate concealments and stratagems of Catholic political activity."[10]

Irish Catholics were hence encouraged when, in 1778, the Irish Parliament passed the first in what Catholics hoped would be a series of acts dismantling the penal laws in the kingdom. The Catholic Relief Act declared that Catholic land was no longer subject to the gavelkind and could be bequeathed in any manner that the proprietor wished, and that Catholics would henceforth be able to hold land on long-term leases of up to 999 years.

The Act was initiated by British officials who, for a number of reasons, wished to extend some measure of relief to Irish Catholics. It is perhaps more difficult to understand how Irish MPs, the majority of whom were as ardently anti-Catholic as their forebears, approved such an Act, even though the concessions granted were quite limited. Why was this Irish Parliament not able to suppress or defuse tolerant legislation as had the assemblies of the 1690s? Changes in the formal and informal institutions surrounding the Anglo-Irish policymaking process help to answer this question.

Formal Institutions Characterizing Anglo-Irish Policymaking in 1778

The two main formal institutions that structured Anglo-Irish policymaking in 1697 were still in effect in 1778. The Irish Parliamentary tradition compelled British monarchs to assemble the Irish Parliament to vote additional supplies and pass other government bills. Poynings' Law remained in place, inflicting Anglo-Irish policymaking with its cumbersome procedures. To these institutions had been added a third: the Declaratory Act.

The Declaratory Act

The Declaratory Act of 1720 established formally that the Irish Parliament was "subordinate unto and dependent upon" the British monarch and the British Parliament, and put an end to the constitutional question, if not the debate, concerning the judicial and legislative independence of the Irish Parliament. The authority of the British Parliament to legislate for Ireland had long been a subject of contention. By the end of the seventeenth century, the Irish Parliament had challenged the authority of the English Parliament to pass legislation binding on Ireland on several occasions.[11] The Irish argument was based on the notion that Ireland was a separate and independent kingdom connected to England in the person of the monarch. Henry II did not conquer Ireland; rather, Irish chiefs submitted voluntarily to the English king in exchange for the benefits of English law and other institutions. Hence, England did not "own" Ireland. The relationship was a contractual one between the Irish people and the sovereign.[12] The English Parliament had no place in that association.

English opinion of the Irish constitutional argument can be discerned from the responses of the English and Irish administrations to the challenges of the Irish Parliament. Parliament's 1460 declaration that all laws applying to Ireland must be sanctioned by the Irish Parliament led eventually to the implementation of Poynings' Law[13]; the Irish judges' response to the "queries" of 1641 questioning the validity of Irish laws not passed by the Irish legislature confirmed that acts passed in England were binding on Ireland.[14] The last decision did not, however, prompt the English Parliament to begin passing policies to confirm its legislative power over the Ireland. It is true that the next several decades saw the approval of a number of directives affecting Irish trade. An act in 1663 restricting the export of Irish goods to the colonies was followed in the same year by English Parliamentary legislation forbidding the export of Irish cattle to England. Another cattle act was passed in 1667. The import of articles from the colonies was restricted in 1671 and 1696. If Irishmen were unhappy with these policies, however, the rulings did not challenge Ireland's status as an independent kingdom.

It was not until 1699 when English MPs passed the Woollen Act, a directive prohibiting the export of Irish wool and woollens to any country but to England, that MPs in the English Parliament exercised what they believed was their right to legislate for Ireland. The Woollen Act was followed by an act of 1710 that required that hops be imported from England only. These directives infringed on what the Irish believed was their constitutional right to control their own economic affairs.[15] Against this understanding was the argument that Ireland, although it was a kingdom, was conquered territory, and as such, was completely subordinate to the government of England. This claim acquired some legal weight when, in 1607,

English judges grappling with the status of individuals born in Scotland after the union of the Crowns of England and Scotland, were obliged to consider Ireland. Their judgment stated that, although Ireland was a separate kingdom, because it had been conquered by Henry II, it was bound by laws passed by the English Parliament.[16] The judges' declaration did little, however, to quell the remonstrations of the Irish constitutionalists.

The Glorious Revolution and the triumph of the English Parliament inspired a resurgence in the debate regarding its jurisdiction over Ireland. The most famous argument for the independence of the Irish assemblies was made by William Molyneux in 1698. His tract, "The Case of Ireland's Being Bound by Acts of Parliament in England Stated," although based on the reflections of earlier writers, became the handbook for generations of Irish patriots. It did nothing but enrage most English MPs.[17] The debate over the legislative independence of the Irish Parliament, although it certainly played a large part in the dialogue preceding passage of the Declaratory Act, was peripheral to the events that gave rise to the legislation. The Act arose out of a series of disputes concerning the right of the Irish Parliament to form the final court of appeal in the kingdom. The first case, that of *The Irish Society v. the Bishop of Derry*, ran from 1691 to 1703 and was concerned with the lease of certain lands and fisheries in the bishop's diocese. When the Irish Court of Chancery ruled in favor of the Society, the bishop appealed the case to the Irish House of Lords, who reversed the court's decision. The Society then asked the English House of Lords for redress, charging that there could be no appeal to the Lords from the Chancery Court in Ireland. Although constitutional issues concerning the status of the Irish Parliament relative to the English Parliament were discussed, it was decided that judgment would be confined to the matter of whether the Irish Lords were permitted to hear appeals from the Chancery. After considering both sides of the matter, the English Lords determined that appeals from the Irish Chancery court should be brought to Westminster, that the judgments of the Irish Lords be voided, and that the Society be permitted to repossess the disputed lands.[18]

Virtually the same series of events occurred in the case of *Ward and others v. The Earl of Meath*, and the same judgment was passed down by the English Lords. This time, however, the injured party, the earl of Meath, approached the Irish Lords for help. The Lords decided to uphold their decision to grant relief to the earl, agreeing to "vindicate the 'honour, jurisdiction and privileges' of their House."[19] They also declared that, as the high court of Parliament in Ireland, the judgments of the Irish Lords were final and that its decisions could not be reversed elsewhere. Thanks to the efforts of the Lord Lieutenant, the Duke of Ormonde and the Lord Chancellor, Sir Richard Cox, who convinced Ward not to pursue the issue and managed to downplay the Lords' resolutions, the dispute ended there.[20]

The matter of appellate jurisdiction was not settled, however, until resolutions were passed concerning the case of *Sherlock v. Annesley*. This time, it was the decision of the Irish Court of the Exchequer in favor of Annesley that was reversed by the Irish Lords. Annesley complained to the British House of Lords, challenging the Irish Lords' judgment and their right to hear appeals from the Exchequer Court. Again, the British Lords ruled that appeals could only be heard in Westminster, and confirmed the Exchequer Court's ruling for Annesley. Mrs. Sherlock then lodged a petition with the Irish Lords. Amidst declarations in defense of their jurisdiction, the Irish Lords decided again to support their "honour, jurisdiction and privileges" and resolved to grant relief to Mrs. Sherlock.[21]

Meanwhile, the Irish Lord Lieutenant, the Duke of Bolton and Viscount Midleton, the Lord Chancellor, did their best to manage the situation, fearful that the dispute might jeopardize passage of the money bills in the Lords. This time, however, their attempts to steer the issue failed. Annesley once more appealed to the British House of Lords, who, once again, ruled in his favor. In response, the Irish Lords drew up a representation to the king. The petition made the case for the judicial independence of the Irish Lords and incorporated many of the arguments of Irish constitutionalists, Molyneux in particular. The British House of Lords considered the representation and once more reviewed the facts of the Annesley case. The proceedings ultimately gave rise to the "Bill for Securing the Dependency of Ireland."

It is obvious from the title and the terms of the bill how little British judges and ministers thought of the constitutional arguments presented by the Irish House of Lords in defense of their position. In accord with past rulings, the bill denied the Irish Lords the right to hear appeals. Beyond this, however, it declared that the British Parliament had the right to legislate for Ireland. Although some British MPs opposed the bill on the grounds that it increased the power of the British Lords, most were in favor of it. The Act passed the Commons on 26 March 1720.[22]

Hence the *formal* institutions governing Irish policymaking were the same in 1778 as they were in 1697, with an addition. The Declaratory Act defined formally the relationship between the British and Irish Parliaments. Now, not only was the Irish Parliament constitutionally subordinate to the British and Irish executives, it was subject to the British Parliament as well. The ire that was raised amongst Irish MPs when this right was exercised meant that British MPs resorted to the Act only rarely during the eighteenth century.[23] Nevertheless, it allowed the British Parliament the authority to curb the power of its Irish counterpart if required.

Formal institutions surrounding Anglo-Irish policymaking in 1778 thus restricted the powers of the MPs in the Irish Parliament more so than in 1697. With such a number of formal constraints on their activities, it would appear that individuals and groups on the "Irish side" of disputes with British officials concerning Irish legislation would have little chance of success. Appearances can be deceiving, however, as became evident during investigation of the conditions surrounding the passage of the Treaty of Limerick ratification bill. In that case informal institutions emerged that compelled English administrators and the Crown to negotiate policy with, and often concede to the demands of, Irish politians despite constitutional guarantees of English supremacy.

Political Actors

The *formal* institutions described above defined the major actors involved in Irish policymaking in the late eighteenth century. The British monarch and the British

Privy Council, the Irish Lord Lieutenant and his council, and the Irish Parliament continued to be the main actors participating in the process. After 1720, the British Parliament was also sanctioned to take part in the policy process as specified by the Declaratory Act. The manner in which pro- and anti-Catholic interests were arrayed amongst these actors had implications for the outcome of policy.

The British Privy Council

By the latter half of the eighteenth century, most of the important tasks assigned to the British Privy Council were conducted by the cabinet. The size of the council had increased steadily during the eighteenth century making it more and more difficult for it to attend to normal administrative duties. In contrast, the number of officials in the cabinet fell, from about twenty-nine at the beginning of George III's reign to about eight or nine by the late 1770s.[24] Although it is difficult to say exactly how many men attended meetings of a body that, as Edith Johnston writes, "was still in a very fluid condition and far from possessing rigidity of form or function" it appears that Irish affairs were usually considered by the First Lord of the Treasury (or Prime Minister), the Secretaries of State North and South and the Lord President of the Council, as well as ministers whose departments were involved in matters being discussed.[25]

A special committee of council was responsible for reviewing bills arriving from Ireland. Like the cabinet, the number of officials sitting on this committee varied. In 1760, thirty-four men signed the committee's recommendation concerning a money bill, including the Irish Lord Lieutenant, the Duke of Bedford, twenty-five peers and seven commoners. Yet only six officials met in May 1778: the Lord President, Lords Hillsborough, Nugent (the vice treasurer of Ireland), Townshend, North (the First Lord of the Treasury) and Charles Townshend.[26]

The approach of these men toward Irish Catholic relief was not driven by personal attitudes. Indeed, many ministers – Lord George Germain, Secretary of State for the Colonies, Attorney General Thurlow, the Northern Secretary Lord Suffolk and the First Lord of the Admiralty, Lord Sandwich, among others – did not hold strong views on toleration.[27] Rather, as Robert Donovan has shown, the ministry's position was influenced heavily by military concerns.[28] By 1778, the British army was suffering for recruits. The surrender of 4,000 men at Saratoga, and an urgent request from Lord Amherst for 30,000 to 40,000 more troops, demanded that the British government find more fighting men, especially for service overseas. Administrators began to look seriously at the large and as yet untapped community of Catholics in Britain as a recruiting source.[29] "Relief as an inducement to enlistment" became an acceptable, albeit undeclared, strategy of prowar ministers.

According to Donovan, Irish Catholic relief was only one component of a larger plan to introduce relief in England, Scotland and Ireland to tap into Catholic manpower.[30] Although discussions surrounding Scottish succour preceded those concerning Ireland, Irish negotiations soon became a priority. Catholics of course made up the majority of the population in Ireland, 70 to 80 percent of the over 4,000,000 inhabitants of the island, as compared to about 8 percent in England and 4 percent in Scotland, a more lucrative source of recruits.[31] As well, gaining the allegiance of Irish Catholics to the British cause, especially after France joined the war in February 1778, became important for security reasons. Offering a modicum of relief to at least the leaders of the Catholic community was a way to foster the loyalty of Catholic subjects.[32]

Lord North and his ministry faced a number of obstacles, however. Changes in the English penal laws were necessary to introduce the relief measures North had in mind for Ireland. Certainly as important was the historically anti-Catholic attitude of the English and Irish Parliaments. It was never intended that "Catholic relief" in England or Ireland would amount to more than a few small concessions to leading Catholics; the strategy was not to overhaul the penal code but to offer some inducement to priests and gentry to encourage enlistment among their lesser followers.[33] But as Donovan writes, many Protestants, in Ireland in particular, "invested an enormous symbolic importance in the code as an emblem of their superiority or, as they put it, their security."[34] Even minor changes to the penal code would certainly elicit an outcry from the Irish Protestants. Indeed, rumors that the British government was considering relief for Irish Catholics had been circulating since December 1777, and had triggered the expected passionate response.[35] To make matters worse, the American war had intensified debate in the Irish Parliament surrounding Anglo-Irish constitutional relations. North needed to find a way to calm the fractiousness of Irish MPs enough to even consider Catholic relief measures. As Thomas Bartlett notes, it was likely no coincidence that the prime minister introduced the idea of commercial concessions to Ireland, modification of hated trade restrictions, in April 1778, just before serious open discussion of Catholic relief in Ireland and England began.[36]

While their attitudes toward Catholic toleration may have been ambivalent, it appears that Lord North and his ministers were committed to securing some measure of Catholic relief in Ireland for military purposes.

The British Parliament

As was discussed in the review of the Quebec Act negotiations, until the latter half of the eighteenth century, the British Parliament was intolerant of Catholic recusants. In 1774, however, the British Parliament passed the Quebec measure, reversing a long history of supporting, actively or passively, anti-Catholicism in the empire. Support of the Quebec Act derived from a number of sources, not the least of which being a concern for the military security of the colony from British and American threats. The Quebec legislation, while its content required that a number of factors and forces specific to the period coalesce to produce its features, demonstrated that practical considerations could sway a majority of MPs in a historically intolerant Parliament to extend concessions to Catholics under the proper circumstances.

In 1778, the North ministry, as part of their larger plan to extend relief to British Catholics to encourage Catholic enlistment, introduced two measures benefiting Catholics. The English Relief Act freed Catholics in England to hear mass, educate their children and buy, bequeath or inherit land. Another repealed legislation enacted during Anne's reign that forbade Catholics from buying forfeited Irish estates, thus abolishing an English restriction on Irish Catholic relief.[37] Both measures were passed by British MPs with little fanfare.

Party politics played an uncertain role in these policy outcomes. The Whigs were the driving force behind the relief policies of 1778. But all the directives, particularly the English Relief Act, won the strong support of Whigs and Tories alike.[38] The personal attitudes of MPs were varied. Edmund Burke, an avid supporter of relief legislation, was well known for his Catholic sympathies and helped the Catholic cause. The address of loyalty presented to George III by a group of Catholics from the three kingdoms initiating the process that led to the English Catholic Relief Act was written by Burke.[39] Not all MPs were so consistent, however. George Savile, the MP who introduced the English Act, actively sought the repeal of the Quebec Act in 1775 and urged revocation of a part of the English Relief Act that he himself had sponsored when the Gordon riots erupted.[40]

As in the Quebec case, the attitudes and party allegiances of MPs did not influence a majority in Parliament to pass these more tolerant measures as much as practical, namely military, considerations. The support of backbench MPs was waning after the defeat at Saratoga when fears that France would join the contest materialized. Suddenly, there was a surge in prowar sentiment in the British Parliament. "By April," Donovan writes, "many in the House of Commons were expressing more fervour for war than was North himself,"[41] a situation that obviously helped the prime minister secure concessions for military purposes and security. Given its support of the English Relief Act, and that they had already taken steps toward instituting some form of relief in Ireland by repealing legislation that would have blocked concessions in Catholic land ownership, it appears likely that the British Parliament would accept a measure of relief in Ireland.

The British Monarch

According to Edith Johnston, "George III took an active and comprehensive interest in every aspect of the government of Ireland."[42] In contrast to many of his royal and ministerial predecessors, the king apparently accorded Irish business a high priority. His approval was, of course, required for all major decisions concerning Ireland. But he chose to involve himself in even the smallest particulars of Irish administration. Always desirous of details concerning the kingdom, George solicited information from a variety of sources, including unofficial ones, such as the private correspondence of his ministers. To the embarrassment of the Irish and British executives, these unofficial communications often informed the king's decisions concerning Ireland, even forming the basis for Irish legislation. He took seriously his responsibility to appoint men who were able and of good character to the Lord Lieutenancy and to military positions. In fact, all things to do with the Irish army, from promotions to the size of recruits, were subject to the scrutiny of the monarch.[43]

If George III's interest in things Irish remained constant throughout his reign, it appears his sentiments concerning Catholic relief did not. The king had of course approved the groundbreaking Quebec Act in 1774, indicating that he was capable of adopting a tolerant stance on the Catholic question. To what extent this stance extended to Ireland, however, is questionable. He refused to emancipate Irish Catholics after Britain's union with Ireland some thirty years later.

Much like the MPs in the British Parliament, George's approval of the Quebec Act suggested that the king would favor concessions under the right circumstances. Matters of imperial security, as they were presented to him by Lord North, convinced George III of the suitability of the Quebec Act. As important as security issues were in 1774, they were even more important in 1778. By this time, the discord between the metropolis and the American colonies had erupted into warfare, dividing a continent once united under the British Crown into a battle-ground pitting a British, but largely French Catholic, Quebec against the rebellious colonials. When France joined the war, the situation became even more critical. Now the enemy was considerably closer to home and the old fears of Irish Catholic collusion with France were again aroused. It is well known that George was determined to maintain military pressure in America and ignored the recommendations and pleas of his prime minister to bring the hostilities to an end. These concerns were to influence George III's position on Ireland significantly.

The Irish House of Commons

As we have seen, by the 1770s, enforcement of the penal laws in Ireland, especially those against Catholic ecclesiastics, had eased. This did not mean, however, that Irish Protestants were ready to repeal these laws. The majority were as committed to maintaining the subject condition of Catholics in Ireland as they had been when the laws were passed. Sixteen-forty one, the reign of James II and the anti-Protestant proclamations of the "Patriot Parliament" were ingrained in the memories of most Protestants. As far as they were concerned, Catholicism was still synonymous with tyranny.[44] Convinced that Catholics were ready to topple the Protestant interest by any means, most Irish Protestants became apprehensive when even the smallest courtesies were shown to Catholics by British or Irish administrators.[45] Any measure that might offer concessions to Irish Catholics would have a difficult time winning the support of the majority of MPs in the Irish Parliament.

The Irish House of Lords

The Irish upper house lost its position as the highest court in Ireland in 1720 with the passing of the Declaratory Act. Despite this loss of prestige, the Lords continued to play an important role in the legislative process. The Poynings' procedure required that they approve all acts of Parliament, and although most legislation originated in the House of Commons, the Lords initiated some bills and handled other political and quasi-judicial matters.[46] The Lords spiritual, who numbered twenty-two in the upper house, were not as active in the latter half of the eighteenth century as in the early 1700s. Whereas they constituted at least one-third of the members attending sessions between 1692 and 1750, their numbers fell to less than a fourth after that date.[47] In contrast, the lay peerage experienced a significant increase in numbers and influence during the reign of George III. Between 1767 and 1785, fifty new peerages were created. Thirty-four of these positions were granted to Irish politicians. The remaining were bestowed on British MPs, many of whom had strong Irish connections.[48]

As in the 1690s the Irish House of Lords was a relatively conservative body. It is true that the Lords gave the Irish administration a difficult time in the years leading up to the passage of the Declaratory Act. A majority of Irish-born "patriotic" peers dominated the upper house during these years, and kept the Irish executive busy trying to downplay to English/British administrators the Lords' constitutional claims.[49] For the rest of the century, however, the Irish administration could usually depend on the House of Lords to support government policy. Of course the fact that members of the upper house were appointed by the Crown on the recommendation of the Irish Lord Lieutenant did much to insure their cooperation with the executive. As well, compliance may have stemmed partly from the religious and familial affiliations of the attending peers. It will be remembered that more than half of the spiritual members serving between 1692 and 1800 were Englishmen. Of those who were born in Ireland, the majority descended from post-Reformation families, the "New English" interest.[50] Although they no longer commanded the House of Lords, the bishops could be counted on to back the administration.[51] The majority of temporal peers, now the leading group in the upper house, had deep roots in Ireland. Most descended from "Old Protestant" families established during the Tudor and early Stuart eras, but some could even trace their ancestry back to Anglo-Norman or Gaelic origins. During George III's reign, these individuals continued to outnumber the peers who descended from the post-1641, "New Protestant" interest.[52]

Thus, many of the Lords in the upper house would have been supportive of an Irish Catholic relief act. English-born spiritual lords and the temporal lords descending from the "Old Protestant" interest had a history of backing most government-sponsored initiatives; lay peers of "Old English" origins may have been, because of their background, sympathetic to Catholic concerns.

The Irish Privy Council

By the middle of the eighteenth century, the task of initiating legislation had been appropriated by the Irish Parliament. But the Irish Privy Council was still bound by Poynings' Law to review and approve all heads of bills submitted by the two Irish houses before they were transmitted to Britain. Councillors apparently took their jobs seriously, reading bills several times, and occasionally amending or blocking proposed legislation.[53]

The nominal membership of the Irish Privy Council grew rapidly during George III's reign. In 1771, there were seventy Privy Councillors; by 1778, there were eighty-four.[54] Given the unwieldy size of this body, most business came to be conducted by a smaller group, the King's Servants in Ireland, a group much like the British cabinet responsible for Irish affairs in number. Usually about ten Irish officials, including the Chancellor, the Attorney and Solicitor General and the Speaker of the Irish House of Commons, would meet in the Lord Lieutenant's or Chief Secretary's quarters.[55]

The sentiments of the council were largely the same as in the early part of the century. More than half of the membership of the council were peers, and more than a third were bishops.[56] The House of Lords was, as a whole, a relatively conservative body, and the bishops were quite consistent in their support of the Irish administration. Although the councillors were known to give advice occasionally that was contrary to the views of the Irish chief governor or British ministers, they usually sided with the executive.[57]

The Irish Lord Lieutenant

The main duties of the Irish Lord Lieutenant were the same in 1778 as in the 1690s. He served as the monarch's personal representative in Ireland and the only official contact between the government of Ireland and the British Privy Council. He was the commander-in-chief of the military and all appointments in the kingdom were made based on his recommendations. But his most important task remained the management of the Irish Parliament, perhaps even more so than at the beginning of the century, as sessions became more regular. The Lord Lieutenant was responsible for insuring that directives approved by the British executive – particularly money bills – were ratified by the Irish Parliament as painlessly as possible.[58]

Except for the Duke of Ormonde, who served as Ireland's Lord Lieutenant under Queen Anne from 1703 to 1707 and again from 1710 to 1713, the majority of eighteenth-century Irish chief governors were Englishmen. George III seemed to have been concerned to appoint able and experienced men to the position. The position remained, however, a political perk, "the consolation prize offered by every new ministry to those whom it wished to conciliate, but exclude from the cabinet, and honourably remove from the scene of political activity."[59] The Irish

Lord Lieutenant was still a creature of the current British administration whose presence and tenure in office had more to do with British politics than with his ability to manage the administration of Ireland.

John Hobart, second earl of Buckinghamshire, was sworn in as the Irish Lord Lieutenant on 25 January 1777. He was to serve in that capacity for four years. Buckinghamshire was cautious in his approach to Irish Catholic relief. When, in October 1777, he was asked to transmit to the king a petition signed by 300 Catholics protesting the restrictions against them, he agreed, but, to the annoyance of the British government, failed to say whether he supported or opposed the address.[60] Later, aside from expressing some sympathy for the Irish Catholics, the Lord Lieutenant remained silent in response to the British Secretary of State's request concerning what sort of relief might best be granted.[61] When pressed finally by the British government to give his opinion of a relief bill prepared by a leading Catholic, Buckinghamshire consulted Protestant supporters of Catholic relief in the Irish Parliament before advising that it would not be prudent to introduce any concessions at that time.[62] Buckinghamshire's sentiments regarding Catholic relief are thus difficult to gauge. Certainly the Lord Lieutenant would have maintained his careful approach during the negotiation and passage of the Catholic Relief Act some months later.

Irish Catholics

At the opening of the eighteenth century, the future facing Catholics in Ireland seemed bleak. Land confiscations under Cromwell and William III had reduced Catholic landownership to 14 percent in 1703; fifty years later, this had fallen to only 5 percent.[63] William's defeat of the Jacobite forces in 1691 had prompted the departure of most of the Catholic leadership, leaving the Catholics that remained unrepresented and powerless. Penal legislation enacted against Catholics by the Irish Parliament placed restrictions on almost every aspect of their lives.

The eighteenth century did not, however, see the ruin of Catholics in Ireland. Quite the opposite: many Catholics actually increased their wealth during the penal era. Although laws prohibited Catholics from owning land outright, some still managed to retain and even expand their landholdings. This was accomplished, legally, by speculating on the thirty-one year leases that Catholics were permitted to hold, and illegally, via the acquisition of "renewable" leases or, as has already been discussed, agreements with Protestant "discoverers."[64]

More significantly, perhaps, Catholic wealth was derived from commercial pursuits. Having been barred from politics, law and the military, ambitious Catholics turned to trade to make their living. Here their opportunities were comparatively open. In fact, there were a number of factors associated with Protestant rule that actually facilitated their commercial success and helped them to accumulate wealth. First, Protestant landowners, secure in their gentry status as long as the penal laws were in place, spurned trade, considering it a lowly occupation; they offered little competition to enterprising Catholics.[65] Second, penal legislation prohibited Catholics from spending their money lavishly. They were not permitted to participate in elections so politics cost them little. They could not legally buy land in Ireland, or build schools or churches, or even give to Catholic charities.[66] Finally, once Catholics had established themselves as important contributors to Irish commerce, the Irish Parliament was hesitant to interfere with their activities. Most of the men in Parliament were landowners and so were resistant to land taxes. When additional supplies were needed to meet the needs of government new taxes were usually levied on trade. The possibility that revenue might be adversely affected discouraged the Irish Parliament from meddling with the Catholic mercantile interest.[67] Their influence on revenue decisions was brought to the attention of Protestant Ireland as early as 1724. Father Cornelius Nary, protesting a measure for banishing priests, declared in a written pamphlet that year, "Now if this bill should pass, all these merchants and dealers would be necessitated to leave the kingdom, to the great diminution of the revenue; and God knows in how many years this could be retrieved, if ever."[68]

These earlier depictions of Catholic commercial wealth and influence in eighteenth-century Ireland have been qualified somewhat in more recent writings.[69] Nevertheless, their economic vitality certainly improved their situation. There were other factors that contributed to their revival as well. Despite their obvious ideological and religious connections with the Jacobites, Irish Catholics failed to take part in the Jacobite risings in England and Scotland in 1715 and 1745. It is possible their burgeoning commercial success discouraged some from disrupting the status quo. In any case, their inactivity did much to enhance their reputations around Dublin Castle and Whitehall, if not with the Irish Parliament.[70] Their standing with government officials was further enhanced by regular declarations of loyalty to the Irish and British administrations and to the king, particularly after 1759.[71] Catholic lords and clergy participated in the suppression of Whiteboys, purportedly mostly Catholic,[72] who committed various of acts of agrarian terrorism in Ireland's south during the latter half of the eighteenth century.[73] A number of leading Catholics even offered to raise Catholic recruits for British service in America. Although Protestant protest pressured the British government to abide by existing legislation[74] and not enlist these troops, officials were nevertheless impressed by Catholic efforts.[75] The death of James III on 1 January 1766, and the pope's refusal to recognize his son, Charles Edward, as the king only helped their cause. With the Stuart threat removed, some of the suspicions against Catholics in Britain and Ireland were allayed.[76]

Another development that helped the Catholics' cause was their decision in 1756 to present to the Irish and British administrations a more united front. Until then, Irish Catholics had tended to handle grievances in smaller groups. This method of protest worked: in the early part of the century, Catholic tradesmen in Cork, Dublin and other towns resisted the quarterage charges levied on Catholics by the corporations.[77] By and large, however, Catholics had not been very successful at persuading administrators to listen to them.[78] In 1756, the Catholic Association, later the Catholic Committee, was established by John Curry, a

Catholic doctor, Charles O'Conor, the son of a Catholic landowner, and Thomas "Bullocks" Wyse, an outspoken and successful Catholic landowner. From the start, the Committee, an association that included Catholic merchants, gentry and clergy, was wracked with disagreement, particularly with regard to how they should present themselves. Some members, especially ecclesiastics, believed that silence and obedience was the best course of action. Others, O'Conor in particular, thought they should take a more active approach, assure the king of their loyalty and press for repeal of the penal laws.[79] In the end, these disagreements were never entirely resolved. The Catholic Committee did, however, manage to unite to affect some legislation. Its members suppressed a number of attempts made in the 1760s and 1770s by Protestant tradesmen to have the Irish Parliament sanction the levying of quarterage, arguing successfully that the charge was illegal and would discourage trade and manufacturing.[80] They were also involved in the formulation of a Catholic "declaration of principles" that eventually served as the basis for a new oath of allegiance that was less objectionable to Catholics than were older oaths.[81] Most importantly, the Catholic Committee demonstrated, to politicians and Irish Catholics themselves, that Catholics were capable of concerted and united political action.

By 1778, Irish Catholics had established themselves as a comparatively powerful force in Irish society, a situation quite different than they had found themselves in in the 1690s.

Irish Dissenters

In the years immediately following the Glorious Revolution, Protestant nonconformists in Ireland, although subject to some restrictions on their activities, supported the Protestant government as beneficiaries of Protestant rule. This changed in 1704 when the bill "To prevent the further growth of popery," much desired by Irish Protestants because it placed severe restrictions on Catholic landownership, was returned to Ireland by the English Privy Council with the addition of a sacramental test clause. By requiring that all Crown servants and borough corporation members be certified as having received the sacrament of the Lord's Supper "according to the usage of the Church of Ireland," the test clause limited the participation of Presbyterians in politics.[82] The test remained in effect in Ireland until 1780.

From 1704 to 1714, the British government vacillated in their stance on the test in Ireland. Whereas the Whigs tried to secure its repeal during their stint in government, the Tories who succeeded them attempted to strengthen restrictions against Irish Dissenters, suspending the payments that nonconformist churches in Ireland had been receiving from the British government (the *regium donum*) and imposing the English Schism Bill, forbidding nonconformists to teach or to keep a school, on Ireland.[83] After 1714 the Whigs acquired firm control of British politics and a more consistently moderate approach toward Protestant Dissent was adopted.

Payments of the *regium donum* were resumed under George I and "Presbyterian agents were accorded sympathetic hearing."[84]

None of this changed the opinions of the MPs in the Irish Parliament, particularly the Anglican bishops who sat in the Irish House of Lords. The Irish Parliament may not have introduced the test but they were ready to oppose any attempt to repeal it or any other laws limiting the activities of nonconformists. In 1719, British ministers apparently concerned with the flow of Irish Dissenters from the north to North America, broached the idea of a toleration bill to ease some of the restrictions against Irish nonconformists. A bill was eventually passed by the Irish Parliament (albeit narrowly in the Lords), but it fell far short of the concessions that British officials had initially intended.[85] Attempts by British officials to revoke the Sacramental Test in 1731 and again in 1733 were scuttled because of the Irish Parliament's opposition to relief for Protestant Dissenters.

Many British officials were baffled by the way in which the Irish of the established church treated the Presbyterians. In a kingdom where Protestants were vastly outnumbered by Catholics, they could not comprehend why the Irish Parliament would not want all Protestants to be on an equal and more secure footing. They had, after all, fought side by side during the revolution. The struggle, however, was about power. Large in number, influential and well-organized, Presbyterians were a threat to the privileged position of the established church. "So long as their toleration was based on favor and connivance rather than on law and so long as they were excluded from public employment, that danger was under control. Remove these checks and the danger would become active. . . . "[86] The Irish of the established church were also aware that the Presbyterians feared the Irish Catholics at least as much as they did. If pressed, Irish Dissenters would join forces with them to repel a Catholic or Jacobite threat. "The explanation, then, of the policy of the [Irish of the established church] is simply this, that the danger of according equal treatment to the presbyterians was great and immediate, while the benefits to be derived from such concessions were, in fact, already secure."[87]

Protestant nonconformists were not outspoken about their mistreatment by the Irish or British governments during the eighteenth century, nor were they active in pressuring the Irish or British governments to lift restrictions against them. They did little to help bring about the Toleration Bill. J. C. Beckett maintains their inactivity stemmed from the fact that the act failed to address the test.[88] The bill only legalized the practical tolerance that Irish nonconformists had long enjoyed.[89] It is true that Dissenters were more active in pressing for repeal of the test. In 1722, some sent addresses and petitions to the king complaining of the grievances they felt they were forced to endure under the provisions of the test clause.[90] In 1731-1733, they sent an agent to London to discuss relief for Protestant nonconformists, a move that motivated British officials to twice try to pressure the Irish Parliament to repeal the test. When both efforts failed, however, Dissenters dropped the matter. Except for a sideways mention of the "S. T." in a letter from the synod to coreligionists in Dublin in 1737, addresses sent to the Irish and British governments by Irish Dissenters focused on Presbyterian loyalty toward the Crown and the Irish administration, and mentioned only their wish that existing conditions be maintained.[91] By 1778, it had been forty-five years since the last serious attempt had been made by Protestant nonconformists to repeal the test, hardly a record of steady dissent.

In spite of the increase in restrictions against Irish Dissenters since 1697, they continued to support the Protestant Ascendancy. Presbyterians benefited from Protestant rule and although they remained subordinate to the Irish of the established church, nothing in their history suggested that they would choose to alter the situation now, especially not on behalf of Irish Catholics.

The sentiments of the major actors in Anglo-Irish policymaking with respect to Catholic relief were varied. As in the case of the Quebec Act, the position of the monarch concerning Catholic relief was somewhat ambiguous. Although perhaps intolerant of Catholics and Catholicism personally, George III was aware of the importance of securing the allegiance of Catholics in the British empire, particularly in this time of war. To predict whether he would maintain this position in the case of Ireland is unclear, particularly in light of the fact that he was to become a strong opponent of Irish Catholic emancipation years later. As for British politicians, MPs, ministers and officials of the Privy Council, the debate on the Quebec Act revealed that many of them continued to hold intolerant attitudes toward Catholics and were adverse to "popish" legislation. Nevertheless, it appears that a majority were prepared to advocate some limited form of relief to Catholics in Ireland, if not for benevolent reasons then for military ones.

In Ireland, most Protestants in power remained opposed to policy that might strengthen the position of Irish Catholics relative to the ascendancy. Catholics of course would have been happy to be granted some relief from the penal legislation that grieved them. They were, further, in a more favorable position now, economically and politically, than in the early years of the penal code to press for concessions.

The situations in 1778 and 1697 were broadly similar, then, with a majority of anti-Catholic Irish Protestant MPs pitted against more charitable British politicians willing to tolerate limited concessions for military purposes. The formal institutional factors surrounding the process in 1778, as in 1697, favored Britain to such an extent that toleration could be expected to triumph.

There appear to have occurred some changes, however, in relations between political actors involved in Anglo-Irish policymaking. Irish government officials, although they obviously held their own views concerning Catholic relief in Ireland, now seemed reticent to express their opinions or embroil themselves in any dispute concerning policy toward Catholics. This is in contrast to Anglo-Irish politicians like Henry Capel at the end of the previous century, who did not hesitate to take a leading role in negotiations with London and Irish MPs, and in formulating policy. These changes did not stem from modifications to the formal institutions surrounding the process, as the formal institutions had not been altered and indeed had been enhanced in some areas. The changes had occurred in the *informal* institutions governing Irish policymaking, modifications to those operational norms and procedures that, while not written down or ensconced in any legal code, nevertheless helped to determine how power was distributed amongst the actors involved in the process, and hence structured their actions and affected policy outcomes.

Informal Institutions Characterizing Anglo-Irish Policymaking in 1778

As in the 1690s, the primary informal institutions influencing the events surrounding the Catholic Relief Act were those that shaped power relations between the Irish executive and the Irish Parliament; the relations between the English executive and the English Parliament; and that structured the policymaking process itself. Since the 1690s, however, these factors had undergone a number of modifications that were to influence policy negotiations and outcomes in important ways.

Informal Institutions Governing Relations between the Irish Executive and the Irish Parliament

In the 1690s Henry Capel had devised a way for the Irish executive to manage the Irish Parliament so that bills arriving from England, especially supply bills, would be passed. As a result of the coming together of a number of contingencies that encouraged its repeated use, Capel's basic strategy – one that rendered to leaders of the Irish House of Commons political perks and anti-Catholic legislation in exchange for a government majority in Parliament and a peaceful session – became institutionalized, that is, became the manner in which Anglo-Irish politics was conducted for the next several decades. This is not to say that the basic relationship did not undergo some modifications. Changes in the nature of Irish Parliamentary politics, for example, altered some of the features of the strategy established by Capel.

The Undertaker System
     In the 1690s, the Irish Parliament split into two factions: the "Country" interest, known for its antiadministration, anti-Catholic views (the anti-Porter, anti-Treaty of Limerick sole right men belonged to this interest) and the "Court" interest, whose adherents typically supported the administration and the established church while taking a more tolerant stance toward Catholics and Catholicism (pro-Porter MPs were members of this faction). By the early eighteenth century, these two groups had developed into Whig and Tory parties, respectively. For the next decade or so, Irish politics was conducted along strict party lines. Tories actively supported the administration and the Church of Ireland, resisting attempts to improve the situation of Irish Dissenters while taking a more lenient (although by no means entirely supportive) position on Catholic legislation. Some "high-flying" Tories, especially clergymen, expounded more extreme Tory sentiments like the doctrines of Nonresistance, Passive Obedience and Hereditary Right, even disputing the validity of the Glorious Revolution. The Whigs on the other hand were more ready than the

Tories to initiate and support penal legislation against Catholics. They also sought the repeal of the sacramental test. In response to Tory ambivalence concerning the Revolution and the right to the English throne, many Whigs became fierce Williamites and supporters of 1688, and spent much of their time after 1709 accusing Tories of being Jacobites. So strong were party divisions during this period that MPs could not avoid taking sides, and found it difficult to change parties once they did. Even family and patronage ties, the "old" ways in which Parliamentary groupings were forged, could not withstand the divisive effects of party affiliation.[92]

After the death of Queen Anne in 1714, the Tory interest, stripped of political office, discredited by its association with Jacobitism and hurt by mass defections to the Whigs, collapsed. With the Whig party in firm control of the Irish Parliament, Irish politics took on a less rigid "Court" versus "Country" character again. Family and patronage connections once more were important. Having operated along fixed party lines for several years, Parliamentary politics became "almost kaleidoscopic, with new combinations forming and dissolving in the space of a session."[93]

These changes did not alter the basic compliance-in-exchange-for-perquisites relationship that Capel had established between the Irish executive and the Irish Parliament in the 1690s. They did, however, influence the nature of negotiations by reducing the number of Parliamentary managers with whom the Irish executive had to deal. In the days of party politics, the Lord Lieutenant was compelled to negotiate with a caucus of party leaders. Chief governors are known to have conferred with seven and eight party rulers in the period leading up to 1714. Once the "rage of party" subsided, however, the number of leaders in the assemblies declined. Now the Lord Lieutenant had only to negotiate with two or three magnates to insure the cooperation of the Irish Parliament, and in most cases one was sufficient. The practice of having just one man in charge of managing the Irish Parliament became the basis for the "undertaker system" of the eighteenth century, a system in which a Parliamentary leader "undertook" to secure a government majority in the Irish Parliament in exchange for the right to distribute royal patronage and other political powers.[94]

The "undertaker system" survived until the late 1760s, but it was not a deliberate creation of either British or Irish administrators. Rather, it developed out of the coming together of a number of contingencies. In addition to the collapse of party politics, the election of William Conolly as the Speaker of the Irish House of Commons in 1715, and his subsequent appointment as both a lord justice and the "first" commissioner of revenue, concentrated in the hands of one man an unprecedented amount of potential power. Conolly was a master at using the influence associated with each of these positions to foster a government majority in the Irish assemblies.[95] His success demonstrated to the Irish and British executives the utility of having an undertaker handling Parliamentary business and encouraged them to maintain the practice. His eventual successor, Henry Boyle, proved himself to be as capable a Parliamentary manager. He delivered to the administration in the 1730s and 1740s two of the most politically uneventful decades in Anglo-Irish relations and established the undertaker as a crucial component in the operation of Anglo-Irish politics.[96] Add to this the fiscal pressures associated with maintaining the military and bureaucracy in Ireland, and there was little incentive or possibility for British administrators to do other than "soothe" the Irish Parliament in the manner established by Capel and institutionalized by his successors.[97]

While the British executive wished to perpetuate the position of undertaker, the system did not allow them anymore power over the Irish Parliament than they had held during Capel's term. The undertaker system was only a modification of the system established by the former Lord Lieutenant in the 1690s; the British and Irish executive were still required to negotiate with the Irish Parliament to insure a peaceful and profitable session. This meant that the executive were compelled occasionally to cede to the Irish Parliament on certain measures. In 1722, for example, Irish MPs took offence when the British government granted a patent to an English ironmaster, William Wood, to coin money for Ireland. No one in Ireland had been consulted on the deal, and when it became known that Wood had obtained the patent through less-than-legitimate means (Wood had apparently paid the king's mistress, the duchess of Kendal, £10,000 to secure the patent), the Irish Parliament turned against the government.[98] All other government business was put aside, petitions complaining of the deal were sent to the king, and Parliament became essentially unmanageable. To appease Irish MPs, the Lord Lieutenant, the duke of Grafton, was recalled and the amount of currency to be issued by Wood was reduced. Nothing calmed the recalcitrant MPs, however, and in September 1725 the administration finally admitted defeat. The Chief Governor, Carteret, informed the houses that "an entire end has been put to the patent formerly granted to Mr. Wood."[99] Anti-Catholic legislation also continued to play a part in Anglo-Irish policy negotiations. Heads of bills for several anti-Catholic measures were forwarded to the British Privy Council during the 1731-1732 session. All were amended by the council to such an extent that the Irish Parliament refused to pass the returned bills. When a piece of anti-Catholic legislation was again proposed in the 1733-1734 session, however, Lord Lieutenant Dorset implored the council to approve the bill. The legislation was returned unchanged.[100] In the 1735-1736 session, the British executive suppressed a measure proposed by the Irish Parliament preventing Irishmen from moving to foreign countries. Still, they were persuaded by the Lord Lieutenant to declare openly their support of the rights of Protestants in possession of forfeited estates in Ireland.[101]

Perhaps the best demonstration of how the Irish Parliament and their representatives could seriously disrupt Anglo-Irish relations was the so-called money bill dispute of 1753. Up until the late 1740s the additional supplies granted by the Irish Parliament every second year to pay for governing costs above the hereditary revenue were not sufficient to cover the administration's expenses. In 1749, however, the situation changed. That year was the first in which the Irish treasury experienced a surplus. But to whom did this surplus belong, the king or the Irish Commons? The Irish administration, along with a faction in the Commons, maintained that it was the Crown who had the exclusive right to determine the disposal of the surplus, and that the king's consent was required before the money could be used. Some in the Commons disagreed. Although they did not insist that they had the exclusive right to apply the surplus – they allowed that the king had some claim to the supplementary funds – they believed that the Commons should be able to dispose of the funds without prior consent.[102] A surplus in 1751 and yet another in 1753 brought the issue to a head. In November 1753, the Irish House of Commons drew up the heads of a bill claiming the right to apply a part of the surplus towards eliminating the Irish national debt. Similar heads had been drafted in 1749 and 1751, but this time the bill made no reference to the king's "previous consent." The British Privy Council took issue with this omission, and returned the bill with the words included. The bill was defeated in the Irish Commons in December.[103]

The Speaker of the House of Commons and Chief Undertaker, Henry Boyle, and his immediates were on the side of what came to be depicted as the "patriot" cause of the opposition. This was not the first time that Boyle had made trouble for the Irish administration. At the beginning of his term, Boyle had locked horns with the Lord Lieutenant, the duke of Dorset. When Dorset refused to back the new Speaker, the Irish Parliament became very difficult to deal with, thanks to Boyle. The troublesome session persuaded Dorset to change his mind; thereafter he gave the undertaker his full support.[104] Granted, the situation surrounding the money bill dispute was somewhat different. This time, Boyle's position was not only being challenged by the administration but by a faction in the Irish Parliament who wanted to replace the Speaker with one of their own representatives. Boyle's own political survival was at stake. In the end, however, the result was the same: Boyle emerged from the fracas victorious. His party succeeded in suppressing the revenue bill, and the Irish Parliament (at least a faction of it) had once again demonstrated its capacity to obstruct government business.

The fall out from the money bill dispute saw Boyle and his supporters replaced by men who had supported the administration on the issue.[105] The undertaker system itself, however, survived the melee. That such a system would be maintained even after a disruptive event like the money bill dispute is usually attributed to the attitude of the British executive. Their main concern was that government business be conducted as smoothly and with as little trouble as possible; beyond that, they were not, at least at the current time, interested in imposing a stricter control over the island's governance.[106] Administrative indifference no doubt goes a long way toward explaining the survival of the undertaker system. But the system's survival is also indicative of the extent to which the relations that comprised the undertaker system, and more generally the perquisites-in-exchange-for-compliance method of Parliamentary management established by Capel in the 1690s, had become institutionalized as the manner in which Anglo-Irish politics was conducted. The undertaker system represented an extension of the basic measures introduced by Capel after the Glorious Revolution. The system that succeeded it, however, was of a different nature entirely.

The Townshend Viceroyalty
    The Parliamentary in-fighting that had characterized the money bill dispute was

factions made it increasingly difficult for the undertaker to deliver to the administration a government majority in the Commons. The undertakers themselves were becoming more difficult to deal with, demanding greater rewards in exchange for their services.[107] Although some administrators recognized that something needed to be done about the situation, Irish affairs were still assigned a low priority by British officials. They had not the time or desire to conceive of a coherent strategy to apply to Ireland.[108] Enter George Townshend. Townshend was appointed to the Irish Lord Lieutenancy in August 1767 and over the next five years transformed the way in which Anglo-Irish politics was conducted down to the Union in 1801. He accomplished this largely on his own, with little help or instruction from the metropolis. Townshend arrived in Ireland assigned with the task of persuading the Irish Parliament to support an increase in the number of troops bankrolled by Ireland. But when the Lord Lieutenant laid the measure before the Commons in April 1768 the leaders of the house, Speaker John Ponsonby, Lord Shannon and John Hely-Hutchinson, succeeded in having the military augmentation rejected. Townshend's failure to acquire the backing of the Commons on the augmentation bill convinced the chief governor that the "undertaker system" had to be broken and he so informed the British administration. British officials were reluctant to sanction a large-scale overhaul of the Anglo-Irish system, however, and for three years cautioned Townshend against using any "extreme measures" to control the opposition, suggesting instead that he try to negotiate and work alongside the powerful leaders of the House of Commons to reach an amiable agreement.[109] In other words, the British administration counseled Townshend to perpetuate the old perquisites-in-exchange-for-compliance method of Anglo-Irish politics that had been in place since the 1690s.

Undeterred, Townshend did his best to consolidate his and the government's power in the face of the influential undertakers in the commons without the support of the British executive. He began to cultivate a government or "Castle" party to counter the opposition, offering rewards and what little patronage he had available to him to independent MPs in return for their backing. He realized in the process that, to retain the support of these men and not lose them to the resident opposition leaders, it was necessary that he remain in Ireland full time and not return to England after each Parliamentary session as his predecessors had done. The next time Parliament sat in October 1769, Townshend had improved the government's position in relation to the opposition. He had not, however, managed to break its majority in the Commons. Not only did this Parliament reject again the military augmentation bill, but, thanks to the contrivances of Ponsonby, Shannon and Hely-Hutchinson, it scrapped a government money bill on the grounds that it had not taken its rise in the Commons. Townshend, faced with a situation much like the one that had confronted Henry Sydney in 1692, reacted like his predecessor and prorogued Parliament.[110]

The rejection of this money bill finally roused British ministers to action. They authorized Townshend to dismiss the leaders of the opposition and their supporters from important positions in the Irish government and replace them with "friends of the Lord Lieutenant." All patronage was removed from the hands of the undertakers and placed under the control of the chief governor. When existing rewards were not enough, new posts and pensions were created and granted. By the time the Irish Parliament reassembled in February 1771, the government was in firm control of the commons.[111] With the British executive at last behind him, Townshend had overpowered the undertakers in the Irish Parliament and instituted an entirely new system of Anglo-Irish politics in the process.

It is true that Townshend himself, his personal commitment to strengthening the position of the Irish executive in relation to the Irish Parliament, was crucial to implementing the new system. But there were other events that occurred during this period that helped to establish Townshend's system. The 1760s were a particularly unstable period in British politics. As ministries rose and fell in Britain in rapid succession, so too did administrations in Ireland. Between 1760 and 1767, Ireland was governed by five different Lords Lieutenant, none whose term lasted more than two years.[112] Independent MPs were initially reluctant to commit to Townshend for fear that a new administration might be appointed that would reverse its stance towards the undertakers. But when Lord North took over the post of Britain's First Lord of the Treasury in January 1770, British politics – and by exception Irish politics – entered an era of relative stability. With Townshend firmly ensconced in Dublin Castle, his actions backed by the British executive, Irish MPs were more comfortable entrusting their support to the government.[113] Townshend could hardly have instituted his changes under the previous erratic conditions. Furthermore, by the time the Irish Parliament met in 1771, serious rifts had developed between opposition groups that diminished their capacity to present a united front against government measures. Doubts among Irish MPs about the sincerity of the opposition leaders, whether their actions were inspired by real grievances or by self-interest, reduced their influence in the Commons.[114]

If these conditions helped to establish Townshend's measures during his tenure in Ireland, their subsistence helped to maintain the system after his departure. British politics remained comparatively stable and so did Irish politics. After serving five years as Lord Lieutenant, Townshend was replaced in 1772 by Simon Harcourt, first earl of Harcourt, who stayed in office until 1777. Moreover, the opposition in the Irish Parliament continued to experience unity and discipline problems that undermined its attempts to reestablish some control over the executive.[115]

This is not to imply that, once Townshend's measures were adopted and institutionalized, the Irish, and by exception the British, executive had an easy time securing the support of a majority in the Irish Parliament. Having eliminated the Irish undertakers, "the wheels still had to be greased." The Lord Lieutenant and his immediates were now responsible for persuading, coddling and seducing fickle Irish MPs to back government legislation.[116] Their indiscipline would occasionally cause problems for the administration. Further, the Irish Parliament's practice of initiating legislation by debating then submitting "heads of bills" to the Irish executive for transmission to England was now the way in which almost all Irish legislation originated.[117] Add to this the fact that the Irish Parliament now met more frequently. After 1695, it granted supplies for only two years. Except for a time at the end of the seventeenth century when no Parliament was called for four years, sessions were held biennially.[118] Nevertheless, there is little question that a shift in power had occurred: the government made no major concessions to the Irish Parliament for the rest of the decade.[119]

Changes to the informal institutions surrounding the relationship between the Irish Parliament and Irish and British administrators over the course of the eighteenth century resulted, by 1778, in a situation very unlike that which existed in the 1690s. Then, Irish MPs exercised considerable influence over policymaking because of the implementation and endurance of the perquisites-in-exchange-for-compliance system of governance established by Henry Capel. Although this system underwent some modifications over the next several decades – the coming together of a number of contingencies encouraged the emergence of the "undertaker system," for example – the informal "rules" governing relations between the executive and the Irish Parliament remained unchanged. It was not until 1767 that the system was altered completely. George Townshend's own determination to establish executive control over the Irish Parliament combined with current political circumstances to produce a relatively rapid change in the informal institutions surrounding Anglo-Irish politics. These new arrangements were maintained after Townshend's departure because of the continuation of those same political circumstances. Whereas in the 1690s informal arrangements had undermined the power accorded to Irish and English administrators by formal institutions like Poynings' Law, by the 1770s informal relations worked for and with formal arrangements to insure that the British executive would dominate the Anglo-Irish policymaking process.

Informal Institutions Governing Relations between the British Executive and the British Parliament

Previous chapters showed that over the course of the eighteenth century the power of the British Parliament relative to the Crown increased. The more influence the British Parliament had over the Crown's choice of ministers and government policy in general, the more colonial policymaking was affected by the disposition of the British House of Commons. The shift had consequences for the informal institutions surrounding colonial policymaking process. The process had been essentially closed to everyone outside the British executive and select groups and individuals. It now allowed a larger number of politicians to participate.

This was true of Anglo-Irish policymaking as well, although the effects were not as apparent as in the colonial case. British MPs did not begin passing legislation binding on Ireland as they did for the colonies after 1760. The power of the British Parliament to legislate for Ireland was actually seldom exercised. Even after the passage of the Declaratory Act, except for matters related to the island's economy and trade and the occasional foray into administrative and religious issues, the British Parliament still left Irish policymaking up to the executive.[120] What did happen, however, was that Ireland, like America, was more readily and openly discussed by British MPs, a change that affected how British officials responded to Irish affairs. British MPs who owned Irish land, were friends of the Irish Lord Lieutenant, or had some other kind of connection to or stake in Ireland, were particularly vocal.[121] As early as 1705, this "Irish interest" succeeded in having legislation that had originated in Ireland, allowing the direct shipment of Irish linen to the colonies, passed by the British Parliament.[122] They also managed to quash a bill to raise the duty on Irish yarn six years later.[123] Although the Irish "lobby" failed in their attempt in 1731 to have removed all British duties on Irish yarn, they did convince the British administration and Parliament to support a bill revising the navigation laws to permit the importation of unenumerated goods from the colonies to Ireland.[124] The opposition of the Irish interest in 1773 to a proposed tax on the estates of Irish absentee landlords was key to the rejection of the bill by the British executive and the Irish Parliament.[125] Their indictments of government policies restricting Irish trade preceded the tabling in the British Parliament in the spring of 1778 of a number of resolutions designed to promote Ireland's commerce.[126]

With the expanded role of the British Parliament in government, the ministers in charge of Irish policymaking were now representatives of the king *and* Parliament and so were compelled to consider the views of the latter on Irish matters when formulating legislation for Ireland. British MPs for their part were much more willing to express their views concerning Anglo-Irish policy. These factors contributed to changes in the informal institutions governing the relationship between the British élite and the British Parliament that made it more acceptable for a wider array of political interests to participate in discussions concerning Irish legislation. This could, of course, be a blessing or a burden to key players in the Anglo-Irish policymaking process. The support of MPs in British Parliament of measures desired by MPs in Ireland was an obvious advantage to the Irish interest, whereas Parliamentary opposition could sabotage their efforts to secure executive approval of favored legislation. Similarly, the disposition of the British Parliament toward government initiatives could help or hinder their cause. Nevertheless, with the addition of so many new voices to the Irish policymaking process, the entire procedure became much more unwieldy, less predictable and more difficult for key players to manipulate and control.

Informal Institutions Governing the Policymaking Process

Anglo-Quebec policymaking was affected by the rise of public opinion and the emergence of new kinds of lobby groups. The eighteenth century saw a similar pattern in the development of Irish popular opinion and interests, although the issues around which they rallied were singularly Irish. The "associational" or "voluntary" groups that Alison Olson describes emerging in England after the restoration also formed in Ireland, as merchants, cattlemen and other interests banded together to lobby the Irish and British governments on issues of common concern.[127] Out-of-doors supporters of the Irish interest in London, churchmen, Irish MPs or officials, represented Irish concerns, although their efforts resembled the more conciliatory and cooperative endeavors of the "earlier" English groups described by Olson.[128] It was not until the second half of the century that Irish lobbies took on a more "radical" flavor, having been preceded by several decades of less focused popular political activity.

Some of the first significant examples of popular protest in Ireland accompanied the Wood's halfpence affair in the 1720s. By 1724, opposition to Britain's granting a patent to Englishman William Wood to produce Irish halfpennies had moved outside the confines of the Irish Parliament and into the public arena. In September, a crowd in Cork threatened to set fire to a ship that had arrived from England carrying seven casks of the new coins. The ship returned to England with the hated halfpence still onboard. Meanwhile in Dublin, wooden effigies of William Wood were being paraded around in the streets by groups of 200 or 300 Dubliners.[129] Encouraged by Irish MPs, and spurred on by the constitutional rhetoric of Jonathan Swift,[130] the populace and their demonstrations caused considerable consternation amongst government officials in Ireland and Britain and contributed to the decision of the executive to back down on the deal.[131]

The money bill dispute of the 1750s spawned further demonstrations of public sentiment. When the money bill was rejected by the Irish Parliament on 17 December, a noisy crowd of 2,000 lit bonfires all over Dublin in support of the opposition and forced government officials to sneak out of the castle by the back door.[132] Anti-government clubs met throughout the city, "and the practice of conveying insults [toward government officials] in toasts was brought to a fine art."[133] In Dublin and elsewhere antigovernment feeling was strong. In contrast, the dismissed officials, Henry Boyle and his associates, were "hailed as martyrs for liberty."[134] Admiration for Boyle and his friends turned to indignation, however, when Dubliners discovered that the "martyrs" had been bought out by the Irish administration. A crowd of 1,000 hanged the speaker in effigy.[135] Events surrounding the money bill dispute had barely concluded when in 1759 rumors of a union of Irish and British legislatures aroused the ire of the public yet again. On the day that the union bill was scheduled to be introduced in the Irish House of Commons, a large crowd assembled around the Parliament building. MPs entering were threatened and forced to swear to oppose the measure.[136] Despite attempts by government officials to restore order, grumbling and disturbances continued until an even larger and more hostile crowd appeared at Parliament house about a week later. This time they invaded the House of Commons and, armed with swords and bludgeons, "abused, struck and otherwise ill-treated" many of the members and pressured them to swear "to be true to the interests of their country."[137] The crowd retreated when troops were sent in to disperse the crowd. When the protesters started throwing stones at the soldiers, the cavalry responded with swords drawn, wounding a number of them and arresting some.[138]

There is evidence of collusion between the populace and the opposition factions in the Irish Parliament during these incidents, especially the events surrounding the money bill dispute. Henry Boyle and his colleagues certainly exploited the popular support of his antiadministration forces. But it was not until later in the century when these largely reactionary and, using John Brewer's terminology, "unfocused" responses to government policy started to develop into a more organized and politically influential popular movement. Parliamentary and out-of-doors "patriots" (so-called because of their support of an independent Irish legislature and their indictment of other English infringements, economic and otherwise) found a champion and figurehead in Charles Lucas, a Dublin apothecary and publisher of the *Citizen's Journal*. In 1749, Lucas was declared by the Irish Parliament an enemy of the country for promoting the patriot cause and was forced into exile. Ten years later, he returned and won a seat in the Commons, where he became a staunch supporter of the patriot opposition.[139] During the decade Lucas served as a member of the Irish Parliament, he did much to help Ireland's, particularly Dublin's, populace focus their political potential. Dublin's commercial interests were especially supportive of the patriot cause. As an MP and a member of the barber-surgeons' guild, Lucas straddled both worlds and solidified the connections between out-of-doors patriots and the Parliamentary opposition.[140]

The similarities between Lucas and John Wilkes were evident to contemporaries. Patriots in Dublin cheered the antigovernment activities of Wilkes and his followers; Lucas drew connections between the situation of Wilkes' common man and that of ordinary Dubliners.[141] Irish patriots were also like their radical counterparts in London in condemning British action in the American colonies. By 1775, patriot societies like the Free Citizens of Dublin were joined by larger, less formal groupings in expressing sympathy for the Americans. Public meetings in Dublin and elsewhere passed resolutions supporting the colonists; petitions were forwarded to the king urging him to make peace with America for the sake of Irish trade.[142] In 1776, Lord Lieutenant Harcourt managed to secure a majority in the Irish Parliament to send to the king an address denouncing American defiance. The patriots put up a strong fight against the address, however, asserting that the colonists were only defending their rights.[143]

The "rise of public opinion" in Britain and in Ireland during the eighteenth century influenced the informal institutions surrounding the formulation of Anglo-Irish policy. Just as the increasing power of the British Parliament over British politics increased the number of politicians who could now legitimately participate in government decisionmaking, the growing influence of public sentiment on the policy negotiations boosted the potential for out-of-doors groups to have an impact on legislation. Again, this could work to the benefit, or detriment, of those traditionally involved in Anglo-Irish policymaking. On balance, it made policy negotiations, already becoming unwieldy with the addition of more politicians to the process, even more difficult to manage for actors involved in the process.

By 1778 and the passage of the Irish Catholic Relief Act the *informal* institutions surrounding the Anglo-Irish policymaking process had changed significantly. The informal "rules" governing the relationship between the Irish, and by exception the British, executive and the Irish Parliament had been transformed, partly by intent through George Townshend, and partly by contingencies that encouraged the persistence and eventual institutionalization of Townshend's measures. They now were in closer concert to the intent and spirit of the *formal* institutions that were in place to insure the subordination of Irish politicians to officials of the British Crown in London and Dublin castle. Further, the policymaking process itself had opened up considerably and was now more susceptible to the views and demands of a larger number of politicians and the public. These factors affected the process surrounding the formulation and passage of the Irish Catholic Relief Act.

The Irish Catholic Relief Act

The matter of Catholic relief was raised in the Irish Parliament in May of 1778 by Luke Gardiner, independent MP for county Dublin. Although some historians have maintained that Gardiner's was a truly private measure, it is possible that he was the North ministry's "unofficial agent" in Ireland, a go-between employed by North to avoid the prime minister being associated with Irish Catholic relief.[144] The relief that Gardiner proposed was nothing like an overhaul of the entire penal code; he stated that his motion would deal only with matters concerning landed property. Nevertheless, the issue sparked heated debate among Irish MPs. After much discussion, it was voted on 25 May that Gardiner be permitted to bring in the heads of a Catholic relief bill.[145]

The proceedings of the last session were well publicized and drew criticism from many in Dublin. Gardiner himself received threats on his life, and could not venture out without being accompanied by armed guards.[146] The public's response alarmed Irish officials and prompted the Lord Lieutenant to appeal to London for instructions. The Southern Secretary, Lord Weymouth, forwarded the details of the English relief bill to Buckinghamshire with instructions to inform the "friends of the Lord Lieutenant" in the Irish Parliament that the king was well disposed to Irish Catholic relief. With the knowledge that the king and the British administration were firmly behind relief, the Irish executive permitted proceedings to continue.[147]

There is evidence to suggest that until around the time of this communication, the Irish executive were not aware of North's plans concerning Catholic relief in England, Scotland and Ireland. It was likely Buckinghamshire himself who finally deduced that an Irish measure was part of a larger scheme that involved relief in the other two kingdoms as well. The Lord Lieutenant was not the only one kept in the dark: apparently not even Weymouth was privy to North's strategy until the matter was well underway.[148] North's secrecy is understandable. Rumors that the British administration was planning to recruit Catholics into the army had caused considerable consternation amongst Irish Protestants in 1777. The notion that the government was planning to arm Irish Catholics to kill Irish Protestant emigrants in the American colonies was distasteful enough. But as Robert Burns writes, "the great and enduring fear that 2,000 disciplined Catholics would return from the American war and train 10,000 of their coreligionists to murder Protestants was no less powerful in 1777 than it had been at any time during the century."[149]

Gardiner returned on 5 June to read the heads of his bill. Objections to the measure continued, and it was at this time that Dissenting MPs voiced their opposition to the legislation. One Dissenter, Sir Edward Newenham, declared that he would introduce the heads of a bill repealing legislation that required Irish officeholders to take the Sacramental Test on 15 June, the day that Gardiner moved for committal of his bill.[150]

By 15 June, Newenham had changed his mind. Instead of introducing a separate bill for repeal of the Test, he decided to offer it as an amendment to Gardiner's relief bill. Supporters of Gardiner's measure were quick to object to the proposed amendment. There was no reason not to introduce repeal of the Test as a separate bill, they argued, unless Newenham was purposely trying to sabotage the relief measure. Despite these charges, the house decided to amend the bill.[151]

Over the next several days, debate over the contents of the bill raged until the small hours of the morning. In addition to the Test clause, the bill contained provisions that would permit Catholics to purchase land without any limitations or restrictions and to bequeath land in any way they liked. (The penal code stipulated that Catholic land was subject to the gavelkind and had to be divided among all heirs.) It was the first provision that concerned the bill's opponents the most. Ownership of land meant that Catholics could increase their political influence if the land they bought carried political rights with it, such as the right to appoint candidates to certain government posts and nominate members of Parliament.[152] If, however, Catholics were limited to leasing land, their political rights would also remain limited.[153] On 16 June, an amendment was proposed by George Ogle, a virulent opponent of the relief measure, that the bill's first clause be struck and replaced with one permitting Catholics to take leases of up to 999 years. It was after midnight when debate was suspended and a vote was taken. Ogle's amendment passed, but by only a small margin: 111-108.[154]

Opponents of the bill were buoyed; perhaps they could defeat the relief measure by "amending it to death."[155] But a cryptic announcement by the Chief Secretary, Sir Richard Heron, near the end of the 18 June session seemed to change the tenor of the proceedings. Earlier in the day, George Ogle had asked Heron about a report that had indicated that the relief issue had become a "Government question." Until then, the Irish government had not made clear its position concerning Catholic relief. It had been thought best by officials in Ireland and in London that the Irish administration restrict their involvement to giving "moral support" to the bill so as not to appear to be interfering in the matter.[156] It was not until later that the Chief Secretary responded to Ogle's query. He said that it was true that the Irish government was behind Catholic relief, but "has by no means presumed what those measures should be."[157] Ogle's condemnation of the government's involvement in "principles of religion" was unequivocal, but it had little effect on subsequent proceedings. No further amendments were made to the long-term lease clause, and an amendment repealing the gavel passed easily.[158]

The next day, the house went through the bill line by line, but there was little dissension concerning its contents until the Test clause came under consideration.

Despite valiant attempts on the part of government officeholders to convince members to strike the Test clause from the bill, the provision remained, passed, as Buckinghamshire reported to Weymouth, "by so large a majority that it was not thought advisable to tell the numbers."[159] Thomas Bartlett maintains that earlier charges that the opposition was trying to sabotage the legislation by including the Test clause were on the mark. The addition of the Test clause to the relief bill was a "no lose" strategy on the part of opponents of the measure. If either of the Privy Councils threw out the clause, the Irish Parliament could vote it down when it returned; if it was allowed to remain, then the bill could be defeated by the bishops in the Irish House of Lords.[160] This is no doubt true, but given the large majority that voted to include the Test clause, perhaps not only opposition MPs were thinking this way. It is possible that the "friends of the Lord Lieutenant" who would normally support government measures saw their endorsement of this clause as a surreptitious way in which to express their aversion – whether it stemmed from intolerance or constitutional principle – towards the bill. That Buckinghamshire was aware of this strategy is suggested in a letter to Weymouth in which he wrote that more councillors would have opposed "the Presbyterian clause, if they had not conceived that it might be more properly rejected in England than on this side."[161] The bill passed a thinly populated Irish Commons on 20 June and was in the hands of the British Privy Council by 2 July.

The British law officers to whom the bill was forwarded for comment were cautious in their approach to the measures. They were disheartened by the lease clause; to prevent Irish Catholics from outright ownership of land would "maintain a principle which preserves an uneasy suspicion."[162] Neither were they pleased with the addition of the amendment repealing the Sacramental Test. Both officers recognized, however, that ridding the bill of either of these terms would risk the failure of the bill in Ireland. They referred the measure to cabinet with only minor revisions.[163]

Not surprisingly, the main discussion in the cabinet revolved around treatment of the Test clause. The concern was that if Irish Dissenters were granted this concession then their coreligionists in England would demand the same. On the other hand, if the clause was struck and the Irish Parliament rejected the bill, it would create a situation that would encourage further "bargaining" between Irish Catholics and Protestant Dissenters for political rights, leading to, as the Lord Chancellor Edward Thurlow put it, a "perpetual nursery of faction."[164] In the end, the British Privy Council returned the bill to Ireland without the Test clause. That the bill would have a difficult time passing the Irish Parliament was recognized by the Irish administration; Edmund Sexton Pery, the Speaker of the Irish Commons, told Edmund Burke that its success depended on its open support by the Irish government. Indeed, the Irish administration did its best to insure that the government's "friends" would back the bill. MPs received letters from the Chief Secretary stating "that your attendance in Parliament on this urgent occasion will oblige him [Heron] and government in the most particular way."[165]

Irish Commons debate on the bill before its transmission to England had focused on the issue of Catholics and property. Now the opposition argued that the bill should be rejected because the British Privy Council's alteration of the measure was unconstitutional. One opposition member urged Irish MPs to throw out the bill and protect "the constitution and the rights of Parliament and laws of the land from violation."[166] The debate was furious, until a government official, John Hussey Burgh, announced in the course of a speech supporting the measure that the Irish government had enough votes in the House to pass the bill. Although the clamor in the House continued there was no further debate on the matter. The bill was put to a vote and passed 129 to 89.[167] It was approved by the Irish House of Lords on 10 August in a 44 to 28 vote, although not without some heated discussion. Just as the Irish administration actively solicited votes in the Commons, the Lord Lieutenant secured proxies from absentees and disinterested Lords and made certain that all in the upper house, the bishops in particular, knew his position on the issue.[168] The bill became law a few days later.

Discussion

Accounts of the proceedings surrounding the passage of the Irish Catholic Relief Act vary in tenor with regard to the certainty of the government's victory. Robert Burns, and to a lesser extent Thomas Bartlett, convey the idea that, once the Irish administration had made known its views on the matter of relief, passage of the act was more or less a foregone conclusion. According to Burns, Heron's 18 June announcement that the government backed Irish Catholic relief was directly responsible for the poor turnout of MPs in subsequent sessions. "Government's intervention had made enactment inevitable, and gentlemen wished only to report some kind of a bill and end the gruelling and interminable sittings of the committee."[169] Bartlett writes: "In 1778 the Irish Parliament was steam-rollered into concession, its inferior status being thereby doubly demonstrated, first by its acceptance of the British initiative, and secondly by its acquiescence in the British deletion of the sacramental test clause."[170] In contrast, Eamon O'Flaherty and Maurice O'Connell emphasize how close the relief measure came to failing. O'Flaherty describes "a definite feeling on all sides of political opinion that the first attempt to remove restrictions on Catholics by the Irish Parliament had been a near-disaster" and makes note of comments by the Lord Lieutenant and other supporters of the bill that suggest that they were annoyed with the way in which the matter was handled.[171] O'Connell points out that the measure was almost defeated in the House of Commons several times and tells of Buckinghamshire's great relief when the issue was finally decided, and his commendation from a London official "having gotten through the longest and most difficult session of Parliament I ever remember in Ireland."[172]

Despite differences in their readings of how strong the Irish Parliament was during these proceedings, they are agreed that the decision on the part of the Irish administration to let their views on the issue be known was crucial to the passage of the Irish Catholic Relief Act. Whereas Burns and Bartlett focus on the failure of

Irish MPs to influence the act in any significant way, O'Flaherty and O'Connell emphasize the number of amendments the Irish Parliament succeeded in adding to the bill. All, however, would concede that it was the open support of the Irish government that proved decisive. The capacity of the government to influence the process and its outcome to this degree was due, in part, to changes in the institutional network surrounding Anglo-Irish relations.

The formal institutions governing the making of Irish policy not only continued to favor the government executive but had been strengthened since the ratification of the Treaty of Limerick. Poynings' Law was still in place, giving the Irish and British executive formal control over the policy process. In 1720, the relationship between the Irish and British Parliaments was finally clarified with the passage of the Declaratory Act, a measure that ruled that the British Parliament had the legal right to legislate for Ireland.

But as the Treaty of Limerick negotiations demonstrated, constitutional predominance did not guarantee that government administrators would dominate Irish legislation. Then, the ability of the English and Irish executives to exercise the power over Irish legislation granted them by Poynings' Law was hampered by informal institutions that allowed Irish MPs to, if not dominate, wield much more influence over Irish policy than they were supposed to. These informal institutions proved most enduring and, although they went through some modifications, conditions facilitated and encouraged their continued use.

By 1778, however, there were mechanisms in place that strengthened the actual power of Irish, and by extension British, administrators over the Irish Parliament. Significant alterations in the informal institutions surrounding executive-Parliament relations in Ireland were introduced by Townshend in 1767 and were perpetuated because of the commitment of succeeding administrations and the subsistence of contingent circumstances favorable to their institutionalization. These changes made it possible for the Irish and British executive to exercise the power over Irish policy that the formal institution of Poynings' Law granted them and were a fundamental factor determining the government's victory in the relief act negotiations.

The picture of Anglo-Irish politics that emerges from accounts of these proceedings, of Crown-appointed officials in Ireland unwilling to allow their support of Catholic relief be known out of concern that their views would unduly influence the House vote, of Irish MPs whose passionate tirades against the measure suddenly cease, indeed, who do not even bother to attend its final readings, after the castle government declares its position, is very different from the picture of politics in the years following the Glorious Revolution. During the Treaty of Limerick ratification bill negotiations and for several decades after, the Irish Parliament was able to dictate to a large degree the nature and content of religious policy in Ireland; the Irish, and by exception the British, administrations were in no position to insist that measures contrary to the disposition of the majority of Irish MPs be adopted in the kingdom. By 1778 this situation had been altered completely. Changes in the institutions influencing Anglo-Irish politics were central to this reversal.

The power of the Irish and British executives to direct Irish policy in 1778 must not be overstated, however. One need only compare the limited nature of the concessions offered to Irish Catholics to those granted to Catholics in Quebec and England to see how Irish MPs were still able to check the capacity of the executive to pass legislation unhindered. Although it is true that changes to the informal institutions governing Anglo-Irish politics had improved the extent to which the executive could control the Irish Parliament, formal institutions, namely the long tradition of participatory politics in Ireland, still required that Irish and British politicians pay heed to the disposition of the Irish Parliament when formulating relief legislation for that kingdom.

Institutional changes also diminished the capacity of the Irish Lord Lieutenant to influence Irish policy independent of the British executive. It is true that the chief governor and his officials were in control of Ireland's governance much more than before. The British executive still relied on the information provided by the Irish executive concerning the state of the kingdom. But the Lord Lieutenant had much less maneuverability as far as negotiation and formulation of Anglo-Irish policy was concerned. In the years following the Glorious Revolution, the chief governor was more negotiator than dictator. Given the power of the Irish Parliament in those days, policy was more flexible because it had to accommodate the demands of Irish MPs. As a result, a strong Irish Lord Lieutenant whose relations with Parliamentary managers were good could inject policy with his own personal and political views. Certainly Henry Capel demonstrated how the Irish chief governor could be the representative of the Crown while still dictating to a large degree the nature of Irish policy. After 1767, the Irish chief governor was more the direct servant of the British government. His management abilities remained important, but the opportunity to influence policy and act independently of the British executive was reduced dramatically. Buckinghamshire's experience and actions during the process leading up to the passage of the Irish Catholic Relief Act provide much evidence of this. The chief governor was unaware of the relief plans of the British executive; information was only given to Buckinghamshire on a "need-to-know" basis. The Lord Lieutenant's urgent appeals to London asking how the Irish administration should approach the matter shows how dependent the chief governor was on British administrators for guidance in the process.

The other figure whose direct role in Anglo-Irish policy negotiations had declined is the monarch. As in the Quebec case, it was the North ministry rather than the king who directed the course of relief legislation in Ireland, another indication that the power of the British Parliament to direct government policy had increased considerably since William and Mary's time. Of course the king could cause difficulties for the ministry, as became evident when the matter of Irish Catholic emancipation was broached after Britain's union with Ireland in 1801. This should not detract from the ministry's strength during the 1778 negotiations, however. While the king supported the relief legislation, it was likely not easy to persuade him to do so.

The changes that Townshend introduced to the informal institutions governing relations between the Irish executive and the Irish Parliament affected the outcome of the process leading up to the passage of the Catholic Relief Act in other less straightforward ways. More specifically, the *interaction* of Townshend's measures with the changes that had occurred in the informal institutions related to British governance had important implications for the capacities of the Irish Parliament and other groups, Irish Catholics in particular, to affect the policy outcome. Townshend's measures in combination with the "opening up" of British politics helped to shape the strategies these groups used to oppose or promote Catholic relief and ultimately helped determine their success or failure in the negotiation process.

The character of the Irish Parliament changed with the institutionalization of Townshend's measures. There had always existed a "separation" between the Irish executive and the Irish Parliament. But before Townshend, conditions demanded that the administration forge cooperative links with Irish politicians. The executive was almost exclusively British, political benefactors of the ministry that happened to be in power. Until Townshend's term, most officials, including the Lord Lieutenant, were nonresident, coming to Ireland only for the sitting of the Irish Parliament, about eight months every two years. Lacking the knowledge and the personal connections necessary to manage the Irish Parliament, the executive really had little choice but to appeal to Irish politicians for help governing the island. After Townshend's reforms, the executive relied less on Irish Parliamentary leaders to rule. It is true that the Lord Lieutenant and his officials were still compelled to negotiate with Irish MPs to achieve desired ends. But that negotiation was now done by executive officials who lived in Ireland, who could develop the political know-how and cultivate the personal relationships to procure a "castle party" on their own. The "middleman" had been done away with and the type of reciprocal links that had once existed between the Irish executive and the Irish Parliament were weakened significantly. This was to have important consequences for Anglo-Irish politics as J. C. Beckett explains:

> So long as government could rely on undertakers to manage the house of commons the true nature of the constitutional conflict between Ireland and Great Britain was obscured. It was so much mixed up in the squabbles of rival groups of self-seeking politicians that the issues seldom stood out clearly. Once the Castle became the real centre of power, exercising a direct control over government supporters in the house, the way was open for a straight trial of strength.[173]

The idea that Townshend's measures led inexorably to the constitutional battles later in the century may be overstated here. But the more distinct separation between the Irish Parliament and the Irish executive that emerged after Townshend's term certainly played a part in the way the Irish Parliament was to approach Anglo-Irish policymaking thereafter.

David Lammey has examined this matter in some detail.[174] Although his purpose is to show that the Irish Parliament was split into distinct administration and opposition parties during the 1770s, his analysis can be used to show how institutions contributed to the failure of the Irish Parliament to block the Catholic relief bill. Lammey agrees with Beckett that the more pronounced division between the Irish executive and Parliament arising out of Townshend's measures brought to the fore constitutional issues once obscured by political posturing. But he also emphasizes that changes in the nature of the constitutional challenges themselves, and the tactics employed by the Irish "patriot" movement both inside and outside Parliament contributed to this focus. Constitutional challenges to the authority of the British Crown and Parliament over Irish affairs were nothing new in Irish politics. But the Wood's halfpence affair and the money bill dispute brought constitutional debate to a new level. The "patriots" in the Irish Parliament realized that there were some distinct political advantages to presenting themselves as defenders of Irish interests.[175] After 1767, their use of constitutional arguments became more regular. Now faced with a virtually "indestructible ministerial majority" in the Commons, constitutional issues became a way in which they could "shake the resolve of ministerialists who were susceptible to the demands of their electorate and thus precipitate a desertion."[176] In other words, by appealing to constitutional issues, the opposition could utilize public opinion in support of their causes and improve somewhat their chances of breaking the Commons majority held by the castle. The opponents of the relief measure adopted exactly this tactic when the Catholic Relief Act returned from London shorn of the Test Act repeal clause. George Ogle also tried to unsettle those MPs who had ignored what he felt was proper constitutional procedure by promising "to move an impeachment against any gentlemen who admitted voting on this question under Government influence."[177] The threat had some effect but not enough to change the vote significantly.

If the activities of the Irish Parliament are considered in the light of the discussion concerning the "opening up" of British politics and the "rise of public opinion" that accompanied and encouraged this process, it becomes evident how Townshend's measures combined with these other institutional changes to shape the strategy adopted by the MPs in the Irish Parliament who were against the relief measure. Opposition MPs, their connections with the Irish administration severed because of the changes put in place by Townshend, responded to their newfound powerlessness by focusing on constitutional issues. They were inspired by and contributed to the simultaneous growth of the influence of "the public" on government policymaking, an experience that was both a response to and a motivation for changes in the informal institutions characterizing British policymaking that encouraged more "openness." Further, the appearance of more "radical" interest groups whose concerns parallelled their own encouraged Irish opposition MPs to adopt many of the same arguments and tactics employed by these public-opinion lobbies: they appealed to a large and diverse public rather than specific interests; they focused on larger, particularly constitutional, matters as opposed to narrower concerns; and they were anything but conciliatory towards government. Given all this, it comes as little surprise that the antirelief forces were made up largely of Irish radicals, the "patriots." All but four in the patriot party opposed the act.[178]

What did all this mean with regard to the capacity of the Irish Parliament to affect the discussions surrounding the Irish Catholic Relief Act? The employment by Irish MPs opposed to Catholic relief of "radical" methods of lobbying rather than the more pliant approaches used by earlier interest groups hurt them. "Radicalism" in Ireland was viewed very differently than radicalism in Britain. The potential of the patriots to cause trouble for the British government was, or perceived to be, much more serious than that of the radicals in Britain. It is true that the Wilkites and other antigovernment groups in London and elsewhere were critical of the Crown and its officials; it is also true that they embarrassed and pressured administrators to listen to and sometimes consider or even concede to their demands. But the Irish patriot cause had much larger political implications than did London radicalism. This became especially clear during the American conflict. There were strong links between Ireland and the American colonies. Most straightforwardly, they shared Irishmen; emigration from Ireland, the north especially, to the "new world" was steady throughout the century.[179] More seriously, Ireland and the American colonies held a somewhat similar constitutional relationship to the mother country, a fact that the patriots in the Irish Parliament were quick to point out when opposing Irish involvement in the war. Patriot leaders warned that the English "understand most perfectly that the cause of America is [ours]. . . . From the highest to the lowest they are all agreed to the point of our dependence; some of them go so far to assert we are theirs by right of conquest. To ask them to prove this point is an insult. Mr. Molyneux's *Case* they have not heard of."[180] Although some modern historians claim that it would have been unlikely that Ireland would go the way of the American colonies and assert their independence from Britain, certainly the possibility of a constitutional conflict of similar proportions in Ireland crossed the minds of British administrators during the American conflict.[181] Suspicions that the Irish would wish "to shake off their dependency on England" had been expressed already in the age of Walpole in response to the constitutional challenges posed by the Irish Parliament. According to Thomas Bartlett, these suspicions were cultivated by successive ministries so that by the 1760s there were many British officials who held serious misgivings about the loyalty of Irish MPs.[182] Expression of their grievances in a more "radical" form would have only contributed to officials' distrust, and had an impact on the latter's views concerning Irish policy and their responses to the demands of the Irish Parliament.

So the "radical" stance taken by Irish MPs to oppose Catholic relief and other government measures did nothing to endear them to British administrators. The question remains whether they would have been able to ward off Catholic relief in Ireland had they been more compromising, less hostile to government officials. The North ministry was behind the bill and was committed to securing some relief measures in Ireland for military reasons. It is unlikely that North and his officials would have delayed or modified the act had the opposition in the Irish Parliament been less bellicose. Furthermore, the Irish Catholic Relief Act was already quite a benign measure. It granted far fewer concessions than did the English Relief Act, and did not come close to including the liberties that had been granted to French Catholics in Quebec. It is difficult to imagine a Catholic relief bill that would have provided for fewer freedoms, unless it was decided to forgo granting any concessions at all. In the end, circumstances were such that the "patriots" in the Irish Parliament would not have considered approaching the Catholic question in a more conciliatory manner. By 1778 the separation that had occurred in Irish politics as a corollary of Townshend's measures, together with the increase in the involvement of "the public" in the policymaking process that was a consequence of the opening up of British politics, had combined with a history rife with constitutional struggles to create an Irish opposition wholly radical in its approach to Anglo-Irish policymaking. By the time the question of Irish Catholic Relief was broached, conciliation was not an option.

The opposition in the Irish Parliament also had to contend with the fact that, given the more open political process, British officials, whether they wanted to or not, were now forced to consider the demands of groups that had traditionally been outside the official policymaking process. The Irish Catholics were the most important out-of-doors interest in these negotiations. It is true that the Catholic Committee in Ireland did not become directly involved in promoting the Irish Catholic Relief Act until the bill had passed the Irish Parliament and had been transmitted to England for approval by the British Privy Council. Then, it sent funds to its London agent, Daniel McNamara, to help convince British officials to support the measure.[183] But Irish Catholic leaders had long been communicating their support of the Irish and British governments, directly, via addresses declaring their allegiance to the king and offers to assist the Crown in recruiting Catholic troops for battle for the British cause, and indirectly, by not participating in the Jacobite risings earlier in the century. The methods used by Catholic leaders and by the Catholic Committee later in the process helped in their efforts to persuade the government to go ahead with plans for Catholic relief. Although there was some disagreement among their ranks concerning how to approach this matter, in the end Irish Catholic leaders made a deliberate decision to adhere to traditional lobbying techniques – private conferences with government officials rather than more public campaigns, insuring the loyalty of their membership and offering help to government in exchange for consideration of their demands as opposed to more aggressive techniques – and it worked well for them. Passage of the Act vindicated those members of the Catholic community who advocated establishing closer links with government officials.[184] Granted, their goals meshed with those of government officials, making it easier for administrators to react favorably to their humble requests for relief. But had they been more belligerent in professing their demands it is doubtful that they would have been as successful in persuading the British government to approve of relief measures.

Irish Dissenters played an indirect yet important role in the Catholic Relief bill process. They did not actively support the Catholic cause, nor did they as a group openly oppose it any more or less than did the Irish Protestants of the established church. But it was a clause repealing the Sacramental Test that proved to be the most controversial portion of the bill. It was the position of the key players on relief for Dissenters and its implications, rather than on Catholic succour, that really decided the fate of the Irish Catholic Relief Act.

In some ways, those most directly affected by institutions, both formal and informal, during the eighteenth century were the Irish Dissenters. The hated test act was introduced in 1704 not as a separate measure but as an amendment tacked onto an anti-Catholic bill by an English Privy Council that some say only added the clause to prevent passage of the bill through the Irish Parliament.[185] The first time repeal of the test was supported by the Irish Parliament it was tabled again not as a separate bill but as an addition to a Catholic Relief bill. Opposition Irish MPs hoped the clause would help bring about the bill's defeat somewhere along the way. In both instances, the fate of Irish Dissenters was being used by key players to try to make the institutions governing the policy process – in this case, Poynings' Law – work to their advantage. In the case of the introduction of the test, the strategy failed, and the bill was passed. In the case of the test's repeal, the scheme failed again. The "no-lose" strategy adopted by the opposition MPs in the Irish Parliament stumbled up against the power of the Irish executive. Institutions helped to shape the experience of Irish Dissenters and contrived to involve them in negotiations concerning Catholic policy, even though they as a group made little concerted effort to participate themselves.

Notes

1. William Burke, *The Irish Priests in the Penal Times (1660-1760)* (Shannon: Irish University Press, 1969), 119-53.

2. Ibid., 219-37; Maureen Wall, *The Penal Laws, 1691-1760* (Dundalk: Dundalgan Press, 1967), 29-31.

3. Wall, *The Penal Laws*, 20, 23-24, 26.

4. W. N. Osborough, "Catholics, Land, and the Popery Acts of Anne," in *Endurance and Emergence: Catholics in Ireland in the Eighteenth Century,* ed. T. P. Power and K. Whelan (Dublin: Irish Academic Press, 1990); Thomas P. Power, "Converts," in *Endurance and Emergence: Catholics in Ireland in the Eighteenth Century,* ed. T. P. Power and K. Whelan (Dublin: Irish Academic Press, 1990), 110.

5. S. J. Connolly, *Religion, Law and Power: The Making of Protestant Ireland, 1660-1760* (Oxford: Clarendon Press, 1992), 308.

6. Thomas Bartlett, *The Fall and Rise of the Irish Nation: The Catholic Question 1690-1830* (Dublin: Gill and Macmillan, 1992), 47-48; R. F. Foster, *Modern Ireland, 1600-1972* (London: Penguin Books, 1989), 205.

7. Wall, *The Penal Laws*, 54.

8. Karen J. Harvey, *The Bellews of Mount Bellew: A Catholic Gentry Family in Eighteenth-Century Ireland* (Dublin: Four Courts Press, 1998); T. P. Power and Kevin Whelan, eds., *Endurance and Emergence: Catholics in Ireland in the Eighteenth Century* (Dublin: Irish Academic Press, 1990).

9. Connolly, *Religion, Law and Power*, 312-13.

10. Foster, *Modern Ireland*, 207.

11. See above, 47.

12. Neil Longley York, *Neither Kingdom Nor Nation: The Irish Quest for Constitutional Rights, 1698-1800* (Washington: The Catholic University of America Press, 1994), 20, 22.

13. Art Cosgrove, "A Century of Decline," in *The Irish Parliamentary Tradition*, ed. B. Farrell (Dublin: Gill and Macmillan, 1973), 64.

14. J. G. Swift MacNeill, *The Constitutional and Parliamentary History of Ireland till the Union* (Dublin: The Talbot Press, 1917), 7-8.

15. Connolly, *Religion, Law and Power*, 107; Francis G. James, *Ireland in the Empire, 1688-1770* (Cambridge: Harvard University Press, 1973), 191-92; Patrick Kelly, "The Irish Woollen Export Prohibition Act of 1699: Kearney Re-visited," *Irish Economic and Social History* 7 (1980): 22-44.

16. J. T. Ball, *Historical Review of the Legislative Systems Operative in Ireland from the Invasion of Henry the Second to the Union (1172-1800)* (London: Longmans, Green, and Co., 1889), 31-32, 66-69.

17. James, *Ireland in the Empire*, 39-41; York, *Neither Kingdom Nor Nation*, 8-38; David Miller, *Queen's Rebels: Ulster Loyalism in Historical Perspective* (Dublin: Gill and MacMillan, 1978), 29. Miller notes the literary hoops through which Molyneux had to jump to avoid the "unavoidable reality" that, if "the Irish Parliament was entitled to powers established by a contract of government between king and people . . . it must have been a contract with ancestors of [Irish Catholics] who had been deprived of their property [by Irish Protestants]." Molyneux tried to sidestep this fact by claiming that the majority of Irish were "the Progeny of the *English* and *Britains*" and that "there remains but a mere handful of the antient [*sic*] *Irish* at this day," a fabrication that did not fool his detractors.

18. Francis G. James, *Lords of the Ascendancy: The Irish House of Lords and its Members, 1600-1800* (Dublin: Irish Academic Press, 1995), 68-69; Isolde Victory, "The Making of the 1720 Declaratory Act" in *Parliament, Politics and People*, ed. G. O'Brien (Dublin: Irish Academic Press, 1989), 10-12.

19. Victory, "The Making of the 1720 Declaratory Act," 12.

20. James, *Lords of the Ascendancy*, 69-70; Victory, "The Making of the 1720 Declaratory Act," 12-13.

21. James, *Lords of the Ascendancy*, 71; Victory, "The Making of the 1720 Declaratory Act," 14-15.

22. Victory, "The Making of the 1720 Declaratory Act," 16-27.

23. David Hayton, "Introduction: the Long Apprenticeship," in *The Irish Parliament in the Eighteenth Century: The Long Apprenticeship*, ed. D. Hayton (Edinburgh: Edinburgh University Press, 2001), 11.

24. Edith M. Johnston, *Great Britain and Ireland 1760-1800: A Study in Political Administration* (London: Oliver and Boyd, 1963), 89-90.

25. Ibid., 92.

26. Ibid., 101.

27. Robert Kent Donovan, "The Military Origins of the Roman Catholic Relief Programme of 1778," *The Historical Journal* 28, no. 1 (1985): 89-90.

28. Ibid.

29. Ibid., 92.

30. Ibid.

31. Ibid., 82.

32. Bartlett, *The Fall and Rise of the Irish Nation*, 87.

33. Ibid., 83; Donovan, "The Military Origins," 84.

34. Donovan, "The Military Origins," 83.

35. Robert E. Burns, "The Catholic Relief Act in Ireland, 1778," *Church History* 32, no. 2 (1963): 185.

36. Bartlett, *The Fall and Rise of the Irish Nation*, 87.

37. Maurice R. O'Connell, *Irish Politics and Social Conflict in the Age of the American Revolution* (Philadelphia: University of Philadelphia Press, 1965), 108-109.

38. Ibid., 109.

39. Bartlett, *The Fall and Rise of the Irish Nation*, 84.

40. Robin E. Close, "The Attempted Repeal of the Quebec Act: the State of the Parliamentary Opposition in 1775," *Past Imperfect* 1 (1992): 83; Robert Kent Donovan, "The Military Origins of the Roman Catholic Relief Programme of 1778," *The Historical Journal* 28, no. 1 (1985): 87.

41. Donovan, "The Military Origins," 88-89.

42. Johnston, *Great Britain and Ireland 1760-1800*, 12.

43. Ibid., 12-16.

44. Bartlett, *The Fall and Rise of the Irish Nation*, 6-9; James Kelly, "Inter-denominational Relations and Religious Toleration in Late-eighteenth-century Ireland: the 'Paper-war' of 1786-88," *Eighteenth-Century Ireland 3*, 40, 66.

45. Burns, "The Catholic Relief Act," 181.

46. James, *Lords of the Ascendancy*, 73, 78-86.

47. Ibid., 131.

48. Johnston, *Great Britain and Ireland 1760-1800*, 257; J. L. McCracken, *The Irish Parliament in the Eighteenth Century* (Dundalk: Dundalgan Press, 1971), 6.

49. David Hayton, "Walpole and Ireland," in *Britain in the Age of Walpole*, ed. J. Black (London: Macmillan Publishers Ltd., 1984), 101; David Hayton, "British Whig Ministers and the Irish Question, 1714-1725," in *Hanoverian Britain and Empire*, ed. S. Taylor, R. Connors and C. Jones (Woodbridge: The Boydell Press, 1998), 49-51.

50. James, *Lords of the Ascendancy*, 148.

51. Ibid., 146; Johnston, *Great Britain and Ireland 1760-1800*, 264.

52. James, *Lords of the Ascendancy*, 99-100.

53. Ball, *Historical Review of the Legislative Systems*, 268-69; James, *Ireland in the Empire*, 282-83.

54. Johnston, *Great Britain and Ireland 1760-1800*, 94.

55. James, *Ireland in the Empire*, 284n; Johnston, *Great Britain and Ireland 1760-1800*, 94-96.

56. James, *Lords of the Ascendancy*, 146.

57. Johnston, *Great Britain and Ireland 1760-1800*, 100.

58. Ibid., 27-28.

59. Ibid., 27.

60. Burns, "The Catholic Relief Act," 184-85.

61. O'Connell, *Irish Politics and Social Conflict*, 107.

62. Burns, "The Catholic Relief Act," 185-86; O'Connell, *Irish Politics and Social Conflict*, 107-108.

63. Foster, *Modern Ireland*, 155.

64. Bartlett, *The Fall and Rise of the Irish Nation*, 46-48.

65. Maureen Wall, "The Rise of A Catholic Middle Class in Eighteenth-century Ireland," *Irish Historical Studies* 11, no. 42 (1958): 97.

66. Ibid., 102-103.

67. Ibid., 96.

68. Quoted in Wall, "The Rise of A Catholic Middle Class," 96-97, n16.

69. David J. Dickson, "Catholics and Trade in Eighteenth-century Ireland: An Old Debate Revisited," in *Endurance and Emergence: Catholics in Ireland in the Eighteenth Century*, ed. T. P. Power and K. Whelan (Dublin: Irish Academic Press, 1990), 85-100.

70. F. J. McLynn, "'Good Behavior': Irish Catholics and the Jacobite Rising of 1745," *Eire-Ireland* 16, no. 2 (1981): 43-58.

71. Bartlett, *The Fall and Rise of the Irish Nation*, 63, 74, 84; Burns, "The Catholic Relief Act," 183-84.

72. Bartlett, *The Fall and Rise of the Irish Nation*, 69. Bartlett writes that the notion that Whiteboy activities were committed by Roman Catholics exclusively was propagated by Irish Protestants at the time. He points out that recent research has determined that Whiteboyism was more "a protest against economic change and innovation in the rural economy" than a purely religious movement. There were some Protestant Whiteboys, and Whiteboy victims were "promiscuously" Protestant and Catholic.

73. J. C. Beckett, *The Making of Modern Ireland* (New York: Alfred A. Knopf, 1969), 176-

79; Burns, "The Catholic Relief Act," 18-83; J. S. Donnelly, "Irish Agrarian Rebellion: the Whiteboys of 1769-76," *Royal Irish Academy Proceedings*, C, 83/12 (1983): 293-331.

74. 2 Geo. I, c. 47 prohibited Catholics from serving in the military. While Catholics were formally barred from service, by 1775 Catholic recruitment was "practiced at large throughout the country." Foster, *Modern Ireland*, 244. Foster notes that by the Napoleonic era possibly a third of the regular army's rank and file were Catholics.

75. J. C. Beckett, "Anglo-Irish Constitutional Relations in the Later Eighteenth Century," in *Confrontations: Studies in Irish History*, ed. J. C. Beckett (Totowa, New Jersey: Rowman and Littlefield, 1972), 57-58; Burns, "The Catholic Relief Act," 183.

76. Wall, *The Penal Laws*, 18.

77. Maureen Wall (MacGeehin), "The Catholics of the Towns and the Quarterage Dispute in Eighteenth-century Ireland," *Irish Historical Studies* 8, no. 30 (1952): 91-102.

78. Bartlett, *The Fall and Rise of the Irish Nation*, 50.

79. Ibid., 60-62; R. B. McDowell, *Ireland in the Age of Imperialism and Revolution, 1760-1801* (Oxford: Clarendon Press, 1979), 186-87; Bartlett notes that O'Conor, along with Curry, had for some time been writing pamphlets in the attempt to revise the Protestant version of Irish history, to counter Protestant representations of 1641, in order to gain support for the repeal of penal legislation. Bartlett 1992: 52-55.

80. Wall (MacGeehin), "The Catholics of the Towns,"

81. Bartlett, *The Fall and Rise of the Irish Nation*, 80-81. Bartlett notes that O'Conor was opposed to the oath that was passed by the Irish Parliament in 1774, largely because he felt it strayed too far from the declaration that he had submitted on behalf of the Catholic Committee. Although he eventually took the oath in 1778, he objected to its content, claiming that it was a Protestant creation designed to divide Irish Catholics. It is true that the oath was much more stringent that the oath that was required of Quebec Catholics. Perhaps O'Conor was correct in his charge that Irish Protestants passed the oath with the hope that Irish Catholics might emigrate to Canada.

82. James I. McGuire, "Government Attitudes to Religious Non-conformity in Ireland 1660-1719," in *The Huguenots and Ireland: Anatomy of an Emigration*, ed. C. E. J. Caldicott, H. Gough and J. P. Pittion (Dublin: The Glendale Press, 1987), 273. The test kept Presbyterians out of Crown and municipal office, but they could still vote as freemen or freeholders, and sit in the Commons or the Lords.

83. J. C. Beckett, *Protestant Dissent in Ireland 1687-1780* (London: Faber and Faber Ltd., 1948), 60; McGuire, "Government Attitudes to Religious Non-conformity," 276.

84. McGuire, "Government Attitudes to Religious Non-conformity," 277.

85. Ibid., 277-78.

86. Beckett, *Protestant Dissent in Ireland*, 17-18.

87. Ibid., 18.

88. Ibid., 78.

89. Ibid., 15.

90. Ibid., 87.

91. Ibid., 91-97.

92. David Hayton, "The Beginnings of the 'Undertaker System,'" in *Penal Era and Golden Age*, ed. T. Bartlett and D. W. Hayton (Belfast: Ulster Historical Foundation, 1979), 42-45.

93. Ibid., 47-48.

94. Ibid., 48.

95. Beckett, *The Making of Modern Ireland*, 189.

96. Ibid., 189-90; James Kelly, *Prelude to Union: Anglo-Irish Politics in the 1780s* (Cork Cork University Press, 1992), 189.

97. Hayton, "British Whig Ministers and the Irish Question," 41-42.

98. Beckett, *The Making of Modern Ireland*, 165.

99. Ibid., 165-66.

100. James, *Ireland in the Empire*, 165.

101. Ibid., 169-70.

102. Declan O'Donovan, "The Money Bill Dispute of 1753," in *Penal Era and Golden Age*, ed. T. Bartlett and D. W. Hayton (Belfast: Ulster Historical Foundation, 1979), 59.

103. J. C. D. Clark, "Whig Tactics and Parliamentary Precedent: the English Management of Irish Politics, 1754-1756," *The Historical Journal* 21, no. 2 (1978): 279; J. L. McCracken, "The Conflict Between the Irish Administration and Parliament, 1753-6," *Irish Historical Studies* 3, no. 10 (1942): 167-69.

104. Hayton, "The Beginnings of the 'Undertaker System,'" 53-54.

105. Boyle and other opposition leaders negotiated with the administration and were eventually bought out with titles and lucrative pensions, further testament to Boyle's continued influence with the executive.

106. Beckett, *The Making of Modern Ireland*, 191; McCracken, "The Conflict Between the Irish Administration and Parliament," 179.

107. Thomas Bartlett, "The Townshend Viceroyalty, 1767-1772," in *Penal Era and Golden Age*, ed. T. Bartlett and D. W. Hayton (Belfast: Ulster Historical Foundation, 1979), 88.

108. Bartlett, *The Fall and Rise of the Irish Nation*, 73; Beckett, *The Making of Modern Ireland*, 198-99.

109. Bartlett, "The Townshend Viceroyalty," 94.

110. Bartlett, *The Fall and Rise of the Irish Nation*, 73; Beckett, *The Making of Modern Ireland*, 201-202.

111. Beckett, *The Making of Modern Ireland*, 202.

112. Johnston, *Great Britain and Ireland*.

113. Bartlett, "The Townshend Viceroyalty," 98.

114. Ibid., 99-101.

115. James, *Ireland in the Empire*, 271-72.

116. Foster, *Modern Ireland*, 230-31.

117. James, *Ireland in the Empire*, 262.

118. Ibid., 16.

119. Bartlett, "The Townshend Viceroyalty," 110; James, *Ireland in the Empire*, 272-73.

120. Beckett, "Anglo-Irish Constitutional Relations," 124.

121. Francis G. James, "The Irish Lobby in the Early Eighteenth Century," *English Historical Review* 81, no. 320 (1966): 556.

122. Ibid., 546-48.

123. Ibid., 548-49.

124. Ibid., 554-55.

125. Johnston, *Great Britain and Ireland*, 294-95.

126. McDowell, *Ireland in the Age of Imperialism*, 250-51; O'Connell, *Irish Politics and Social Conflict*, 53-55.

127. Alison Olson, *Making the Empire Work: London and American Interest Groups 1690-1790* (Cambridge: Harvard University Press, 1992), 26.

128. Francis G. James, "The Irish Lobby in the Early Eighteenth Century," *English Historical Review* 81, no. 320 (1966): 556.

129. Connolly, *Religion, Law and Power*, 101.

130. James, *Ireland in the Empire*, 120. Swift, under the pseudonym "The Drapier," published four letters in 1724, the last of which linked the Wood's halfpence controversy to the

more general (and explosive) issue of Ireland's political independence from England.

131. Connolly, *Religion, Law and Power*, 101-102. According to Sean Connolly, these were the only demonstrations of public hostility toward the Wood's halfpence that occurred. But the severity and number of public protests were exaggerated by English observers, reports that no doubt contributed to the executive's belief that the patent should be revoked.

132. Bartlett, "The Townshend Viceroyalty," 64; McCracken, "The Conflict Between the Irish Administration," 169.

133. McCracken, "The Conflict Between the Irish Administration," 170.

134. Ibid., 172.

135. Ibid., 177.

136. Beckett, *The Making of Modern Ireland*, 195; Sean Murphy, "The Dublin Anti-Union Riot of 3 December 1759," in *Parliament, Politics and People*, ed. G. O'Brien (Dublin: Irish Academic Press, 1989), 54.

137. Quoted in Murphy, "The Dublin Anti-Union Riot," 54.

138. Ibid., 54-56.

139. Beckett, *The Making of Modern Ireland*, 192, 198; James, *Ireland in the Empire*, 183-85.

140. Seamus Cummins, "Extra-parliamentary Agitation in Dublin in the 1760s," in *Religion, Conflict and Coexistence in Ireland*, ed. R. V. Comerford et al. (Dublin: Gill and MacMillan, 1990), 118-20, 125, 126-27, 133.

141. Ibid., 120.

142. R. B. McDowell, *Irish Public Opinion 1750-1800* (London: Faber and Faber, 1944), 43-44.

143. O'Connell, *Irish Politics and Social Conflict*, 27.

144. Bartlett, *The Fall and Rise of the Irish Nation*, 85-86. According to Thomas Bartlett, North frequently made use of agents; it was "his preferred tactic for dealing with tricky policy issues with which his government could not appear to be directly involved."

145. Burns, "The Catholic Relief Act," 189-90, 191-92.

146. Ann K. Kavanaugh, *John FitzGibbon, Earl of Clare: Protestant Reaction and English Authority in Late Eighteenth-Century Ireland* (Dublin: Irish Academic Press, 1997), 27.

147. Bartlett, *The Fall and Rise of the Irish Nation*, 88-89; Burns, "The Catholic Relief Act," 192-93.

148. Bartlett, *The Fall and Rise of the Irish Nation*, 85, 86, 87-88.

149. Burns, "The Catholic Relief Act," 185.

150. Ibid., 193.

151. Ibid., 193-94.

152. O'Connell, *Irish Politics and Social Conflict*, 117.

153. Bartlett, *The Fall and Rise of the Irish Nation*, 88.

154. Burns, "The Catholic Relief Act," 195-96.

155. Ibid., 196.

156. O'Connell, *Irish Politics and Social Conflict*, 118; Burns, "The Catholic Relief Act," 190. Burns maintains that the government had decided to support the bill by 22 May. Although there was no official announcement of their position, the fact that the press coverage of recent house debates on the issue was "unusually detailed" and focused on the English act was an "unmistakable sign" of the government's feeling.

157. Quoted in Burns, "The Catholic Relief Act," 197.

158. Ibid., 197-98.

159. Quoted in Bartlett, *The Fall and Rise of the Irish Nation*, 88.

160. Bartlett, *The Fall and Rise of the Irish Nation*, 88.

161. Quoted in Burns, "The Catholic Relief Act," 198-99.

162. Quoted in Bartlett, *The Fall and Rise of the Irish Nation*, 89.

163. Ibid., 89.

164. O'Connell, *Irish Politics and Social Conflict*, 119-20.

165. Bartlett, *The Fall and Rise of the Irish Nation*, 89-90.

166. Quoted in Burns, "The Catholic Relief Act," 202.

167. Bartlett, *The Fall and Rise of the Irish Nation*, 90.

168. Burns, "The Catholic Relief Act," 203.

169. Ibid., 198.

170. Bartlett, *The Fall and Rise of the Irish Nation*, 91.

171. Eamon O'Flaherty, "Ecclesiastical Politics and the Dismantling of the Penal Laws in Ireland, 1774-82," *Irish Historical Studies* 26, no. 101 (1988): 38.

172. O'Connell, *Irish Politics and Social Conflict*, 122-23.

173. Beckett, *The Making of Modern Ireland*, 202-203.

174. David Lammey, "The Growth of the 'Patriot Opposition' in Ireland During the 1770s," *Parliamentary History* 7, no. 2 (1988): 257-81.

175. Ibid., 263.

176. Ibid., 275.

177. Quoted in Burns, "The Catholic Relief Act," 199.

178. O'Connell, *Irish Politics and Social Conflict*, 123.

179. Ibid., 28.

180. McDowell, *Irish Public Opinion*, 45-46.

181. O'Connell, *Irish Politics and Social Conflict*, 30-31.

182. Thomas Bartlett, "The Origins and Progress of the Catholic Question in Ireland, 1690-1800," in *Endurance and Emergence: Catholics in Ireland in the Eighteenth Century,* ed T. P. Power and K. Whelan (Dublin: Irish Academic Press, 1990), 6.

183. Eamon O'Flaherty, "Ecclesiastical Politics and the Dismantling of the Penal Laws in Ireland, 1774-82," *Irish Historical Studies* 26, no. 101(1988): 39.

184. Ibid., 40.

185. See above, 62.

Chapter 7

Conclusion

The aim of this study was twofold. First, to analyze closely using the institutional approach the events surrounding the formulation of three pieces of legislation affecting Catholics in the British empire in the eighteenth century to determine how formal and informal institutions helped to shape each policy process and ultimately each policy outcome. The second objective sought to explore how the specific policy events contributed and were linked to the more general tendency on the part of British administrators to favor Catholic relief over more repressive measures as time went on. The intent was to supplement existing studies that have focused on *why* policy toward Catholics became increasingly charitable as the century progressed, with an investigation of *how* a more tolerant approach to Catholics was established and perpetuated in an era preceded by generations of legislated anti-Catholicism.

The Institutional Approach and Policy Outcomes

Policymaking in each case took place in an institutional context. Institutions provided the structure that helped to determine the actors who were sanctioned to take part in the policymaking process, as well as what those individuals and groups were authorized to do within that process. By providing the fundamental bounds within which policy decisions were made, institutions both formal and informal influenced the nature of the resulting policy.

This is not to say that institutions *determined* the policy outcome. Rather institutions *guided* the process, by arraying factors and forces in such a way as to encourage individuals and groups promoting certain legislative alternatives to gain ground relative to others. Thus, Henry Capel and the sole right men of the Irish House of Commons did not succeed in dismantling the original intent of the Treaty of Limerick *because of* the institutions in place; institutions did not cause this outcome in any direct way. Instead, institutions helped to arrange pro- and anti-Catholic interests in a manner that encouraged mutilation of the Treaty rather than its acceptance. Similarly, institutions helped to array factors and conditions so that Guy Carleton and other supporters of a more charitable policy in Quebec were able to affect legislation more than their detractors, and gave those favoring relief in Ireland an advantage over those who opposed it.

How institutions structured the policymaking process in each case was a complicated matter, one made even more complex given the *density* of the institutional network. Institutions seldom worked in isolation from one another. More often, institutional effects were overlapping, with the result that some effects were lessened or negated, or enlarged, depending on the direction of the influence. In some cases, institutions were complementary and worked together to structure the process. This was the situation in some respects in 1778, when the formal institutions in place to subordinate the Irish Parliament to British power were supplemented by informal institutions that enabled the Irish executive to dominate MPs in the Irish House of Commons. At other times, the institutions worked at cross-purposes, as in 1697 Ireland when those same formal institutions were undermined by informal institutions that allowed Irish MPs more control over the legislative process than the formal structure granted.

Of course, in each of these cases, there were other institutions in operation that could further confound the process. In 1697, informal institutions structuring political relations in England, procedures that established the power of the king and his ministers relative to the English Parliament, as well as the place in the process of politicized groups out-of-doors, benefited the Crown by limiting the influence of other political actors, and so gave greater weight to the monarch's legislative preferences. In 1778, the informal institutions characterizing these areas were no longer so supportive of the Crown, allowing as they did the participation of MPs and out-of-doors groups alike, and so had the potential to undermine the policy options favored by the executive. Yet in the first case the institutions, although they complemented the formal institutions in place, did not insure the passage of the Treaty of Limerick in its original form as may have been predicted. In the second case, the Irish Catholic Relief Act was passed despite the sanctioned participation of a variety of anti-Catholic forces both inside and outside the walls of government.

The institutional context within which the Quebec Act was formed was perhaps the most convoluted. The *mutability* of the institutional network discouraged the emergence of any clear pattern of strength during formulation of the act: the Declaratory Act made official the power of the British Parliament over the colony, but the informal procedures affiliated with "government by instruction" granted considerable autonomy to colonials; the Crown determined the form of governance in conquered regions such as Quebec (as stipulated by *Calvin's Case*), yet these powers were restricted by the British Parliament (by the ruling of *Cambell v. Hall*, and informal procedures sanctioning the participation of MPs in British policymaking) and out-of-doors groups (by means of procedures permitting politicized groups a voice in legislation); those supporting a more traditional, less charitable, stance toward Quebec Catholics had institutional precedent on their side, but other institutions (those structuring power relations between the major political actors in Britain in particular) were such that they tended to reduce the authority of these actors within the negotiations. Who would triumph was far from clear.

The Quebec and the Irish cases hence demonstrate that identification of the institutions surrounding the policymaking process was not sufficient to understand the policy outcomes. While it was possible to infer institutional "advantage," the density and mutability of institutional networks gave rise to interactive effects that often steered events in directions contrary to what that advantage predicted. When combined with other factors and forces unique to each situation, institutions gave rise to some unexpected results. William III's personal predilection for international warfare and his disinterest in domestic matters helped to strengthen the impact of those institutions that favored anti-Catholic Irish MPs and downplay the influence of the institutions that had the potential to defeat them; longtime informal institutional precedents associated with colonial rule were overcome and formal institutions were made more salient in the Quebec case in large part because of the worsening of American hostilities and to some degree by Guy Carleton's persuasive nature and weighty political connections. The American war also encouraged British administrators to look favorably upon Irish Catholic relief and granted them some of the legitimacy required to push through the legislation despite a number of strong institutional barriers. Individual interests and concerns, the unfolding of events outside negotiations of the policy proper, unexpected turns of events, interacted with institutions to result in that unique legislative experience.

Recognition that the institutional context was not sufficient to account for policy outcomes should not, however, suggest that institutions were only one of many equally influential factors affecting policy. They were, rather, fundamental to the unfolding of the policy process. The institutions of the state are what define certain activities as *political* and others not, hence their role is integral to an understanding of policy outcomes. This can be missed by researchers who focus primarily on the characteristics of individuals and groups involved in the political process to explain government legislation. Thus, the origins of more charitable policies toward Catholics are located in the hearts and minds of enlightened state officials; Catholic relief is represented as a rational response by those same officials to the requirements of empire. "The state" plays little if any role in these decisions apart from providing the mechanisms for their promulgation.

Change the perspective to an institutional one, however, and the state is revealed as a requisite of the outcome. A policy of toleration in Quebec, whether based on charity or pragmatism, first had to overcome the inertia contained in nearly a century of legislated anti-Catholicism; similarly, Catholic relief in Ireland depended upon the existence of institutions that favored pro-Catholic forces in the executive. The capacity of individuals and groups to influence government policy was contingent upon more than their numbers or their material resources. By the latter half of the eighteenth century, the situation of many Irish Catholic élites had improved as a result of their having taken up commercial pursuits. Here was a group whose collective resources had increased to the point where they could afford to begin to demand political concessions of the Protestant ascendancy. It is conceivable that their opportunities would have been more restricted, however, had institutions surrounding the policymaking process not changed to become more open to groups and individuals outside the government executive and select others. Catholic commercial interests may not have been as successful at convincing government officials partial to landowning élites to consider their grievances had these institutional modifications not taken place. Irish Catholics may have been less likely to come together in associations like the Catholic Committee had this kind of political action not emerged as an acceptable, or at least tolerable, way to press for concessions as a cause and consequence of institutional changes. The "busy, elbowing scene" to which Charles O'Conor referred in 1759 when advising his son that the system could be used to advantage encouraged Catholics to act and administrators to pay heed.[1]

If institutional changes helped Irish Catholics to influence government policy during Relief Act negotiations, institutions lessened the influence of once-powerful Anglo-colonial merchant groups in the period leading up to the passage of the Quebec Act. In this case, changes in the institutions surrounding colonial policymaking conspired to reduce the impact that the merchants may have had on the policy process. The decline in the influence of the promerchant Board of Trade and its officials relative to other administrators and offices; the rise of "mass" politics and the concurrent "opening" of the policymaking process that increased the number of individuals and groups competing for the attentions of ministers, while discouraging some officials from consulting with merchants once conciliatory but now apt to adopt more "radical" (and less palatable) methods to let their desires be known; the formalization of the guidelines governing metropolis-colony relations granting officials of the metropole authority over decisions taken concerning colonial affairs; all curtailed merchant influence independent of their personal or collective resources, which were considerable. Donald Creighton is correct when he writes that "Lord North's parliamentary machine rolled over [merchant] protests . . . unhesitantly, . . . solidly"[2]; the capacity of North's government to do this, however, was dependent upon an institutional context that permitted such concerted action. In both this and the case of Irish Catholics, it is necessary to examine how institutions structured political pursuits and affected the relative power of the individuals and groups involved to understand the ability (or inability) of people to affect the political process.

While institutions clearly affected the capacity of individuals and groups to promote their pro- and anti-Catholic interests in each case, they comprised more than the "rulebook" to which actors referred while engaging in political pursuits. The situations were not such that actors, come to the political arena already equipped with their respective agendas, competed in accordance with the procedures defined by institutions, then emerged either defeated or victorious. Institutions helped to define the agendas themselves. Institutionalization of Henry Capel's bargaining method encouraged intolerant MPs and officials in the Irish Parliament and government to become more demanding of anti-Catholic legislation as their power grew, entrenching further Capel's approach to Anglo-Irish policy-making. The fall in power of the Lords Commissioners of the Board of Trade and

Anglo-colonial merchants that accompanied changes to informal institutions structuring British policymaking compelled some of them to modify their demands to include Catholics on the Quebec representative assembly that they so desired. And institutional changes introduced by George Townshend deepened divisions between the Irish Parliament and the executive, encouraging Irish MPs to adopt a more combative stand toward government, a position that did little to endear them to officials or further their interests. Differences in institutional mutability also affected the strategies and actions of political actors in each case. The institutions surrounding colonial policymaking were not well defined with respect to the Quebec situation, and allowed for discussion and consideration of a wider array of novel solutions. In Ireland, the institutions placed greater restrictions on what both the (majority) British and Irish sides of the debate could do and not do; the options available and the resulting legislation were also more restrictive.

This does not mean that the institutional context *produced* the views promoted by political actors or the strategies that they adopted to achieve those ends; institutions did not oblige individuals and groups to approach the matter in a particular way. Rather, institutions helped to encourage or discourage certain positions and courses of action over others, thereby affecting the complexion and range of legislative alternatives open to policymakers.

The Institutional Approach and Policy Change

Of concern here, however, was more than how institutions impacted on these three measures at the time of their passing. It was also to gauge how institutions affected the emergence of a *trend* in British policymaking, the turn toward policies more charitable and less repressive of Catholics in the empire. Over the course of the eighteenth century, British policy toward Catholics changed; so did the institutions surrounding Anglo-Irish and colonial policymaking. Were these two processes related and if so, how?

With respect to Ireland, although the *formal* institutions surrounding Anglo-Irish policymaking remained fairly constant during the eighteenth century, the *informal* ones experienced considerable alteration. Changes in informal institutions – in particular, those that surrounded the actual and practical operation of formal institutions, the procedural norms that parties followed while trying to satisfy (or undermine) constitutional and legal directives like Poynings' Law and the Declaratory Act – had a significant impact on the distribution of power in Irish policymaking and, consequently, on policy outcomes.

Modifications to Anglo-Irish policymaking introduced by George Townshend in 1767 appear to coincide with a "punctuated equilibrium" model of institutional change. Townshend could certainly be understood in the context of Clemens' and Cook's description of a *"deus ex machina* smacking into [the] stable institutional arrangements" characterizing the undertaker system and creating an indeterminancy that ultimately led to a shift in power away from Irish MPs toward the executive.[3]

While there is certainly some value to such an image, more was needed to institutionalize Townshend's measures. Contingencies such as the stabilization of British governance and the steady support of British officials and future Irish chief governors were crucial to the perpetuation of these modifications. The increasing radicalization of Irish "patriot" MPs, their radicalism born, to a large degree, of these self-same changes, only contributed to the maintenance of institutions that curbed the power of the Irish Parliament. By 1778, the fundamental institutions surrounding Anglo-Irish policymaking had become *complementary* rather than operating at cross-purposes, as they had at the beginning of the century; the informal institutions structuring Anglo-Irish politics were now consistent with the substance of the formal institutions which sought Irish subservience and British control. These institutional changes were crucial to the passage of the Irish Catholic Relief Act. It is difficult to imagine how the British-led initiative to allow some concessions to Irish Catholics could have succeeded had these changes not taken place. The legislation had a difficult time passing the Irish House of Commons; it is doubtful that the Act would have been approved had the informal procedures characterising Anglo-Irish politics earlier in the century still been in effect.

Institutional change was also central to the creation of the Quebec Act. But whereas institutional change preceded policy in the Irish case, it was in the process of the negotiation of the act itself that the institutional modifications necessary for its passage were formulated. Institutionally-entrenched procedures – those that comprised the "government by instruction" method of colonial rule certainly – needed to be overcome for the terms of the Act to be discussed, let alone passed and implemented. Further, institutions that structured power relations between pro- and anticoncessions forces both inside and outside government changed to favor proponents of change over supporters of the status quo. The difference was, however, that the institutions in the Quebec case changed in a manner less direct than in the case of Ireland. Quebec had no George Townshend to come in and "clean house" and purposefully reconstruct the informal institutions structuring political relations, no formal institutions to which informal procedures could be fashioned in accordance. As a result, Quebec institutions changed in a more incremental manner, gradually rather than suddenly. There was a realization on the part of political actors involved in the process that the existing (informal) institutions governing metropolis-colony relations were unsatisfactory in this case, but that realization came about slowly, as governments and personnel fell and came to power, as reports were commissioned, forgotten, then resurfaced, as actors supportive of a new policy were given a voice, as a war raged on and the strategies and demands of various politicized individuals and groups were expressed. It was an institutional deconstruction project that by no means was finished with the passage of the Quebec Act, as the Act was replaced in succeeding years with the Constitutional Act (1791), the Union of Upper and Lower Canada (1840), the creation of the first Canadian Parliament (1841) and finally the British North America Act (1867), which established the Dominion of Canada and the attainment by the colony of responsible self-government. Quebec served as a model for Crown colony rule in Britain's new and ever-expanding empire, and Britain's experiences there helped to fill the institutional "vacuum" created decades earlier when the procedures that had structured colonial rule for more than a century became redundant in an empire suddenly less uniform, less homogenous, than before.

Thus changes to the institutions surrounding the policy process in each case were crucial to the success of the proponents of relief in each case. But whence the trend? The Quebec Act and the Irish Catholic Relief Act were the first major legislative departures from Britain's anti-Catholic tradition. How did they contribute to, indeed help to initiate, the more protracted movement toward more inclusive policies?

There is little question that the Quebec Act formed an important precedent to the English and Irish Catholic Relief Acts that were to follow four years later. It is not the case, however, that once administrators had "broken the ice" and instituted a more liberal Catholic policy in Quebec that it was easier, even inevitable, that Catholic relief would follow in other areas of the empire, because this was not the case. Rather, the Quebec Act was important to the later relief acts because its proponents had framed Catholic relief in such a way that it could be marketed in a similar manner in these other situations.

Generous terms were granted to Catholics in Quebec as part of a larger scheme concocted by Guy Carleton and supported by his proponents that stipulated the terms were necessary to secure the loyalty of the Catholic population in case America or France threatened. The notion that relief could be exchanged for allegiance was not new. Certainly William III knew this when he extended generous terms to the surrendering Jacobites in the Treaty of Limerick. What was new, or at least relatively untried and certainly contentious, was the proposition that Catholics should be actively and publically encouraged to join the British army. This, advocates of the Quebec Act argued, could be accomplished by offering inducements to those whom they saw as the leaders of the Catholic community in Quebec, the landholding *seigneurs* and Catholic clerics. Concessions would bind them to the Crown and they would in turn encourage their *habitant* followers to take up arms against any potential enemies, including America and France. It took time, but because of the mutability of the institutional structure surrounding colonial decisionmaking at the time, combined with concerted lobbying on the part of Guy Carleton and his supporters and a fortuitous turn for the worse in the American situation, British officials came to accept that such a controversial approach was required. Although the connection between concessions and troops was a contentious one when the terms of the Act were being drafted, by 1775 enough of the House had accepted the idea for North to announce openly that "if the refractory colonies . . . [could not] be reduced to obedience by the present force, he should think it a necessary measure to arm the Roman Catholics of Canada, and to employ them in that service."[4]

When the circumstances surrounding the passage of the Irish Catholic Relief Act are examined those same justifications were used to extend relief in Ireland four years later. The terms of the Act were much more limited than in Quebec, largely because existing institutions constrained the range of legislative options available to proponents of relief and prevented administrators from ignoring the opposition to the Act as completely as they did in the Quebec case. The Act merely made it easier for wealthier Irish Catholics to own and inherit land. Nevertheless, it was hoped that these small concessions would encourage leading Catholics to persuade lesser Catholics to join the British army, which was suffering for troops.

That the reasons behind the extension of relief to Quebec and Irish Catholics were so strictly defined in these two cases helps to explain why the "trend" toward Catholic relief was not immediately discernible, and policy toward Catholics continued to vary to such an extent across the empire after these measures were passed. Relief was not offered in and of itself but as one part of a "package" prepared out of and for very specific circumstances. These circumstances did not exist elsewhere so other alternatives and solutions came to be applied. It also helps to account for a number of matters that continue to puzzle historians of this period. It helps to explain how Lord North managed to convince an otherwise intolerant George III to approve of the measures taken in Quebec, something that strikes historians writing about the Quebec Act as nothing short of miraculous, as well as his compliance to later relief Acts in England and Ireland. It also helps to account for the king's seemingly inconsistent behavior toward Irish Catholic emancipation in later decades, which he so strongly opposed. Concessions and emancipation were not synonymous. The first offered toleration, the second rights commensurate with followers of the established church. George was clearly against emancipation. As Charles Fedorak writes, the king "considered the established church as vital to the security of the realm and believed that granting further privileges to Catholics would violate the Coronation Oath [that stated that the monarch would uphold the established church] that he took seriously."[5] Perhaps more importantly the concessions offered in the 1770s were linked to the defense of the empire in such a way that made relief more palatable to the king, politicians and a public that held strong anti-Catholic views.

Hence, the Irish Catholic Relief Act was in some ways an extension of the Quebec Act, but not in any straightforward manner. The institutions structuring Anglo-Quebec policy combined with circumstances to allow for the formulation of Quebec legislation in which relief played a major but highly contingent role. Many of the same circumstances that had served as the bases for the Quebec measure, namely the American and French threats, still existed, indeed had worsened, by 1778. This encouraged policymakers to conceive of Catholic relief in Ireland in much the same way as in the Quebec case. Meanwhile, institutions had developed so as to permit British administrators to secure the passage of a more limited relief measure through the Irish Parliament despite virulent opposition there.

What this suggests about the general movement toward Catholic relief in the British empire is that chance and circumstance played a significant role in the establishment of early relief efforts. Toleration was not a policy that emerged naturally out of the Seven Years' War; nor does it appear that it was an approach that British administrators intended to become established. At most, the Quebec Act and the Irish Catholic Relief Act seem to have represented temporary solutions to immediate problems. This is indeed evident in the Quebec case. Although the public Act was unprecedentedly generous, the governor's private instructions revealed metropolitan officials had no intention of allowing these conditions to prevail indefinitely. "Contrary to the dictates of the Act, Governor Carleton was to have his council introduce *habeus corpus* into the colony and consider the introduction, by ordinance, of English laws concerning debts, promises, contracts and agreements. He was to undermine the Catholic religion by gradually imposing restrictions on the bishop, the seminaries, the male religious orders, and the missionaries."[6] It was Carleton himself that decided to keep the instructions hidden, preventing the establishment of a system that in many ways resembled the traditional pattern of British colonial rule more than it differed from old forms of governance. While the Quebec Act is now considered a watershed in the "movement" toward Catholic relief and emancipation, there is little evidence that contemporary British administrators envisioned such a movement becoming established.

Of course, once Catholic relief was institutionalized in the legislation pertaining to Quebec and later Ireland, the option of extending more concessions to Catholics in Ireland and elsewhere in the empire gained ground relative to other courses of action available to British administrators. Toleration was henceforth a formal legislative alternative. It did not, however, gain so much ground that other options were not still considered and implemented, as French Catholics in Grenada were to discover in 1784 when they were stripped of the rights they had held before the French interregnum there and a stringent policy of anglicization was put into place,[7] and as Irish Catholics realized when forced to wait another three decades for their emancipation.[8] Nor did it lead to an immediate decline in hostility toward Catholics in the British Isles, as the Gordon Riots were to so clearly demonstrate. Thus at what has been deemed the start of the long-term trend toward Catholic relief in the British empire there were few indications that any sort of trend would emerge. The tendency for British administrators to favor toleration over other kinds of measures did increase but only gradually. It was by no means a sudden change but a result of the accumulation of a number of specific policy outcomes whose connections with the relief legislation that came before may have been less than straightforward. Close study of subsequent measures would reveal the factors and forces, institutional and others, that combined to further the process.

Notes

1. Quoted in R. F. Foster, *Modern Ireland, 1600-1972* (London: Penguin Books, 1989), 209.

2. Donald Creighton, *The Empire of the St. Lawrence* (Toronto: The MacMillan Company of Canada Ltd., 1956).

3. Elisabeth Clemens and James Cook, "Politics and Institutionalism: Explaining Durability and Change," *Annual Review of Sociology* 25 (1999): 447.

4. Colin Haydon, *Anti-Catholicism in Eighteenth-Century England, c. 1714-1780: A Political and Social Study* (Manchester: Manchester University Press, 1993), 197.

5. Charles John Fedorak, "Catholic Emancipation and the Resignation of William Pitt

in 1801," *Albion* 24, no. 1 (1992): 54.

6. Susan Mann Trofimenkoff, *The Dream of Nation: A Social and Intellectual History of Quebec* (Toronto: Gage Publishing Ltd., 1983), 37-38.

7. See above, 15n23.

8. The Irish Catholic Relief Act of 1778 was followed by further concessions to Irish Catholic worship and religious orders in 1782, an act that also allowed Catholics to acquire lands on virtually the same terms as Protestants. In 1792, legislation was enacted that allowed Catholics admission to the legal profession, and in 1793 an act was passed that permitted Catholics to bear arms under certain conditions and restore to them the 40s. county franchise on the same terms as Irish Protestants. Thomas Bartlett notes that it was here, however, that "the cycle of concessions to Catholics [came] to an abrupt end"; further relief measures were not forthcoming until Catholics were emancipated in 1829 (Bartlett 1990, 16).

Selected Bibliography

Adams, George Burton. *Constitutional History of England.* New York: Henry Holt and Co., 1956.

Atkinson, Michael M. and William D. Coleman. *The State, Business, and Industrial Change in Canada.* Toronto: University of Toronto Press, 1989.

Ball, J.T. *Historical Review of the Legislative Systems Operative in Ireland from the Invasion of Henry the Second to the Union (1172-1800).* London: Longmans, Green and Co., 1889.

Bartlett, Thomas. "The Townshend Viceroyalty, 1767-1772." Pp. 88-112 in *Penal Era and Golden Age,* edited by T. Bartlett and D.W. Hayton. Belfast: Ulster Historical Foundation, 1979.

————. *The Fall and Rise of the Irish Nation: The Catholic Question 1690-1830.* Dublin: Gill and Macmillan, 1992.

Bayse, Arthur Herbert. *The Lord Commissioners of Trade and Plantations Commonly known as the Board of Trade 1748-1782.* New Haven: Yale University Press, 1925.

Baxter, Stephen. *William III.* London: Longmans, 1966.

Beckett, J.C. *Protestant Dissent in Ireland 1687-1780.* London: Faber and Faber Ltd., 1948.

————. *The Making of Modern Ireland.* New York: Alfred A. Knopf, 1969.

————. "Anglo-Irish Constitutional Relations in the Later Eighteenth Century." Pp. 123-41 in *Confrontations: Studies in Irish History,* edited by J.C. Beckett. Totowa, N.J.: Rowman & Littlefield, 1972.

————. "Introduction: Eighteenth-Century Ireland." Pp. xxxix-lxiv in *A New History of Ireland, Volume IV: Eighteenth-Century Ireland, 1691-1800,* edited by T.W. Moody and W.E. Vaughan. Oxford: Clarendon Press, 1986.

Bradley, James E. *Popular Politics and the American Revolution in England: Petitions, the Crown and Public Opinion.* Macon, Ga.: Mercer, 1986.

Bradshaw, Brendan. "The Beginnings of Modern Ireland." Pp. 68-87 in *The Irish Parliamentary Tradition,* edited by B. Farrell. Dublin: Gill and Macmillan, 1973.

Brebner, John Barlet. *New England's Outpost: Acadia Before the Conquest of Canada.* Hamden, Connecticut: Archon Books, 1965.

Brewer John. *Party Ideology and Popular Politics at the Accession of George III.* Cambridge: Cambridge University Press, 1976.

Brooke, John. *King George III.* New York: McGraw-Hill, 1972.

Browne, G.P. "James Murray." Pp. 569-78 in *Dictionary of Canadian Biography, Volume IV, 1771-1800.* Toronto: University of Toronto Press, 1979.

———. "Guy Carleton." Pp. 141-55 in *Dictionary of Canadian Biography, Volume V, 1801-1820.* Toronto: University of Toronto Press, 1983.

Bullion, John L. "Security and Economy: the Bute Administration's Plans for the American Army and Revenue, 1762-1763." *William and Mary Quarterly* 45, no. 3 (1988): 499-609.

Burke, William. *The Irish Priests in the Penal Times (1660-1760).* Shannon: Irish University Press, 1969.

Burns, Robert E. "The Catholic Relief Act in Ireland, 1778." *Church History* 32, no. 2 (1963): 181-206.

Burt, Alfred Leroy. *The Old Province of Quebec.* Toronto: The Ryerson Press, 1933.

Campbell, John. "Recent Trends in Institutional Political Economy." *International Journal of Sociology and Social Policy* 17, no. 7 (1997): 15-56.

Canny, Nicholas. *Kingdom and Colony: Ireland in the Atlantic World, 1560-1800.* Baltimore: Johns Hopkins University Press, 1988.

Christie, Ian R. "George III and the Historians – Thirty Years On." *History* 71, no. 232 (1986): 205-21.

Clarke, Aidan. "The History of Poynings' Law, 1615-41." *Irish Historical Studies*, 18, no. 70 (1972): 207-22.

Clark, J.C.D. "Whig Tactics and Parliamentary Precedent: The English Management of Irish Politics, 1754-1756." *The Historical Journal* 21, no. 2 (1978): 275-301.

Clark, Samuel. "International Competititon and the Treatment of Minorities: Seventeenth-Century Cases and General Propositions." *American Journal of Sociology* 103, no. 5 (1998): 1267-1308.

Clemens, Elisabeth and James Cook. "Politics and Institutionalism: Explaining Durability and Change." *Annual Review of Sociology* 25 (1999): 441-66.

Close, Robin E. "The Attempted Repeal of the Quebec Act: The State of the Parliamentary Opposition in 1775." *Past Imperfect* 1 (1992): 77-91.

———. "Toleration and Its Limits in the Late Hanoverian Empire: The Cape Colony 1795-1828." Pp. 299-317 in *Hanoverian Britain and Empire*, edited by S. Taylor *et al.* Woodbridge: The Boydell Press, 1998.

Connolly, S.J. "Religion and History." *Irish Economic and Social History* 10 (1983): 66-80.

———. *Religion, Law and Power: The Making of Protestant Ireland, 1660-1760.* Oxford: Clarendon Press, 1992.

Cosgrove, Art. "A Century of Decline." Pp. 57-67 in *The Irish Parliamentary Tradition*, edited by B. Farrell. Dublin: Gill and Macmillan, 1973.

Coupland, R. *The Quebec Act.* Oxford: Clarendon Press, 1925.

Creighton, Donald. *The Empire of the St. Lawrence.* Toronto: The MacMillan

Company of Canada Ltd., 1956.

Cullen, Louis. "Catholics Under the Penal Laws." *Eighteenth-Century Ireland* 1 (1986): 23-26.

Cummins, Seamus. "Extra-Parliamentary Agitation in Dublin in the 1760s." Pp. 118-34 in *Religion, Conflict and Coexistence in Ireland*, edited by R.V. Comerford, *et al*. Dublin: Gill and MacMillan, 1990.

Dearlove, John. "Bringing the Constitution Back In: Political Science and the State." *Political Studies* 37, no. 4 (1989): 521-39.

Dickerson, Oliver Morton. *American Colonial Government, 1696- 1765: A Study of the British Board of Trade in its Relation to the American Colonies, Political, Industrial, Administrative*. New York: Russell & Russell, 1962.

Dickson, David J. 1990. "Catholics and Trade in Eighteenth-Century Ireland: An Old Debate Revisited." Pp. 85-100 in *Endurance and Emergence: Catholics in Ireland in the Eighteenth Century*, edited by T.P. Power and K. Whelan. Dublin: Irish Academic Press, 1990.

————. *New Foundations: Ireland 1660-1800*. Dublin: Irish Academic Press, 2000.

Domhoff, W. *The Power Elite and the State*. New York: Aldine de Gruyter, 1990.

Donnelly, J.S. "Irish Agrarian Rebellion: The Whiteboys of 1769-76." *Royal Irish Academy Proceedings*, C, no. 83/12 (1983): 293-331.

Donovan, Robert Kent. "The Military Origins of the Roman Catholic Relief Programme of 1778." *The Historical Journal* 28, no. 1 (1985): 79-102.

Dugger, William. "Comparison of Marxism and Institutionalism." *Journal of Economic Issues* 28, no. 1 (1994): 101-27.

Eccles, W.J. *Essays on New France*. Toronto: Oxford University Press, 1987.

Edwards, R. Dudley and T.W. Moody. "The History of Poynings' Law: Part I, 1494-1615." *Irish Historical Studies* 2, no. 8 (1941): 415-24.

Ellis, E.L. "William III and the Politicians." Pp. 115-34 in *Britain After the Glorious Revolution*, edited by G. Holmes. London: Macmillan and Co. Ltd., 1969.

Ethington, Philip J. and Eileen L. McDonagh. "The Common Space of Social Science Inquiry." *Polity* 28, no. 1 (1995): 85-90.

Farrell, Brian, "The Patriot Parliament of 1689." In *The Irish Parliamentary Tradition*, edited by B. Farrell. Dublin: Gill and Macmillan, 1973.

Fedorak, Charles John. "Catholic Emancipation and the Resignation of William Pitt in 1801." *Albion* 24, no. 1 (1992): 49-64.

Fitzpatrick, Martin. "Toleration and the Enlightenment Movement." Pp. 23-68 in *Toleration in Enlightenment Europe*, edited by O.P. Grell and R. Porter. Cambridge: Cambridge University Press, 2000.

Foster, R.F. *Modern Ireland, 1600-1972*. London: Penguin Books, 1989.

Garner, John. "The Enfranchisement of Roman Catholics in the Maritimes." *Canadian Historical Review* 34, no. 3 (1953): 203-18.

Gipson, Lawrence Henry. *The British Empire Before the American Revolution, Volume IX: The Triumphant Empire: New Responsibilities Within the Enlarged Empire, 1763-1766*. New York: Alfred A. Knopf, 1956.

Goldstein, Judith. "Ideas, Institutions, and American Trade Policy." *International Organization* 42, no. 1 (1988): 179-217.

Greene, Evarts Boutell. *The Provincial Governor in the English Colonies of North America.* New York: Russell & Russell, 1966.

Greene, J.P. *Peripheries and Centre: Constitutional Development in the Extended Polities of the British Empire and the United States, 1607-1788.* Athens: University of Georgia Press, 1986.

————. *Negotiated Authorities: Essays in Colonial Political and Constitutional History.* Charlottesville: University Press of Virginia, 1994.

Grenstad, Gunnar. "Cultural Theory and the New Institutionalism." *Journal of Theoretical Politics* 7, no. 1 (1995): 5-27.

Hall, Peter. *Governing the Economy: The Politics of State Intervention in Britain and France.* Cambridge: Polity Press, 1986.

————. *The Political Power of Economic Ideas.* Princeton: Princeton University Press, 1989.

Hall, Peter and Rosemary Taylor. "Political Science and the Three New Institutionalisms." *Political Studies* 44, no. 5 (1992): 936-57.

————. "The Potential of Historical Institutionalism: A Response to Hay and Wincott." *Political Studies,* 46, no. 5 (1996): 958-62.

Harvey, John T. "Symbolic Interactionism and Institutionalism: Common Roots." *Journal of Economic Issues* 26, no. 3 (1992): 791-812.

Harvey, Karen J. *The Bellews of Mount Bellew: A Catholic Gentry Family in Eighteenth-Century Ireland.* Dublin: Four Courts Press, 1998.

Hay, Colin and Daniel Wincott. "Structure, Agency and Historical Institutionalism." *Political Studies* 46, no. 5 (1998): 951-57.

Haydon, Colin. *Anti-Catholicism in Eighteenth-Century England, c. 1714-1780: A Political and Social Study.* Manchester: Manchester University Press, 1993.

————. "Parliament and Popery in England, 1700-1780." *Parliamentary History* 19, no. 1 (2000): 49-63.

Hayton, David. "The Beginnings of the 'Undertaker System.'" Pp. 32-54 in *Penal Era and Golden Age*, edited by T. Bartlett and D.W. Hayton. Belfast: Ulster Historical Foundation, 1979.

————. "Walpole and Ireland." Pp. 95-119 in *Britain in the Age of Walpole* edited by J. Black. London: Macmillan Publishers Ltd., 1984.

————. "The Williamite Revolution in Ireland, 1688-9." Pp. 185-213 in *The Anglo-Dutch Moment: Essays in the Glorious Revolution and its World Impact*, edited by J. Israel. Cambridge: Cambridge University Press, 1991.

————. "Constitutional Experiments and Political Expediency, 1689-1725." Pp. 276-305 in *Conquest and Union: Fashioning a British State, 1485-1725,* edited by S. Ellis and S. Barber. London: Longman, 1995.

————. "British Whig Ministers and the Irish Question, 1714-1725." Pp. 37-64 in *Hanoverian Britain and Empire*, edited by S. Taylor, R. Connors and C. Jones. Woodbridge: The Boydell Press, 1998.

————. "Introduction: the Long Apprenticeship." Pp. 1-25 in *The Irish Parliament in the Eighteenth Century: The Long Apprenticeship,* edited by D. Hayton.

Edinburgh: Edinburgh University Press, 2001.

Higham, C.S.S. "The General Assembly of the Leeward Islands, part II." *English Historical Review* 41, no. 163 (1926): 366-88.

Hill, Jacqueline. "Religious Toleration and the Relaxation of the Penal Laws: An Imperial Perspective." *Archivium Hibernicum,* 44 (1989): 98-109.

Hoksberger, Roland. "Postmodernism and Institutionalism: Toward a Resolution of the Debate on Relativism." *Journal of Economic Issues* 28, no. 3 (1994): 679-713.

Horwitz, Henry. *Parliament, Policy and Politics in the Reign of William III.* Newark: University of Delaware Press, 1977.

Humphreys, R.A. "Lord Shelburne and the Proclamation of 1763." *English Historical Review* 49, no. 194 (1934): 241-64.

Iguarta, Jose. "A Change in Climate: The Conquest and the Marchands of Montreal." Pp. 255-72 in *Readings in Canadian History: Pre-Confederation,* edited by F. Douglas and D.B. Smith. Toronto: Holt, Rinehart & Winston of Canada Ltd., 1990.

Ikenberry, G. John. "Conclusion: An Institutional Approach to American Foreign Economic Policy." *International Organization* 42, no. 1 (1988): 219-43.

James, Francis G. "The Irish Lobby in the Early Eighteenth Century." *English Historical Review* 81, no. 320 (1966): 543-57.

————. *Ireland in the Empire, 1688-1770.* Cambridge: Harvard University Press, 1973.

————. "The Active Irish Peers in the Early Eighteenth Century." *Journal of British Studies* 18, no. 2 (1979): 52-69.

————. *Lords of the Ascendancy: The Irish House of Lords and its Members, 1600-1800.* Dublin: Irish Academic Press, 1995.

Johnston, Edith M. *Great Britain and Ireland 1760-1800: A Study in Political Administration.* London: Oliver and Boyd, 1963.

————. *Ireland in the Eighteenth Century.* Dublin: Gill and Macmillan, 1974.

Kavanaugh, Ann K. *John FitzGibbon, Earl of Clare: Protestant Reaction and English Authority in Late Eighteenth-Century Ireland.* Dublin: Irish Academic Press, 1997.

Kearney, H.F. "The Political Background to English Mercantilism, 1695-1700." *Economic History Review* 11, no. 3 (1959): 484-96.

Keith, A. Berriedale. *Constitutional History of the First British Empire.* Oxford: Clarendon Press, 1930.

Kelly, James. "Inter-Demoninational Relations and Religious Toleration in Late-Eighteenth-Century Ireland: The 'Paper-War' of 1786-88." *Eighteenth-Century Ireland* 3 (1988): 39-67.

————. "The Genesis of 'Protestant Ascendancy': The Rightboy Disturbances of the 1780s and their Impact upon Protestant Opinion." Pp. 93-124 in *Parliament, Politics, and People: Essays in Eighteenth-Century Irish History,* edited by G. O'Brien. Dublin: Irish Academic Press, 1989.

————. *Prelude to Union: Anglo-Irish Politics in the 1780s.* Cork: Cork University Press, 1992.

―――. "Monitoring the Constitution: The Operation of Poynings' Law in the 1760s." Pp. 93-127 in *The Irish Parliament in the Eighteenth Century: The Long Apprenticeship*, edited by D.W. Hayton. Edinburgh: Edinburgh University Press, 2001.

Kelly, Patrick. "The Irish Woollen Export Prohibition Act of 1699: Kearney Revisited." *Irish Economic and Social History* 7 (1980): 22-44.

―――. "Lord Galway and the Penal Laws." Pp. 239-54 in *The Huguenots and Ireland: Anatomy of an Emigration*. edited by C.E.J. Caldicott, H. Gough and J.-P. Pittion. Dublin: Glendale Press, 1987.

Kennedy, W.P.M. *The Constitution of Canada 1534-1937: An Introduction to its Development Law and Custom*. New York: Russell & Russell, 1973.

Kerr, William. "The Stamp Act in Quebec." *English Historical Review* 47 (1932): 648-51.

Koehn, Nancy F. *The Power of Commerce: Economy and Governance in the First British Empire*. Ithaca: Cornell University Press, 1994.

Krasner, Stephen. "Approaches to the State: Alternative Conceptions and Historical Dynamics." *Comparative Studies in Society and History* 26, no. 1 (1984): 223.

Labaree, Leonard Woods. *Royal Government in America: A Study of the British Colonial System Before 1783*. New Haven: Yale University Press, 1930.

Lammey, David. "The Growth of the 'Patriot Opposition' in Ireland During the 1770s." *Parliamentary History* 7, no. 2 (1988): 257-81.

Lawson, Philip. "'Sapped by Corruption': British Governance of Quebec and the Breakdown of Anglo-American Relations on the Eve of the Revolution." *Canadian Review of American Studies* 22, no. 3 (1991): 301-23.

―――. *The East India Company: A History*. London: Longman, 1993.

―――. *The Imperial Challenge: Quebec and Britain in the Age of the American Revolution*. Montreal & Kingston: McGill-Queen's University Press, 1994.

Leder, Lawrence H. *America – 1603-1789: Prelude to a Nation*. Minneapolis: Burgess Publishing Co., 1978.

Leighton, C.D.A. *Catholicism in a Protestant Kingdom: A Study of the Irish Ancien Regime*. New York: St. Martin's Press, 1994.

Long, J.C. *George III*. London: Macdonald & Company Ltd., 1962.

McCracken, J.L. "The Conflict Between the Irish Administration and Parliament, 1753-6." *Irish Historical Studies* 3, no. 10 (1942): 159-79.

―――. *The Irish Parliament in the Eighteenth Century*. Dundalk: Dundalgan Press, 1971.

McDowell, R.B. *Irish Public Opinion 1750-1800*. London: Faber and Faber, 1944.

―――. *Ireland in the Age of Imperialism and Revolution, 1760-1801*. Oxford: Clarendon Press, 1979.

McGrath, Charles Ivar. "Securing the Protestant Interest: The Origins and Purpose of the Penal Laws of 1695." *Irish Historical Studies* 30, no. 117 (1996): 25-46.

―――. *The Making of the Eighteenth-Century Irish Constitution*. Dublin: Four Courts Press, 2000.

McGuire, James I. "The Irish Parliament of 1692." Pp. 1-31 in *Penal Era and Golden Age*, edited by T. Barlett and D.W. Hayton. Belfast: Ulster Historical

Foundation, 1979.

———. "Government Attitudes to Religious Non-Conformity in Ireland 1660-1719." In *The Huguenots and Ireland: Anatomy of an Emigration,* edited by C.E.J. Caldicott, H. Gough and J.-P. Pittion. Dublin: The Glendale Press, 1987.

McLynn, F.J. "'Good Behaviour': Irish Catholics and the Jacobite Rising of 1745." *Eire-Ireland* 16, no. 2 (1981): 43-58.

MacNeill, J.G. Swift. *The Constitutional and Parliamentary History of Ireland till the Union.* Dublin: The Talbot Press, 1917.

March, James G. and Johan P. Olsen. "The New Institutionalism: Organizational Factors in Political Life." *American Political Science Review* 78, no. 3 (1984): 734-49.

Marshall, Peter. "The Incorporation of Quebec in the British Empire, 1763-1774." Pp. 43-70 in *Of Mother Country and Planations: Proceedings of the Twenty-Seventh Conference in Early American History,* edited by V.B. Platt and D.C. Skaggs. Bowling Green, Ohio: Bowling Green State University Press, 1971.

Martin, F.X. "The Coming of Parliament." Pp. 37-56 in *The Irish Parliamentary Tradition,* edited by B. Farrell. Dublin: Gill and Macmillan, 1973.

Maseres, Francis. *An Account of the Proceedings of the British and other Protestant Inhabitants of the Province of Quebec in North America in order to Obtain an House of Assembly in that Province.* London, 1775.

Metzger, C.H. *The Quebec Act: A Primary Cause of the American Revolution.* New York: The United States Catholic Historical Society, 1936.

Milobar, David. "Quebec Reform, the British Constitution and the Atlantic Empire: 1774-1775." Pp. 65-88 in *Parliament and the Atlantic Empire,* edited by P. Lawson. Edinburgh: Edinburgh University Press, 1995.

———. "The Origins of British-Quebec Merchant Ideology: New France, the British Atlantic and the Constitutional Periphery, 1720-70." *The Journal of Imperial and Commonwealth History* 24, no. 3 (1996): 364-90.

Miquelon, Dale (ed.). *Society and Conquest: The Debate on the Bourgeoisie and Social Change in French Canada 1700-1850.* Toronto: Copp Clark Publishing, 1977.

Moody, T.W., F.X. Martin and F.J. Byrne. *A New History of Ireland VIII: A Chronology of Irish History to 1976.* Oxford: Clarendon Press, 1982.

Murphy, Sean. "The Dublin Anti-Union Riot of 3 December 1759." Pp. 49-68 in *Parliament, Politics and People,* edited by G. O'Brien. Dublin: Irish Academic Press, 1989.

Neatby, Hilda. *Quebec: The Revolutionary Age, 1760-1791.* Toronto: McClelland and Stewart Limited, 1966.

O'Connell, Maurice R. *Irish Politics and Social Conflict in the Age of the American Revolution.* Philadelphia: University of Philadelphia Press, 1965.

O'Donovan, Declan. "The Money Bill Dispute of 1753." Pp. 55-87 in *Penal Era and Golden Age,* edited by T. Bartlett and D.W. Hayton. Belfast: Ulster Historical Foundation, 1979.

O'Flaherty, Eamon. "Ecclesiastical Politics and the Dismantling of the Penal Laws in Ireland, 1774-82." *Irish Historical Studies* 26, no. 101 (1988): 33-50.

Olson, Alison. *Making the Empire Work: London and American Interest Groups 1690-1790.* Cambridge: Harvard University Press, 1992.

Osborough, W.N. "Catholics, Land, and the Popery Acts of Anne." Pp. 21-56 in *Endurance and Emergence: Catholics in Ireland in the Eighteenth Century,* edited by T.P. Power and K. Whelan. Dublin: Irish Academic Press, 1990.

Ouellet, Fernand. *Economic and Social History of Quebec, 1760-1850.* Ottawa: Gage Publishing/Institute of Canadian Studies, Carleton University, 1980.

Parkman, Francis. *France and England in North America. 10 volumes.* Boston: Little Brown & Company, 1851-1892.

Pares, Richard. *King George III and the Politicians.* London: Oxford University Press, 1967.

Peters, B. Guy. *Institutional Theory in Political Science: The 'New Institutionalism.* London: Pinter, 1999.

Power, Thomas P. "Converts." Pp. 101-27 in *Endurance and Emergence: Catholics in Ireland in the Eighteenth Century,* edited by T.P. Power and K. Whelan. Dublin: Irish Academic Press, 1990.

Power, T.P. and Kevin Whelan (eds.). *Endurance and Emergence: Catholics in Ireland in the Eighteenth Century.* Dublin: Irish Academic Press, 1990.

Reid, Allana. "Representative Assemblies in New France." *Canadian Historical Review* 27, no. 1 (1946): 19-26.

Rollmann, Hans. "Richard Edwards, John Campbell, and the Proclamation of Religious Liberty in Eighteenth-Century Newfoundland." *Newfoundland Quarterly* 53, no. 2 (1984): 4-12.

Rutman, Darrett B. *The Morning of America.* Boston: Houghton Mifflin Company, 1971.

Quinn, David. "Parliaments and the Great Councils in Ireland, 1461-1586." *Irish Historical Studies* 3, no. 9 (1942): 60-77.

Sainsbury, John. *Disaffected Patriots: London Supporters of Revolutionary America, 1769-1782.* Kingston: McGill-Queen's University Press, 1987.

Shortt, A. and A.G. Doughty (eds.). *Documents Relating to the Constitutional History of Canada, 1759-1791, Volume I.* Ottawa: J. de L. Tache, 1918.

Simms, J.G. *The Williamite Confiscation in Ireland 1690-1703.* Westport, Connecticut: Greenwood Press, 1976.

———. "The Jacobite Parliament of 1689." Pp. 65-90 in *War and Politics in Ireland, 1649-1730,* edited by D.W. Hayton and G. O'Brien. London: The Hambledon Press, 1986.

———. "Williamite Peace Tactics, 1690-1." Pp. 181-202 in *War and Politics in Ireland, 1649-1730,* edited by D.W. Hayton and G. O'Brien. London: The Hambledon Press, 1986.

———. "The Treaty of Limerick." Pp. 203-24 in *War and Politics in Ireland, 1649-1730,* edited by D.W. Hayton and G. O'Brien. London: The Hambledon Press, 1986.

———. "The Bishops' Banishment Act of 1697." Pp. 235-50 in *War and Politics in Ireland, 1649-1730,* edited by D.W. Hayton and G. O'Brien. London: The

Hambledon Press, 1986.

———. "The Making of a Penal Law." Pp. 263-76 in *War and Politics in Ireland, 1649-1730*, edited by D.W. Hayton and G. O'Brien. London: The Hambledon Press, 1986.

Skocpol, Theda. *Protecting Soldiers and Mothers: the Political Origins of Social Policy in the U.S.* Cambridge, Mass.: Belknap Press of Harvard University Press, 1992.

Skogstad, Grace. "The State, Organized Interests and Canadian Agricultural Trade Policy: The Impact of Institutions." *Canadian Journal of Political Science* 25, no. 2 (1992): 319-47.

Smith, Goldwin. *A Constitutional and Legal History of England*. New York: Charles Scribner's Sons, 1955.

Stanbridge, K.A. "The French-Canadian Bourgeois Debate: History and the Ideology of Colonialism." *International Journal of Comparative Race and Ethnic Studies* 1, no. 1 (1994): 127-33.

———."England, France and their North American Colonies: An Analysis of Absolutist State Power in Europe and in the New World." *Journal of Historical Sociology* 10, no. 1 (1997): 27-55.

Steele, Beverley. "Grenada, an Island State, Its History and Its People." *Caribbean Quarterly* 20, no. 1 (1974): 5-43.

Steele, Ian K. *Politics of Colonial Policy: The Board of Trade in Colonial Administration 1696-1720*. Oxford: Clarendon Press, 1968.

———. "The British Parliament and the Atlantic Colonies to 1760: New Approaches to Enduring Questions." Pp. 29-46 in *Parliament and the Atlantic Empire*, edited by P. Lawson. Edinburgh: Edinburgh University Press, 1995.

Steinmo, Sven, Kathleen Thelen and Frank Longstreth (eds.). *Structuring Politics: Historical Institutionalism in Comparative Analysis*. Cambridge: Cambridge University Press, 1997.

Szechi, Daniel and David Hayton. "John Bull's Other Kingdoms: The English Government of Scotland and Ireland." Pp. 241-80 in *Britain in the First Age of Party, 1680-1750*, edited by C. Jones. London: The Hambledon Press, 1987.

Taswell-Langmead, Thomas Pitt. *English Constitutional History*. London: Stevens & Haynes, 1890.

Thomas, P.D.G. "The Cost of the British Army in North American, 1763-1775." *William and Mary Quarterly* 45, no. 3 (1988): 510-16.

Thomson, Mark A. *A Constitutional History of England, 1642-1801*. London: Methuen & Co., Ltd., 1938.

Tilly, Charles. *Popular Contention in Great Britain 1758-1834*. Cambridge, Mass.: Harvard University Press, 1995.

Tousignant, Pierre. "The Integration of the Province of Quebec into the British Empire, 1763-91, Part I: From the Royal Proclamation to the Quebec Act." Pp. xxxii-xlix in *Dictionary of Canadian Biography, Volume IV: 1700-1800*. Toronto: University of Toronto Press, 1979.

Trofimenkoff, Susan Mann. *The Dream of Nation: a Social and Intellectual History of Quebec.* Toronto: Gage Publishing Ltd., 1983.

Troost, Wouter. *William III and the Treaty of Limerick (1691-1697): A Study of His Irish Policy.* Leiden: Wouter Troost, 1983.

————. "William III and Ireland." Pp. 225-58 in *Fabrics and Fabrications: The Myth and Making of William and Mary,* edited by P. Hoftijzer and C.C. Barfoot. Amsterdam: Rodopi, 1990.

Valentine, Alan. *Lord North.* Norman: University of Oklahoma Press, 1967.

van den Berg, J. "Religion and Politics in the Life of William and Mary." Pp. 17-40 in *Fabrics and Fabrications: The Myth and Making of William and Mary,* edited by P. Hoftijzer and C.C. Barfoot. Amsterdam: Rodopi, 1990.

Victory, Isolde. "The Making of the 1720 Declaratory Act." Pp. 2-29 in *Parliament, Politics and People,* edited by G. O'Brien. Dublin: Irish Academic Press, 1989.

Wall (MacGeehin), Maureen. "The Catholics of the Towns and the Quarterage Dispute in Eighteenth-Century Ireland." *Irish Historical Studies* 8, no. 30 (1952): 91-114.

————. "The Rise of a Catholic Middle Class in Eighteenth-Century Ireland." *Irish Historical Studies* 11, no. 42 (1958): 91-115.

————. *The Penal Laws, 1691-1760.* Dundalk: Dundalgan Press, 1967.

————. "Catholics in Economic Life." Pp. 85-101 in *Catholic Ireland in the Eighteenth Century: Collected Essays of Maureen Wall,* edited by. G. O'Brien and T. Dunne. Dublin: Geography Publications, 1989.

Weir, Margaret. "Ideas and Politics: The Acceptance of Keynesianism in Britain and the United States." In *The Political Power of Economic Ideas,* edited by P. Hall. Princeton: Princeton University Press, 1989.

Wight, Martin. *The Development of the Legislative Council 1606-1945.* London: Faber & Faber Ltd., 1946.

York, Neil Longley. *Neither Kingdom Nor Nation: The Irish Quest for Constitutional Rights, 1698-1800.* Washington: The Catholic University of America Press, 1994.

Zucker, Lynn. "Institutional Theories of Organizations." *Annual Review of Sociology* 13 (1987): 443-64.

Index

About the Author

Karen Stanbridge is an Assistant Professor with the Department of Sociology at the Memorial University of Newfoundland, St. John's, Canada. Her work has appeared in *The Sociological Quarterly, The Journal of Historical Sociology* and *The International Journal of Comparative Race and Ethnic Studies.*